The Diary of a Victorian Squire

Extracts from the Diaries and Letters of
Dearman & Emily Birchall

Dearman Birchall. Portrait by F.G. Cotman, 1877

The Diary of a Victorian Squire

Extracts from the Diaries and Letters of
Dearman & Emily Birchall

**Chosen and Introduced
by
David Verey**

ALAN SUTTON
1983

Alan Sutton Publishing Limited
17a Brunswick Road
Gloucester   GL1 1HG

First published 1983

British Library Cataloguing in Publication Data

Birchall, Dearman
    The diary of a Victorian Squire.
    1.   Birchall, Dearman   2.   Upton St. Leonards (Gloucestershire)
    i.   Title   ii.   Verey, David
    942.4'14'0924   DA565.B/

    ISBN   0 86299 055 6

Typesetting and origination by
Alan Sutton Publishing Limited
Photoset Garamond 10/11
Printed in Great Britain
by Redwood Burn Limited, Trowbridge

In Memory of Lindaraja

What things I have missed today, I know very well,
But the seeing of them each new time is miracle.
Nothing between Bredon and Dursley has
Any day yesterday's precise unpraised grace.
The changed light, or curve changed mistily,
Coppice, now bold cut, yesterday's mystery.
A sense of mornings, once seen, forever gone,
Its own for ever: alive, dead, and my possession.

Ivor Gurney

Acknowledgements

I am most grateful to my cousin Peter Birchall for his kindness in allowing me to publish our grandfather's diaries. He has also generously enabled me to use our grandfather's watercolours of Bowden and the china collection, taken from our grandparents' superb catalogue, as illustrations for this book. I would also thank his wife Ruth for the interest she has shown in the enterprise.

My thanks are due to Mrs. Galvin for her skill in typing the manuscript, to Sandra Raphael for reading it and to Peter Turner for taking the excellent coloured and other photographs, and to Peter Clifford of Alan Sutton Publishing, who was always patient with my whims. Finally, I would thank Alan Sutton for his support and my wife Rosemary for encouragement.

David Verey

Illustrations

Frontispiece: Dearman Birchall by F.G. Cotman

4 Dearman Birchall as a tall young man and before he came to Gloucestershire.

9 John Jowitt; Deborah Jowitt; Clara Birchall; Edward Birchall; Benson Jowitt.

38 Barwick Lloyd Baker; Sir John Dorington; Thomas Gambier Parry; St. John Ackers.

56 Dearman and Emily on honeymoon in Naples.

97 The hall at Bowden Hall.

125 Emily Birchall.

146 Jack, Percy, Violet and Lindaraja.

159 Emily and daughters in Russian costume.

165 Bowden Hall; Mr Keen and the gardeners.

194 Dearman on his tricycle.

200 The Birchall family at Dinard.

207 Family group with Bruno the St. Bernard; Percy under gunnera leaves at Bowden.

211 Vivian, Lindaraja and Violet on ponies; Jack, Clara and Percy standing at the front door Bowden Hall; Clara driving her cobs with Archer in attendance.

215 Dearman's portrait by Collier; Bishop Ellicott; Clara Sophia Birchall; Eliza Sibon Birchall.

225 Dearman as High Sheriff; Thomas Dyer-Edwardes on his Egyptian donkey.

230 Linda Birchall.

235 Adela Wykeham; Jack Birchall; Noëlle Dyer-Edwardes; Violet Birchall.

237 Indoor staff at Bowden; Upton people.

Colour Plates

Emily Birchall by F.G. Cotman.

Bowden Hall : Upton St. Leonards churchyard.

The hall and library at Bowden.

Illustrations from Dearman Birchall's catalogue of his china collection.

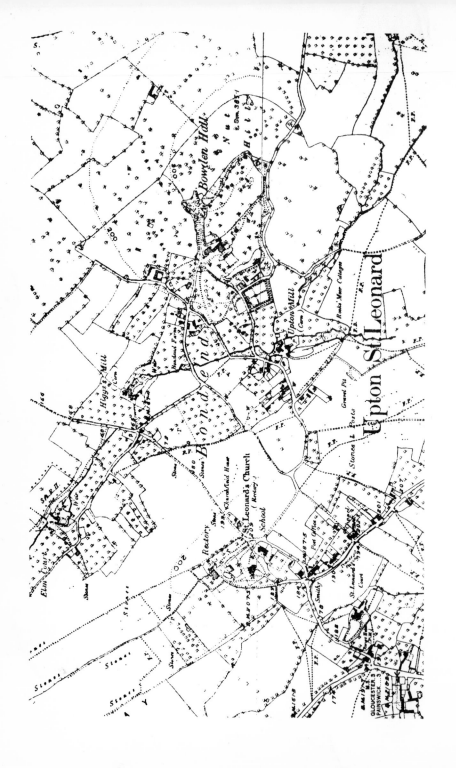

Introduction

The Squire was not a native of Gloucestershire, but the product of Victorian Leeds, where his father and grandfather were successful and respected merchants of that city. They were strong Quakers and married into Quaker families. As so many professions were closed to Quakers, the sons of Quakers followed their fathers in trade and it was not unusual for Quaker families to acquire considerable wealth. The Birchalls and their relations the Jowitts were no exception. Wealth opened the door to various developments. Country estates could be bought in the north (or even the south) by those whose inclinations led them towards the traditional sports of the upper classes. At the same time the cultural life of these great cities offered intellectual rewards to the more serious minded who could attend lectures on art and science from the most learned professors. By the 1860s Ruskin, Rossetti, Burges and Norman Shaw were all familiar figures in Leeds and Bradford. John Dearman Birchall developed in both directions, with the artistic and intellectual interests eventually taking over.

From his father Samuel Jowitt Birchall he inherited his fresh colour, fair complexion and blue eyes and from his mother Sophia Dearman's family his good features and height. He was 6 ft. 1 in. He was born at Springfield House, Leeds on August 6th 1828. His mother died when he was 9 and his older half-sister Eliza gave him careful religious instruction, and remained his closest and most faithful friend for the whole of his life. He was educated at small private schools in York and Croydon, and when he left he took lessons in "dancing, riding and foreign languages".

Not very much is known about his early business career. His daughter Clara Sinclair in her biography of her father says that he went into business in the cloth trade and entered the house of Messrs William Smith & Son, merchants of Cookridge Street, Leeds. Mr Smith is said to have taken him abroad on several occasions and we know he went to Germany. In 1853, when he was 25 he started his own business, which terminated practically when he moved into Gloucestershire in 1869, and actually when he sold his share as sleeping partner in the concern twenty two years later. As sleeping partner in J.D. Birchall & Co. he retained the biggest share, and was able to be fairly dictatorial to his partners. He increased his personal wealth by judicious investments. According to Clara Sinclair his success was not due to his practical knowledge of manufacturing but to his judgement and skill as a merchant or buyer and seller of goods. He never seems to have been very concerned with his mill at Armley. It was also said that his pessimism hampered his partners occasionally in conducting business.

His attention to "dancing, riding and foreign languages" combined with the fact that many ladies thought him the handsomest man they had ever seen, made him very acceptable in society, and for his part he could never resist the fascinations of a pretty woman. His future sister-in-law Susie Howard said he had a "tall, slender, well-knit, well-proportioned figure with beautifully formed hands and feet, a bright complexion, clear blue eyes, and singularly expressive mouth". Emily, when she married him, was surprised at the smallness of his hands, and it seems strange that such beautiful feet should have suffered so excessively from gout.

His artistic temperament was useful in business for he was fertile in giving ideas to manufacturers especially in the combination of colours. His descendants' colour-blindness comes from Emily's family. His firm won prizes for their cloth at the International Exhibitions in London in 1862, Paris 1867, Vienna 1873, Philadelphia 1876, Paris 1878 and Sydney 1879.

All the time he was collecting, collecting beautiful objects, particularly Chinese porcelain and Persian fabrics for his private delight. He does not often mention his acquisitions in his diary which is a disappointing fact; but Clara, who knew him better than anyone, considered his most prominent characteristic was acquisitiveness followed closely by caution. His beautifully illustrated catalogue of his china collection shows his artistic skill and his great knowledge and appreciation of the subject.

Dearman's father died in 1854, leaving three sons and two daughters by two marriages. The elder family were Sam and Eliza, the younger Dearman Sophie and Edward. In 1860 the family broke up. Sophie married William Atkinson, a civil engineer. Sam married the heiress of the Whiteholm estate on the Yorkshire Fells, and Edward went into Sir Gilbert Scott's office as an architect in London.

On April 25th 1861 Dearman married Clara Jane Brook, daughter of William Leigh Brook of Meltham Hall and Mills. In order to do this Dearman left the Quakers, and was baptized into the Church of England on March 30 in Leeds Parish Church. He was confirmed at the Woodhouse Church on April 3rd, and took his first Communion with his fiancée at Meltham Mills church which had been built by her family. This was a love-match which ended in tragedy. Their daughter Clara Sophia was born on April 3rd 1862 but Clara Jane died of consumption the next year aged only 21.

In January 1864 Dearman's brother Sam died from a chill collected while out shooting and his widow retired to her estate near Slaidburn. Springfield House, therefore, was sold and Dearman took his half-sister Eliza with his motherless baby to live at Hill House, Scarcroft, 8 miles from Leeds.

Dearman hunted with the Bramham hounds, and joined with his late wife's Armitage uncles to take a moor near Doncaster.

In 1868 he bought Bowden Hall, near Gloucester, a stuccoed Georgian house in exceptionally beautiful surroundings on a southern slope of a small spur of the Cotswolds. Trees of considerable size were planted about the grounds in front, and on a steep slope behind, and a long terrace walk terminated in a vista cut through the trees with a view of Gloucester Cathedral. There were sloping lawns whose trees and shrubs half hid the winding lake below.

Beyond, the park-like meadows extended over a narrow valley and climbed the opposite hills, till they merged in the old park of Prinknash or skirted the base of Painswick Beacon. Thomas Gambier Parry declared it the prettiest place in the country.

Inside the house, the rooms though not large were well-proportioned and comfortable. Edward Birchall, the architect, made some necessary alterations and constructed a billiard room at the top of the house. Aldam Heaton arranged the interior decorating. Accommodation was made for Dearman's collection of blue china, which he had been making during the past years. He had employed as his agent in the Netherlands a Dutch Jew called Duveen[1] whose chief trade was in forage but who also dealt in china and became the father of one of the most famous dealers of all time.[2] He learnt about Nankin from Dearman, who also bought rare textile fabrics and embroideries and Bowden was full of them. He bought pictures by Rossetti, Solomon, Birket Foster, Elijah Walton, Ziem and a window by Burne-Jones and William Morris. His valuable library was said to be "sumptuously housed" by Aldam Heaton.

A landscape gardener, Marnock, whom Dean Hole considered "the most accomplished artist we have had in the design or the development of a garden", was employed to advise on planting and cutting. Dearman moved there in August 1869 with his sister and seven year old daughter.

It was not a shooting estate but Dearman was not a keen sportsman. It was near Gloucester where Dearman could exercise his business talents on boards and committees. There were plenty of congenial neighbours. He enjoyed putting his little estate in order and then adding to it, a 500 acre farm at Upleadon, and the beech woods at Cranham. Upton St. Leonards was one of the last parishes to retain the open field system. Dearman bought several of these pieces of land.

On January 22 1873 after a few escapades in Gloucestershire and elsewhere, Dearman married for the second time. All his life he had been intimate with his second cousins the Jowitts of Harehills, Leeds. They, like him, were of Quaker origin but by this time most of the younger members of the family had become Church of England. Dearman was especially attracted to Emily, the fourth daughter described by Clara as "a striking personality, handsome in a dark and aquiline style, vivacious and brilliant in manner, of untiring energy and immense ability (the cleverest woman I ever met, said one M.P.) and considerably Dearman's junior. In some ways she was the exact opposite to him. One great charm about him was his perfect openness; she, on the other hand, was extremely reserved and self-contained. She disliked anything approaching gush or emotionalism. She was very fond of general society as was natural in one so fitted to shine in it. He, on the contrary, preferred a narrow circle of intimate friends. The marriage, however, was very happy, and their love and admiration

---

[1] Afterwards Sir Joseph Joel Duveen (1843–1908). Settled in Hull, 1866.
[2] Lord Duveen.

for one another grew steadily year by year". Clara's view of her young step-mother is not wholly reliable. Emily was far ahead of Dearman and Clara intellectually. She was only 20 when she married having just sat the Cambridge Examination for Women in which she obtained first class honours, distinguished in divinity, literature and French. She wrote the most perfectly open letters home to her family full of unreserved affection. Her letters particularly those written in Moscow and Gibraltar are probably the most interesting part of this book.

Well known Victorians, Norman Shaw, Ruskin, Oscar Wilde, the Duke of Rutland, Matthew Arnold, Thomas Gambier Parry, Sir Michael Hicks Beach, Professor Huxley, Sir John Collier and even Beatrice Webb say a word to Dearman as they flit across the pages of his diary and disappear, along with prominent men in Gloucestershire like Lord Ellenborough, Sir John Dorington, Lord Ducie, Thomas Bazley, St. John Ackers, Barwick Lloyd Baker, Thomas Dyer Edwardes, Bishop Ellicott and the Cathedral hierarchy of dean and canons.

After Emily's untimely death Dearman depended greatly on Clara's companionship and after her marriage his life seems to become more superficial and uninteresting.

It was very sad for the five children of Dearman and Emily that their clever mother did not survive; but they all grew up to become remarkable people.

Jack (Sir John Birchall) was Conservative M.P. for N.E. Leeds from 1918 to the second World War. He was Ecclesiastical Commissioner 1923–1929 and a member of the Church Assembly.

Percy was killed in action near Ypres on 23 April 1915, when commanding a Canadian contingent, and was recommended for the V.C.

Vivian (sometimes called Edward and at other times Thomas) was killed in the Battle of the Somme on August 10th 1916, and awarded the D.S.O. When in his twenties he founded the National Association of Guilds of Help. Before he died he left a note to a friend, S.P. Grundy, "If I am scuppered I am leaving you £1,000 to do some of the things we talked about". This scrap of paper, a symbol of the idealism of a lost generation, is preserved in the Imperial War Museum in London, and the legacy founded the National Council of Social Service.[3]

Violet lived all her life after Jack's marriage at Saintbridge House, Gloucester and ran a Men's Bible Study Class for 50 years.

Linda spent her life as the devoted wife of a parish priest.

---

[3] A History of the National Council of Social Service by Margaret Brasnett, 26 Bedford Square, London, W.C.1.

DEARMAN BIRCHALL'S FAMILY TREE

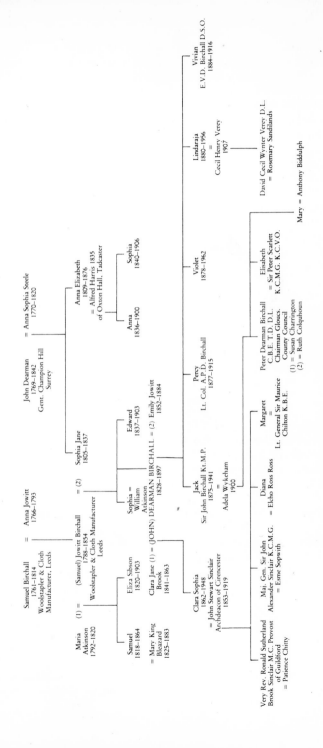

CLARA BROOK'S AND EMILY JOWITT'S FAMILY TREES

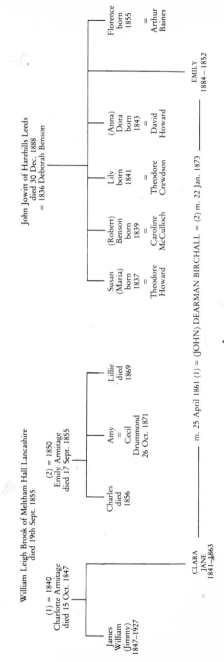

William Leigh Brook of Meltham Hall Lancashire
died 19th Sept. 1855

(1) = 1840
Charlotte Armitage
died 15 Oct. 1847

(2) = 1850
Emily Armitage
died 17 Sept. 1855

James
William
(Jimmy)
1847–1927

Charles
died
1856

Amy
=
Cecil
Drummond
26 Oct. 1871

Lillie
died
1869

CLARA
JANE
1841–1863

m. 25 April 1861 (1) = (JOHN) DEARMAN BIRCHALL = (2) m. 22 Jan. 1873

Dearman Birchall

John Jowitt of Harehills Leeds
died 30 Dec. 1888
= 1836 Deborah Benson

Susan
(Maria)
born
1837
=
Theodore
Howard

(Robert)
Benson
born
1839
=
Caroline
McCulloch

Lily
born
1841
=
Theodore
Crewdson

(Anna)
Dora
born
1843
=
David
Howard

Florence
born
1855
=
Arthur
Baines

EMILY
1884–1852

EMILY
1884–1852

The Diary of a Victorian Squire

Extracts from the Diaries and Letters of Dearman and Emily Birchall

(John) Dearman Birchall was born on August 6, 1828 at Leeds, and died on June 11, 1897 at Bowden Hall, Gloucester.

We open the diary in 1861. On Good Friday, March 29 Dearman wrote "Spent this day quietly at Gledhow with Eliza". Eliza Birchall was Dearman's older unmarried half-sister. She later accompanied him to Gloucestershire and eventually resided in Cheltenham. "Went to Chapeltown church in the morning. Evening to Leeds Parish Church and afterwards saw the vicar, James McCheane to talk over the subject of to-morrow, my Baptism".

Having been baptised into the Church of England, the next day, Easter Sunday, he took his first Communion with his fiancée Clara Brook at Meltham Mills church. He was confirmed at the Woodhouse church on April 3 and on the 25th married Clara at Meltham Mills. We have to rely on a newspaper cutting for a description of the wedding.

> The bride was the daughter of the late William Leigh Brook and his first wife Charlotte Armitage. He and his second wife Emily Armitage, sister of his first wife, died of cholera within days of each other in 1855. The children of both marriages were brought up by their uncle Charles Brook and his wife at Meltham Hall, Lancashire. Of the first marriage there survived Clara Jane, the bride, and her brother James William, and of the second two girls Lillie and Amy, whose appearance in their dresses of white attracted considerable attention. The bride wore a dress of rich white satin, lace veil and wreath of orange blossom. The bridegroom was accompanied to the altar by James William Brook, the Rev. James McCheane of Leeds and Edward Birchall his brother.
>
> The prettiest scene of all, and one which will not soon be forgotten by the villagers was that which awaited them on leaving the church. No sooner had they passed the doors than they were met by the girls in white, each bearing a basket of flowers; two and two they walked before the happy pair, whose faces were radiant with pleasure, strewing their path with flowers and thus embalming, as it were, the first moments of their matrimonial life with the odorous sweets of hearty good wishes. The crowd around expressed their congratulations by raising a shout of applause, which continued until the pair had entered the carriage.
>
> As yet, despite the few threatening clouds, no rain had fallen; on the contrary the sun had continued most auspiciously to shine; but now "a shower" as acceptable as it was sudden startled the spectators. On either hand the bridegroom threw handfuls of silver coin from the carriage amongst the gladdened spectators, never before was there such a "silver shower" experienced at Meltham Mills, and on few occasions has there been more liberality manifested. The scene at this point was

very animating. The bells of Meltham church rang out their merry peal, and combined with the enlivening music produced by the band, the huzzas of the multitude, to make up an effect both pleasing and imposing.

The wedding party having returned to the Hall, sat down to a luncheon of the most *recherché* description, at which a large number of guests were present. At 3 o'clock, the Sunday, Week-day and Infant schools — numbering about 550 and 50 teachers, were marched from the National school play-ground to Meltham Hall to give a parting cheer to Mr & Mrs Birchall who left shortly after for the 5 o'clock train at Penistone en route for the Continent.

A present of 12 pocket handkerchiefs, in a handsome box of white American wood, nicely ornamented with gilt, was made to Mrs Dearman Birchall by the mistress and girls of the Meltham Mills School, and a polyglot bible and prayer book superbly finished was also presented by the teachers of the Sunday school. From the park the children walked to the dining-hall where they all partook of tea, each one being allowed a bun and an orange to take home. The teachers and elder scholars, numbering about 170, took tea in the Infant School, after which Mr Brook, in a brief but graphic manner, kindly thanked them for the gratitude manifested and the handsome testimonial presented to his niece, expressing the hope that the same kind feeling may long continue. The festivities concluded with a grand concert by the Meltham Mills choir and the celebrated Meltham Mills brass band. The audience returned to their homes delighted with the evening's entertainment and the day was one that time will not soon erase from their memory.

After the party had returned to the house an accident occurred to an empty carriage belonging to J.W. Carlile Esq which was returning down the drive. The horses took fright and ran away, and the coachman was seriously injured, but we are happy to hear he is progressing favourably.

1862 and 1863

Dearman and Clara's daughter Clara Sophia was born on 3 April 1862. All that year Dearman's young wife was very ill and he devoted his entire time to nursing her. On September 26 they went to Bonchurch, Ventnor, Isle of Wight, and took Pulpit Rock House for six months. Clara Jane died of consumption on 4 March 1863, aged only 21. She was buried at Bonchurch. "I gave way to a grief which was consuming and could not take a spiritual view. All my misery seemed to culminate at leaving sweet Clara out in the field."

The next day Dearman left Bonchurch and went to London with his brothers Sam and Edward. And on the 12th he went by train to see his sister Sophy Atkinson who was living at Builth. "I went into Gloucester Cathedral;" he writes, "from Hereford by coach to Hay, whence in carriage and pair post to Builth, the 4 miles took more than six hours. Found Sophy and baby very well.

William (Atkinson) had arrived at home the day previously." Next day "William and I drove to Newbridge and then walked the four miles to see a bridge he is constructing over the Wye . . . Sophy's baby is larger and stronger than ours, and more forward, but not near so interesting looking". The next day was Sunday. "Heard Mr. Harrison, very depressing preacher, quite a hypochondriac."

On March 17 he went home to Leeds. "Mrs Jowitt [but evidently not his future mother-in-law] has been so kind and entered so unexpectedly into my feelings. She described the triumphant death of her husband who died the day I proposed to Clara, also the quiet sinking away of my mother at which she was also present". On the 20th he went to London to meet Webb, his partner in business, and then back to Bonchurch where Mr & Mrs Venables dined with him. "If there are saints on earth, these beloved ones deserve the title; good Christian souls running over with the milk of human kindness." On the day Clara Jane died, Dearman wrote, "Dear Mr Venables [afterwards, Precentor of Lincoln,] spent some time with me in the presence of the dear remains, he spoke to me very earnestly on the one thing needful and that I should not forget it when again mixing in the busy scenes of life. He prayed and wrestled with God for me and my sweet baby . . ."

1864

In 1864 Dearman made some sporting arrangements with his late wife's Armitage uncles. He wrote in his diary on April 8 "Accepted J.T. Armitage's proposal to take the vacant ticket. Shooting over Cantley manor. John, J.T. and Edward Armitage, 4 guns, 4000 acres, average killed 2000 head during season; expense £100 year, entrance £20-25. New cottage — This gives a share of the furniture and pays for wine and everything."

He was also anxious about his young brother-in-law. "*Nov. 12.* Went to Scarborough. Saw Jimmy Brook.[4] This evening he looked half demented, and as if he could not bear the light — and he had been howling and larking on horseback with Miss Hirst. *Nov. 13.* Jimmy seemed quite rational today and did not strike me as nearly so odd. He is very plump in the face — memory seems pretty good."

1865

March 4. News of the fall of Charleston makes the failure of the Confederates more probable than ever. Anniversary of the "saddest day of my life".

Oct 23. I proposed to Mary Tucker[5] and was refused, and next day I was persuaded it was for the best, fearing she was delicate like my first wife.

---

[4] Dearman's brother-in-law. No explanation is given for Jimmy's madness except that Dearman later speculates about Jimmy's father being epileptic.
[5] Tried again 1867. The Tuckers lived at Pavenham. Dearman thought Bedford very dull.

Dearman Birchall as a tall young man. Photograph by P.P. Skeolan miniature painter and photographer, 14 Commercial St., Leeds

Dearman Birchall before he came to Gloucestershire

Oct 28.   I hunted all day with my black mare. Glorious gallops through Harewood Park.

Nov 9.   Dined with the Jowitts[6] to meet Benson and his wife. The latter is jolly and has fine eyes but rather gross, heavy looking and very stout.

Dec 15.   I went to Paris. Visited the gallery opposite the Tuilleries gardens, Dessoi, 5 years in Yokohama. Asked for Japanese books by Osci, but didn't buy imitations which are of no value. Made many notes on buying stocks and shares. I am proposed at the Junior Carlton supported by Lord Nevill.

1866

Feb 22.   We took James William to consultation Dr. Watson. On returning to the hotel he was very violent, feared treachery, spoke of murder and suicide and seemed to take a terrible horror of me and his uncle. He threw bread violently at Lillie calling her a murderess. He said he was W. Leigh Brook of Meltham and had twice attempted his life. The medical man said the best establishment in England was Dr. Newington's at Ticehurst near Tunbridge Wells. Terms 12 gns. a week. 100 acres of pleasure grounds, nearly 100 servants. Lord Carlisle and Lord Hay's brother are there, among the 56 patients.

Christmas Day.   I have one of my most overpowering headaches. In fear of the gout I have been teetotal.

Dec 27.   Consulted Dr Burrows in London. He strongly urged the desirability of my again marrying and without delay. Advises me not to be a teetotaler.

1867

1867 was spent by Dearman in furthering his business interests, adding to his collections and visiting the Paris Exhibition. He was also thinking of leaving Leeds.

1868

Sept 20.   Arrived at Gloucester 4.15 a.m. Sunday. Took the sacrament at the Cathedral, which is newly restored and very pretty. In afternoon to Bowden Hall, Upton St. Leonards, beautiful drive 4 miles. Church and graveyard very pretty. Hall appearing at a distance on the side of a hill surrounded by fine timber, large bow-windowed house. Views of finely timbered fields; *tout ce qu'il y a de beau.*

[6] His future in-laws.

Sept 21.   Caught 7.40 train to Cirencester. Scenery through Stroudwater Valley exceedingly lovely and apparently undefiled by smoke. Earl Bathurst's Park opposite station at Cirencester has majestic and most glorious timber. The Agricultural College most picturesque Gothic building with broken outline. Mr Constable and his amiable wife drove me through Stroud to Bowden Hall calling on Mr Hyett at Painswick House on our way. We were delighted with Bowden. Mansion with 215 acres, 8 cottages, 2 sets of farm buildings £2,000 worth of timber, the whole for £25,000. Its proximity to Cheltenham and Gloucester, its church, and the society make me sorely tempted.

Bowden Hall 4 miles from Gloucester and 8 from Cheltenham.

Reasons for.   Situation between two desirable places and reasonable distance. Good society and extra good chances of introductions. Agreeable country. Lovely situation and surroundings of the house; to my mind views from the estate are very fine, soil prolific, timber old and handsome, house plain but convenient. Cheltenham affords good masters for Clara and more congenial society for her, and more to my mind than the Tennants and Harrisons who form the children's circle at Scarcroft.

Against.   Could not be let for 2 years and I am not disposed to leave here (Scarcroft) for at least a year. Charles Brooke Hunt, proprietor desires to go abroad for a time and does not accede to my suggestion that he should remain as a tenant for 2 years. My lease of Scarcroft lasts until Oct. 1st 1871 and owing to the badness of trade could not be let at present. Some doubt whether it might be damp from amount of trees and the clay soil which exists in the valley. My new engagements in Leeds make it undesirable I should leave at present — shooting in neighbourhood. A good deal to do at the house, being brick plastered and colour-washed, the windows numerous with old and ugly glass.

1869

Jan 14.   Came to Bowden Hall. Delightful children's party at Dr. Ancrum's. The little Ancrums are sweet looking children. Party elegantly conducted.

Jan 15.   Ball at Gloucester. I was introduced to . . . [all the county]. I never saw a more lovely party of ladies, a greater want of stewards, a narrower ball-room, a rougher floor, or half so many falls. Relics of torn dresses filled every corner.

Callers at Bowden included Dr and Mrs Ancrum. Col. & Mrs Prevost (neé Keble). Mr Barwick Baker (Hardwicke) of Reformatory notoriety. Stantons (Stroud). Mrs & Miss Somerset (cousin of Beaufort) of Upton. Gambier Parry (Highnam). Mrs St. John Ackers (Prinknash). Ackers' father was a Liverpool merchant who bought Prinknash. Mrs Price (Tibberton). Samuel Bowly (Horse Pools). Curtis Hayward (Quedgeley). W.H. Hyett (Painswick Ho.) Mrs Ellicott, wife of Bishop.

Feb 13.   Went to Ticehurst where we met Commissioner Barlow who examined James William, and also Dr. Newington. Edward Armitage's proceedings very short because his interview with Jimmy seemed to satisfy him. Dr. N. told me the children of an epileptic father nearly always go wrong [this suggests that William Leigh Brook was epileptic]. Jimmy past abusing himself, is taking large doses of Bromide of potassium and may live a good age.

The findings of the Commissioner were that he was of unsound mind, and unable to take charge of his affairs.

The sole heiress and sole next of kin is his niece Clara Sophia Birchall. James William Brook was 21 years of age on 18 Sept. 1868.[7]

Feb. 15,   I was in London. Saw Siamese twins. Born in Siam — visited England 1829. They are farmers in North Carolina, and are here to repair their loss of fortune by American war. All the surgeons concur in advising them not to attempt an operation. Chang has 6 girls and 3 boys. Hang has 6 boys and 3 girls. They have a melancholy cast of countenance but brighten up when spoken to. They walk with arms folded in what looks a painful position but is described as being "perfectly comfortable".

Scarcroft

Feb. 25.   I have walked to Leeds 3 times this week. Today I contrived to repeat 21 hymns during the two hours this pedestrian feat occupied me.

[7] His half-sister Amy was declared illegitimate owing to the fact that her mother was her father's deceased wife's sister. Family tradition always maintained that James William's lunacy was caused by his having been hit on the head by a cricket ball at Eton; but there is no mention of such a thing in the diaries. He inherited a considerable fortune. He lived to be 80 so Clara did not inherit it till 1927.

Feb. 26.   Uncle and Aunt Harris, Anna and Sophia came for a few days.[8]

Feb. 27.   Sophia and I went to meet at Kidhall Lane. We had a good run of 45 minutes without a check — very fast. We hunted again on March 1st; intensely satisfied with our two days performances.

March 29.   I agreed to let Hill House Scarcroft from 1st July. Mr. Salomé comes to take Clara's portrait — 20 gns.

April 8.   Dined at Bowden Hall. Arrived 6.30. I arranged with Mrs Brooke Hunt to take all the plants, odds and ends about farm, garden and carpenter's shop at a valuation by Bruton & Knowles; in the yard the Cobourg and suitable harness. Mr Hunt says my tenant Edwards is thoroughly respectable and dependable and may be consulted about cattle and what not with perfect safety.
   Servants I have engaged at Bowden.
   George Clapham. £60 p.a. with cottage. Milk, vegetables and coals.
   Henry Wastley, under-gardener 16/- per week but pays rent for cottage.
   Henry Wastley's nephew 9/- week.
   R. Jones. Farming man 11/- but pays for his cottage.
   Betteridge 2nd ditto, the same, only temporary.
   1 woman 5/- a week.

April 11.   I took train yesterday to Ashchurch and Evesham, posted across country to Stratford-on-Avon; put up at Rhine Hill. We had a glorious summer day, very hot indeed 90° in sun at 12 o'clock. Swallows appeared for the first time today and we watched a kingfisher darting across the Avon. Drove to Warwick in evening, attended parish church (it was a Sunday) and caught night train from Birmingham to Leeds. The old rector Mr Lucy at Hampton Lucy was very kind in morning, took me round the church and explained all the windows which are mostly by Hardman.

April 18 at Scarcroft.   We had a dish of asparagus from our own garden and a dish of strawberries from the hot house. Warburg says Salomé is a brutal husband and treats his very pretty wife disgracefully. She was a maid of all work at Doncaster. He saw her washing the steps, fell in love with her, sent her to school and married her.
   Miss Van has now been with us as Governess for some time and I thought it right to have a little conversation with her. At present, thank God Clara is a picture of health, so was her mother at her age, can we be successful in

[8] Alfred Harris b. 14 Ap. 1801. Senior partner in Old Bank Bradford. Of Steningford, later of Oxton Hall nr. Tadcaster. J.P. DL. Not a Quaker. d. 11 April at Oxton Hall 1880 m. Anna Elizabeth Dearman, died 1876. They had daughters Anna Jane 1836 died 1900 at Oxton Hall. Sophia 1840–1906. Dearman's uncle Harris was a great friend to him. Mrs Harris was sister to Dearman's mother Sophia Jane Dearman.

John Jowitt of Harehills

Deborah Jowitt, his wife

Clara Birchall
by
Antoine de Salomé

Benson Jowitt, the Jowitts'
only son

Edward Birchall, Dearman's
architect brother

training and bringing her up to withstand those difficulties under which her dear mother succumbed at the age of 21. Dr Newington says "Do not excite the brain until fully developed, do not call for any mental exertion until at least a child is near ten years of age."

Aldam Heaton[9] has agreed to go with Edward [Dearman's architect brother] and myself to Bowden. We went on April 27, and carefully went into all the house arrangements.

May 28.   We dined with the Jowitts at Harehills, quite a family party. Lily Crewdson, Mrs Benson, Edward and ourselves.

May 29.   We have truly enjoyed having Sophy this week [his sister Sophy Atkinson] — our last at Scarcroft.

May 31.   The library furniture was dismantled, the books packed and they began with the wine.

Dearman then went to London and on June 5 reports "In evening to hear Traviata with Miss Nilsson as Violetta. Verdi's music is distasteful to me and I don't think I shall spend 1½ gns. again very shortly at the Italian opera."

By the 9th he was at Bowden for a night. "We are cutting our grass in Gloucester to the surprise of folks here", he writes on his return to Scarcroft. "I brought home some ripe strawberries and garden peas".

July 5.   Went with Shaw to see Morris & Co. 26 Queen St. Bloomsbury. We selected the yellow paper for morning room ceiling and looked at designs for 1 pane (17 in. by 13⅞) in each of the 3 windows. The manager at Morris & Co. being a morbid sort of medieval man, married Madeline Smith the poisoner, who had a sensational trial in Edinburgh.

July 15.   I came to Bowden yesterday. Thermometer 110. It is awfully hot here. Took a long walk to Coopers Hill and Prinknash.

July 17.   Left Bowden for Manchester. The hottest day I ever knew. I left my coat off and had only a dust coat on, no hat and still as the train swiftly passed through the air the wind and dust were as the blast of a furnace. . . . I hate Manchester.

July 22.   Returned to Bowden. Clara came from Whiteholme. She looks well and happy and was very affectionate, and has had a delightful visit at Auntie Bia's [his widowed sister-in-law].

[9] Aldam Heaton was a textile designer who married a governess, not an easy thing to live down in the closed social circles of Leeds. He therefore moved to Bradford, and became later a friend of Ruskin, Rossetti, Burges and Norman Shaw. He also became High Church, an advanced Goth and very influential as an interior decorator in London where he was frequently employed by Norman Shaw.

July 23. All going on very slowly. I am still confined to housekeeper's rooms.

Aug. 14. Eliza and I called on widow Browning who has a bad leg and is a sort of pensioner, also at the cottage I rent in which are widow Green, widow Pitt and Vaughan's father and son.

Aug 15. Mr Green gave us a high church sermon dwelling on the high office of Christian ministers.

Aug 26. Mrs Charles Sumner called yesterday and asked us to tea on the grass. Harescombe Grange has a lovely view. It was built by Lucy of Gloucester and has cost a heap of money. Sumner, son of Bishop of Winchester, a judge, the county court at Stroud. He gave £12,000 for house and some 30 acres. He has laid out some thousands in increasing the house and has added 8 bedrooms and has 12 children.

Aug 31. Yesterday Eliza, Clara and I mounted for a ride. I slipped Clara's leading rein over my wrist. My horse started. Clara's pony was as immovable as a milestone, and I was pulled off my horse backwards way.

Today we went to a croquet at home at Barwick Bakers, Hardwicke Court. The son and his bride, formerly Miss Lascelles, were there, two Misses Gordon Canning and brother of Hartpury House, Miss Stuart daughter of Lady Stuart of Stratford House, the Sumners and Mrs Curtis Hayward. Tea, coffee, claret cup and next to nothing to eat.

Sept 2. About 4 o'clock I found a large hornet in one of the bottles of decoction hung up to destroy wasps. He was too far gone to fly so I took him out with a stick and trod upon him on the soft bed until I thought he was dead. On bringing him into the house he bit and stung with insane fury. About 6 o'clock I cut his head off and drew out his sting with a pair of tweezers. The poor denuded body was not very active, but the head with its two legs and feelers resented the treatment and ran about biting at everything, even the tweezers, which hard material it only relinquished with a perceptible crack in its teeth at 8.

Sept 17. Mrs Clapham says Georgie [Somerset] was terribly in love with Charles Hunt [previous owner of Bowden]. She would be continually hanging about the place as early as 5 in the morning, and really be got to keep out of the way. She picked the strawberries and made herself more at home than anybody desired. She said to me, coming from church; "I have never been abroad, scarcely out of Gloucestershire. I should have liked to have gone with the Hunts. Mrs Hopkinson [the Somersets' married daughter] was very much admired at the ball in London. She did not care much for gaiety, indeed none of us do. We all love our own county supremely."

Oct 5.   Mrs Hyett said, "I never heard anything against the moral character of young Somerset. He has been extravagant and the Duke has paid his debts. I suppose the Hopkinsons want £300 p.a. for Edgeworth. It is too much. I said, "Is not Mrs H. much quieter than the others". "Oh no, Miss S. will make quite a staid matron. She has the most in her and is the only one who can manage her father, who is hot hasty but he has a kind heart."

William Atkinson (his brother-in-law) said (October 12 letter) "I see what a dangerous position you are in with Miss Somerset. You look as if you admired her, and she looks as if she knew it". The position is embarassing; her proximity, her constant calls for one object or another, unlimited intercourse without meeting where we could have any prolonged conversation. It is dangerous for one's piece of mind to be much with so sweetly fresh a girl. In her favour are her transparent honesty, off-handedness and sprightliness, love of home and the poor, apparent love to her sisters. Against: parentage means — so much needed by her nearest relatives, her taking possession of us and making so very free and in the circumstances perhaps we would have admired her more if she had not made herself so cheap, her passion for riding or doing anything and feeling of weariness with inactivity. Personally I like the girl but is she what I should desire as a mother for Clara. Is she capable of loving me for my own sake and as warmly if I lived in a cottage, or is Bowden Hall with its reminiscences the bait which allures her. The worst suspicion which can occur is she playing for the Hall or capable of so base a game.

Oct 8.   Elizabeth [a maid] came and complained that Elwood Gell had taken some liberty with her on 14 Sept. She thought he had drunk some beer and had only proceeded as far as giving her a kiss. On Saturday evening he came into the laundry and stood about, someone else being there as well as Elizabeth. When they left he came and threw her on to the ground, got on to her and did his utmost to commit a rape. She wonders now that she had sufficient strength to scream or breathe. William Moulding stood outside looking on and dare not render any assistance. Elwood said he had set his mark on her and would have her. She is afraid of his taking her life. On consulting Thomas I found he was convinced that the account given me by Elizabeth was essentially correct. It surprised him the more because Elwood had stood aloof from the servants never sitting in the kitchen or joking with them, in fact he had invariably conducted himself with the utmost propriety. As Elizabeth had not mentioned this until Thursday and it occurred last Saturday and we are engaged to go to the Diocesan Conference tomorrow I delayed dismissing him until our return.

Oct 9.   Elwood drove us into Gloucester and while we were at the meeting in the Shire Hall effected some shopping and then drove as far as Capt. Arthur Stewart's (Saintbridge) to meet Clara and Miss Van. They noticed he drove them very wildly to the station to which place they proceeded to meet the Newloves who were passing through on their way home. While there

Elwood drove away. He was very drunk and on getting to the Bell came into collision with a haycart, bent the lamp and slipped off his box. The head hostler got him into a cab and sent him home and I drove our party (which included the vicar Mr Green) from the meeting. When we got to the King's Head (just outside Upton) the cab was standing at the door and Mr Green kindly volunteered to go in and see Elwood Gell. I also directed the cabman to take him to his cottage. I forestalled him there and saw his wife, in a few words putting her in possession of the above particulars. She said it was one of the first times he had misconducted himself when out with carriage or horses but when intoxicated he was a raving lunatic and he had so ill-treated her on Saturday last that she and her son had spent the night in the fields. His brutality was such she was determined to see him no more so I sought an asylum for her at George Clapham's and so when Elwood returned the bird had flown.

Oct 10. Elwood was apparently very penitent and looked respectable though sad and depressed. I warned him off the premises. He gave the key of the house to me for his wife after trying to induce her to join him he went away. I hear they have £150 in the Bank in Gloucester, the remains of £300 he got with her as a marriage portion, left by a grandmother. I suppose he will bag this and drink it. Mrs Clapham seems to think Mrs Gell is now repenting not going with him.

Oct 16. It appears probable Elwood Gell has taken his departure for America. He drew £95 out of the Bank.

Oct 15. This day called on James Stanton, the Culls, near Stroud, out, and the Dickinsons at Browns Hill. Mrs Dickinson a daughter of Mr Hyett, a very bright cheerful, jolly person.
Dinner at 7 at Barwick Bakers. The decoration of flowers lovely. Young Baker seems a pleasant enough fellow.

Oct 17. Mr Green gave us a very severe sermon urging the farmers and owners of property to see to the children going to school and many other things. He offends his parishioners and seldom visits them. He seems not to appreciate the good that can be done by sympathy and loving tender action.

Oct 20. Last night there was a terrible frost. Fortunately I put out my thermometer and it registered 21°F or 11 degrees of frost. Bedding plants, vines, figs, fuchsias, beans, dahlias etc all as so much dung this morning. The blight is magical, I never saw its equal in my life.

Oct 27. The whole place is covered with snow and yesterday we had a hailstorm and very cold wind. Letters from Leeds report fine warm weather — like Madeira.

Nov 15.   Resolved but without vow to devote two hours of every day to prayer and meditation, and the study of religion. God grant a blessing on this place. Dined again at the Bishop's Palace. Hunted with the Cotswold from Air Balloon.

I had a long talk with Mr Stewart about farming. He strongly advises me to take no more than 35 acres which is quite enough for all amusement. Without a practical acquaintance with the matter, the losses, annoyance and worry are never repaid. Bailiffs unless first class highly paid men are constantly creating suspicion and with good cause. He says I should get a good rent and have that safe.

I have agreed to let the farm but with the right of selecting certain lands at £3 per acre.

Nov 18.   Visited Bishop of Hereford. Dinner party. Lady Emily Foley called "The Queen of Herefordshire", and the Saye and Seles.

Nov 29.   Dinner at Curtis Haywards, Quedgeley. I sat between Mrs Peters and Miss Somerset and was not much pleased with either of them. (Dinner parties every day now).

Mr Jones, Whitley Court, thinks Mr Wylliams would dispose of the hill behind my house at a fancy price — say £200 an acre — there are 10½ acres.

Dec 7.   I enjoyed a run with the Berkeley hounds immensely. We found in a covert near the meet at Hardwicke Court and ran past Robins Wood Hill across the valley up on to Painswick Beacon and down into Prinknash where we lost our fox. We walked down to Upton and I left them.

Dec 11.   Dined at Arthur Stewart's at Saintbridge.

Dearman spent Christmas with his wife's Brook uncle at Enderby Hall, Leicester. "I feel in very low spirits. We had a quiet day. Mrs Brook suffered from her remembrances . . ." of Lillie. Amy played the organ very well.

Dec 27.   I shot with Mr Brook. We had a good walk but did little execution in blinding snow.

Dec 28.   Ripon Ball. I danced with great energy.

1870

Jan 13.   County Ball, Spread Eagle, Gloucester. Nothing could be more successful. I danced with Carrie and Georgie Somerset.
     Mrs Somerset told me that her maternal grandfather was Capt. Bligh of the Bounty.

Jan 20.   Sent my horse on to Berkeley last night. Took 8 train this morning. Large meet doomed to disappointment due to non-arrival of Prince of Wales. We hunted round Rockhampton, Thornbury, Hill and near the Severn. I rode home and must have done near 40 miles.

Jan 25.   Hunted with the Berkeley from Norton. Had a very hard day, the country being exceedingly heavy. We ran round Tewkesbury Park. Dr Ancrum's horse fell and kicked him on the head and four horses were killed or died.

Jan 26.   Attended the Stewarts' sale. To Exeter by train. Met with the Bishop of Ripon and his family en route for Torquay where they are to visit Miss Burdett Coutts.

Jan 27.   Spent morning at Lucomb and Pinces, Alphage Road and Veitchs. I spent £20 at the former and purchased a beautiful collection of coniferae, shrubs and especially the fruiting Aucuba. Met with the Brooks at Royal Hotel, Torquay. Amy looks well but has a cold. She is staying with the Blomfields.

Jan 28.   Dined with Fred Blomfield. He has taken The Larches, a capital house. St. Luke's church built by Blomfield's brother; very satisfactory and not costly.

Feb 6th.   Meet at Sir Lionel Darell's, Fretherne Court, a man who has become suddenly enriched. We got very wet and I came home early, having gone after the wrong fox at Frampton. Mrs Brook writes Amy has had another attack of hysteria and is giving considerable anxiety.

Feb 8.   Meet at Hardwicke. Morning without much excitement. Elmore, etc. After trying coverts round house and partaking of a capital lunch we went to Stonehouse Court and had sharp run to Whitminster where we ended without killing our fox. Many casualties and very hard riding. Mrs Clifford rode well.

Feb 9.   I lunched with Mr Hyett. Showed me his dyed woods — his tiles.

Feb. 12.   Dined with the Gambier Parrys. Capt. & Mrs Noel of Clanna Falls, Lydney . . . and many others of whom I did not even hear the name.

Feb 13. Miss Somerset at church after a month's visiting, looked very coldly at us and seemed very indifferent even to my sister. We cannot understand them.

Feb 14. I went to town. Slept at Lewis's Private Hotel, 84 Jermyn Street. Saw *Ages Ago* & *Cox & Box* . . . very amusing.

Feb 25. Our first party. The success was unmistakeable. The guests were Mr, Mrs and three Miss Sumners, Canon & Mrs & Miss Harvey, Rev. & Mrs & Miss Green, Mr & Mrs Granville Baker, Mr Hayward, Louis Oxley & Capt. Stewart. The dining room was decorated with a mass of flowers, our camellias coming in so well. The dinner was better cooked and more to my mind than the one at Prinknash where they had engaged a French cook. We had Dudman and another to wait and nothing could be better. Mrs Harvey, my partner, told me her grandson said to the Canon "Dear grandpapa, it's our last day at home, don't let us have any prayers."
Louis Oxley is staying. I had written to him repudiating the Valentine which I thought had been concocted with his assistance or by his connivance. I pointed out its injustice, said how seldom I had met Miss Somerset and how chilling her reception of me had always been after an absence. He was rather surprised how little we had met, and denied any complicity in the Valentine. I think I convinced him of my not having given up all thoughts of Miss Somerset; but I thought she had some secret objection to me by her coldness, not only when we met after long absence but out at dinner at the Curtis Haywards. He said she was not to be trifled with and she wisely held aloof in society from showing any fondness. He thinks all her actions show she is in love with me, he believes it firmly and he watched her most carefully the evening she dined here. On Tuesday I was out hunting and I talked a good deal with Mrs Clayton who said what a lovable child Miss Georgie was but she had not the strength of character of Carrie, and the latter was so unselfish, so thoughtful and good natured, no wonder she visited so much, she was so beloved and was so nice in a house. She loved riding but always gave up when there was one horse to her sister. What a self-denying life she must have, so much to put up with by such resources in herself. Oh that if anything ever comes of this I may prove worthy of her. I implore God's blessing on her from my heart.

Feb 28. We called on the Somersets and then went to the Cathedral, lunching at Canon Harvey's. We invited Col. Somerset & Mrs Clayton to dine tomorrow.

March 1. The Somersets dined with us to meet Oxley, who with me had been hunting in their company all the morning. Mrs Clayton was with us. She is an exquisite rider, poor girl she told me she had been married 7 years; but omitted that she had left her husband owing to his brutality. Carrie was charming and looked lovely.

Ash Wednesday.   I enter into a vow this day to devote at the rate of 2 hours a day or 14 hours a week during Lent to communion with God and study of Heavenly Things and to be very circumspect in my living.

March 7.   Meet at Prinknash. Home to lunch and drove to call at Sir W. Guise, Elmore, and to see St. Lucy's House and the children's hospital. Service at the Cathedral, and so home. The children's hospital is admirably conducted and very pleasing.

March 8.   Hunted at Hardwicke.

March 9.   Mrs Clayton and Miss Somerset came to lunch. The former owing to fatigue from hunting yesterday or unhappiness in her circumstances was very depressed. Miss S. had a severe cold, Eliza ditto. Everything hung fire. The tone of conversation, and want of appreciation from Carrie made me feel very flat about her: the same chill that occurred at the Curtis-Haywards. Her music book exclusively contains the most affecting and melancholy songs of lovers dead and in heaven. She is a mystery.

March 15.   Meet at Whitminster. We hunted round Standish Park. I had a long talk with Dr. Evans. He could not feel any sympathy with Col. Somerset, his fondness for his children had spoiled them. Miss S. was much the best of them. They were singularly proud and suffered from it. He recommends men to remain single till they are 50 and then to marry with sweet 18.

March 22.   I went to Brockworth on foot. Met Col. Somerset's hounds with Mr. Moore. He told me a good deal about the Col.'s family. The son is in destitution, spoiled. The father awfully passionate and abuses everybody. Miss S. has a temper, indeed is a Somerset.

March 27.   Called on Mr Hyett. His son,[10] aged 25, is going to marry Miss Carpenter, aged 29, plain looking and worth no fortune. He told me about Earl Ducie's gardener Mr Cam taking apprentices. They turn out very thorough gardeners. He would give me a note to him if I do not succeed. He got his late gardener from Mr Lindley[11] who was head of Horticultural garden in London and who had a collection of clever young men to whom he paid 12/- per week and from which Paxton was selected by the Duke of Devonshire. Mr Hyett's gardener got advanced from that to £100 a year when he died having managed all the estate.

March 30.   Came up to town during night and met a number of gardeners by appointment at the Junior Carlton. My choice fell on Thomas Bevan,

---

[10] Sir Francis Hyett, Gloucestershire Bibliographer.
[11] John Lindley (1799–1865) eminent botanist, F.R.S.

aged 25, married 6 months, pupil Royal Horticultural Society and Jardins de
la Ville de Paris. He was also sometime at Lord Lyttelton's. He seemed
pleasant and unassuming but very plain, is to be paid £60 a year and cottage,
coals and garden staff.

April 10. Thirty eight confirmed at Upton church including two of our
maids. Had a cup of tea at the Greens with the Bishop and Mrs Ellicott
afterwards. His address was mostly on the words "May we be Thine for
ever".

April 15. Good Friday. Church in morning. Afterwards I walked and
called on James Hutchinson at Cowley Manor. He is about 70, a martyr to
gout, and very genial. Summers Clarke, the architect, there. They prevailed
on me to stop for dinner and I did not get home till 10 o'clock at night. Mr
Hutchinson well remembers that gentlemanly old man John Dearman and
his two beautiful daughters. He told me he had called last week at Edgeworth
and Mr & Mrs Clayton, who had come to a reconciliation, were there, and
Mrs Somerset and Miss S. with Mrs Hopkinson.

Easter. Took the sacrament at Upton. Afterwards called on the Somersets.

April 18. Squire Bubb to lunch. He told us a good deal about pears which
with other fruit are his speciality. He is grafting Josephine Desmoulins on to
Whitehorn and sends us some to try on a hedge. Apples are grafted on crabs
or kernel apples, i.e. those grown from the seeds of apples. It really has been
summer heat for some days. We have had no rain for more than a month.
    We heard the cuckoo first on Easter Sunday. The leaves are coming on but
grass grows most sparingly.

April 21. Lunch at Jex Blake's, Cheltenham College, where we met Mr &
Mrs Philpott, tutor of Rugby. The athletic sports which we witnessed
during the afternoon were very amusing and somewhat exciting.

April 26. I saw yesterday in the garden a yellow looking bird like the
yellow hammer but much larger and today I find a letter in the Times saying
that a large number of golden orioles have arrived in Cornwall. It was the
size of a thrush of which family it is the most gaudy member. Called at
Edgeworth taking Mrs Somerset with us.
    Mr Stratton's advice with regard to Alderneys. About a week before
calving give them ¼ lb. of flour of sulphur mixed with 3 lbs of treacle and a
little milk. If the cow drops give her ½ pint of brandy in milk or gruel
everyday until she gets up and no medicine. Send Alderneys to the bull at 15
months. They go 9 months and calve at 2 years.

May 6. The Tinlings lunched with us. Canon Tinling thinks very badly of
the Prince of Wales having heard a great deal of him from Lord Granville's

sister-in-law. He has made some investigation into prostitution in Gloucester and found it unusually prevalent. In a population of 30,000 there are 400 known prostitutes. He is in favour of the contagious diseases bill. He meets no sympathy in his Evening Services from the Chapter.

May 13.   I left Paris 8.40 last night and arrived in Turin midnight.

> "Give no quarter to bad habits
>   Or they'll propogate like rabbits."

May 16.   Stayed with the Venables at Stresa.

June 4.   Returned to Bowden.

June 8.   John Jowitt[12] is said to be worth many hundreds of thousands of pounds; the enormous business he is doing giving colour to the opinion. Spent this morning at Brook & Batteys (Leeds). They are preparing a memorial to Court of Chancery showing they will have to pay about 44 or 45 thousands personalty over to the Crown on behalf of Lillie Brook. They have also memorials to the Lords of the Treasury to make a regrant of this sum to the three survivors[13] in thirds. The reason of the amount being so large is that in addition to Clara's share there is the income which has accumulated.

June 13.   Dr Smythe preached on the triune ascription of praise Glory be to the Father and to the Son and to the Holy Ghost, as it was in the beginning is now and ever shall be, world without end Amen, dates from the 5th Century and is universally in use in all the churches of Christendom.

June 15.   Commenced cutting hay.

June 19.   Walked with Col. Somerset to Brockworth church. A very earnest young man preached. The church was filled to overflowing with farmers, labouring men and their families.

June 23.   Dined at the Deanery. 7 p.m. the night before the Cathedral audit. All the canons present. Sir John Seymour, Tinling, Evans, Harvey, Minors, James, Foster, (brother-in-law to Sir J. Seymour) Boevey-Crawley. The Dean is a much more hearty looking individual than I had been given to understand. Mr & Mrs Bathurst took the ends of the table.

June 24.   Sadly worried with servants. Jones and Williams Moulding leave on 30th. They are not replaced and I want a gardener. Bevan is not a

---

[12] His future father-in-law.
[13] Amy Brook, the mad Jimmy, and Clara.

manager with other servants I fear. We seem the only people with no strawberries or cherries, or nice salad or young potatoes or young ducklings. I wish the place was smaller and the birds and snails could not get everything.

June 25.   Sale of Saintbridge at the Bell. Whole extent about 200 acres. 1st lot 109 acres including House. 2nd Farm and mill, 80 acres. 1st lot £12,900 bid, withdrawn at £17,500. 2nd lot bid £6,000, withdrawn at £7,200. Remainder small lots in common fields of which a few sold amounting to about £600.

July 1.   Samuel Bowly's Fete seems for the lower orders the festivity of the year. Every game and amusement that can be thought of. Kiss in the ring, football, bazaars, beautiful speaking by the Rev^d. Mr Hewlett, the chaplain to the forces at Woolwich (he was formerly curate to Lord William Somerset, father of the Colonel).

July 10.   During Eliza's absence I have to call at Archdeacon Prevost, Stinchcombe, and Capt. Graham, Dursley; Mr Grey on road to Frampton. The Cliffords abroad; but leave cards, Eliza's. Hutchinson, Cowley Manor; Rolts of Miserden; and Sherringhams of Standish.

July 11.   At Dickens Sale (Christie & Manson) all wished a momento of the great man and the prices fetched were truly ridiculous. A stuffed raven brought £120. Dolly Varden by Frith costing £20 fetched £1,000 from Agnew. Trifles of Dresden costing 12/6 sold for 18 gns. and a poor small portrait by Maclise 660 gns.

July 13.   Archery at Capt. de Winton's at Wallsworth Hall. About 50 sat down to a very nice collation.

July 14.   Dined at Prinknash. Met Mr Booth of Shorthorn notoriety.

July 15.   The Curtis-Haywards' Ball.

July 16.   War declared against Prussia by France. All grades of opinion in the English newspapers. Concur in calling it an unprovoked aggression. The Times says the greatest national sin which has occurred since Napoleon 1st.

July 18.   Picnic in Cranham Woods. A pleasant day and enjoyed most thoroughly the delightful concert of glees and catches prepared for our delectation.

July 20.   Attended the Royal Agricultural Show and found it very interesting. Mr Booth told me he had that morning been offered £2,000 for his best cow. Arthur Stewart (of Saintbridge) got 1st place for a Berkshire Sow, the

2nd was given to Cirencester College to a descendant of one of Stewart's sows.

Wrote to William Tanner offering him 15/- a week, cottage and garden. He to manage farm and have the assistance of his wife with the poultry and to be accommodating with gardener.

July 22.   To Leeds by mid-day train. An examination of the books rather reassured me. Mr Webb very well. Mr Campbell at Arran in Scotland.

Amy Brook looks well but her uninteresting manner and dull habits made Mr & Mrs Brook nervous and uneasy about her.

Aug 5.   Eliza and Clara returned home, sadly disappointed with the look of our garden which was shameful.

Aug 6.   I never spent a more unhappy birthday for scarcely had I received the felicitations of my sister (Eliza) and Clara than the former found something to bicker about which made me wretched.

Went to Clearwell Court, late Countess of Dunraven. Her second son's eldest son is heir but he is only 13. Clapham has taken the garden to farm it till he comes of age. He sells his best stuff, and finds cucumber strangely in demand.

Aug 11.   Agricultural Society Show at Mr Hakewell's park at Stroud. It was very inferior to the Yorkshire Show and of course to the Royal but the beauty of the park made up for the paucity of exhibition in each department.

Aug 13.   Garden Party at Bowden. Had Militia Band.

Aug 22.   Heavy rain. We have not had a drop this month, and only one thunder-storm last month. It has been universally fine; not one garden party has failed for want of fine weather.

Aug 23.   Hereford Festival. Went to stay with the Bishop and Mrs Atlay until the 27th.

Aug 24.   I took Mrs Ellicott into dinner two days running. Was amused by her opinion of our neighbours. Said she thought I'd have fallen in love with Miss Somerset. Supposed my objection must be to the family. "Mrs Curtis Hayward", she said, "we always call the old sheep. Her daughters are not at home in society, dull, bad manners, and smile because they have nothing to talk about". She likes the Sumners very much but does not admire the eldest — the orifices of her nose are so marked she thinks she could almost see the brain working. Great admiration for Miss Stewart. She likes Mr & Mrs Gambier Parry but thinks they have spent very heavily in London this season, had a house in Portland Place and kept much company though rather mixed.

Morning performance Elijah, which we enjoyed very much.

The Prince and Princess Christian[14] spent day at the Palace, coming at 11. He is addressed Your Royal Highness, she as Ma'am. He is a great light-haired elderly German-looking man with bald retreating forehead, rather good looking but with furtive wandering eyes, and awkwardly moving restless eyebrows, a dissatisfied look and cold calculating expression not often lightened by a smile. The Princess is a very good tempered happy looking girl. Her dress and bonnet and petticoat were all of a delicate pale mauve, ornamented with lace and in her bonnet she had a few white flowers. She has a little likeness to the Queen in days gone by; but the fancied resemblance between the Prince and Prince Consort is ridiculous. The next day the Princess was dressed in cerise silk with many flounces edged with maroon velvet. She is a cheerful bright pleasant creature but speaks in a foreign accent. "Lady Croft", said she "those animals grazing what you call de cow". We shortly went into luncheon which was most exquisitely laid for 30, the roses obtained from Cranstons were matchless. She sat with the Bishop in the middle of the table and looked artless and pleasing. She said she had always admired Mendelssohn songs; her father's great love for them had induced her early appreciation. The Prince does not inspire particular interest. We then formed a procession and went into the cathedral. The Prince gave her a coin both days for the collection which she concealed in her glove. In the afternoon on returning from the cathedral a most exquisite arrangement of tables was made in the garden with one for ice and sweets, another fruit of every delicious colour, another with tea and coffee. Many more came than we had at lunch. Nothing could be prettier than the sight of the lawn and many brilliant dresses, gay flowers and animated conversation.

At 6 p.m. we had dinner. Lord Edward and Lord Arthur Somerset joined us, two nice fresh interesting young men. Lord Edward said he was passionately fond of music and spends three nights a week at the Opera during the season. He counts it a holiday before going in to Parliament. The dinner circle composed of those staying in the house was unusually genial and in the evening Lord and Lady Bateman and I went to the Ball; nothing very particular, it was only a poor affair.

Sept 2. [Staying at Enderby with the Brooks.] Pleasant days shooting partridges. I missed two hares shamefully; plenty of game but bad shots.

Sept 11. All the world are gasping with anxiety to hear the first news of either an armistice or the commencement of a seige of Paris. Most of the respectable inhabitants have fled and there seems as much fear of the rampant reds, escaped convicts, thieves and murderers in Paris as of the invading force of Prussians said to be 500,000 strong.

---

[14] Princess Christian was the daughter of Queen Victoria and married Prince Christian of Schleswig-Holstein in 1866. She was 24 in 1870.

Sept 12.   Received a note from Lord Ducie asking me if I was agreeable to be placed on the Commission of the Peace to send him my name in full. In reply I said never having sought such an appointment I should not hesitate to accept the position so courteously proposed.

Sept 21.   School feast. I sent some cotton thread to be distributed which gave great pleasure, also some toys but these were held over until next week. Eliza and I went to town, and spent the day amongst the carriage builders. Ordered a light Park Phaeton with spring cushion pole and bar, £56 net cash.

Oct 22.   Took a drawing lesson with Mr Kemp[15] in the afternoon.

Dec 17.   Hunted with the Cotteswolds. The meet was at the Kennels at Cheltenham and we rode on the magnificent downs on the summit of Cleeve Hill. We passed by Postlip Hall and had a famous gallop.

Dec 20.   Meet at Fretherne Court. Found in covert behind the House. Soon lost; but picked up another at Withy Bed, Frampton. Ran him with great speed to within 2 miles of Sharpness Point, a fine sight on the sands. A most enjoyable day, 9 hours in the saddle, about 40 miles.

Dec 21.   Conversazione at Cirencester — Constable's — very pleasant evening. Prof. Church lectured on the colour and copper obtained from the Touraco's wing, another gentleman on deep sea dredgings especially new sponges. The exhibition of jewellery of the 17th century was much admired. Constable astonishes with the boldness of his ideas and general liberality of sentiment.

Dec 27.   Clara's Christmas Tree at Upton School, with Moody Bell's Magic Lantern; latter very poor, but the evening was a delightful one. All our neighbours assisted and the tree was a genuine success. 148 children bringing with extra ones the presents up to about 200.

Dec 30.   Party charades at the Hyetts at Painswick. Francis Hyett, Mr Dickinson, Miss Wolley, Mr Walace and Miss Hyett acted *Slasher and Crasher*, a very amusing play; but the finest fun was in an exhibition of automation wax works, the Marquis of Lorne and Princess Louise kissing hands especially good, and Miss Wolley's singing a Chinese song accompanying herself on a banjo infinitely amusing.

All the week the pond has been frozen and we have had large parties of skaters. As many as a dozen came in to lunch one day including the Sumners. On Wednesday we sat down 14 to dinner, Miss Somerset and Georgie and the Ackers etc, nothing could go off better.

---

[15] John Kemp, master at the Gloucester Art School.

1871

Jan 4. The Gambier Parrys' ball, a mixture of juveniles and adults. The dancing was most spirited and I danced with a very pretty girl a Miss Noel, also with two Misses Guise and Carrie Somerset. Amy was very giddy during the Lancers but I attribute it more to the heat of the room than to anything else. She enjoyed the party and seemed quite well afterwards. On our way home she confessed her penchant for the Rev. Mr Berry whom she met in Northampton.

Jan 14. Dined at Canon Tinling's. The Bishop expects a severe attack on the church and especially cathedrals next session. He says the former will have more defenders than the latter. The Bishop has withdrawn from visiting St. Lucy's home because he cannot approve the religious ceremonies which now take place there. The Bishop told me he had determined to speak plainly to the Ritualists; they were getting most overbearing.

Jan 29. Attended service at St. Paul's Cathedral. The preacher said St. Paul's is the metropolitan church of the greatest city in the world and the most prominent representation of the English Church. He pleaded earnestly for its completion according to the designs of its architect Sir Christopher Wren.

Jan 31. Meeting of the committee of the Gloucester and Bristol Diocesan Association to which I was invited but being in London I could not attend. I learn that they appointed me Vice President of the Society.

Feb 21. Meet at Claypits, 2 miles beyond Whitminster Inn. We went on to Fretherne and tried the coverts. One fox took us around by near Frampton, round the Park and back to its home. The same or another ran down to Arlingham. We had there a very pretty view of Newnham on the opposite bank of the Severn. We ended again at Fretherne without a kill. I lunched at Hardwicke. My horse carried me nobly.

Feb 24. Lunched with the Doringtons at Lypiatt Park. Mrs Stoughton (Owlpen House), Mrs Bengough (The Ridge) and her sister Miss Cornwall daughters of Mr Cornwall of Ashcroft House, Rector of two or more livings. The house is a most interesting old English structure, kept up with marvellous taste. Mrs Dorington (nee Speke) has a passion for flowers and china and her exposition of each does her credit. The garden is very pretty and in splendid order. In the conservatory they had in bloom lilacs, Deutsias, amaryllis, hyacinths, cyclamen, tulips, primulas, cinerarias, camellias, and salanums. It made me ashamed of my own conservatory where I have a large stock of hyacinths costing much and little else.

Feb 28. The children of Sir Alexander Dixie came to luncheon driving themselves in a wagonette and four in hand, a most lovely team of little ponies. The weather was bad and we played pool most of the morning.

March 2.   The entry of the French capital by Germans is the news of the day and the dramatic sitting of the national Assembly at Bordeaux where by a majority of near 3 to 1 they confirmed this iniquitous treaty and deposed the Bonaparte family for ever. These and other striking scenes fill one's mind to the exclusion of all ordinary topics.

March 17.   We had a tremendous frost last night; fortunately my apricots which are all in bloom are well protected.

March 28.   I hear that the Hopkinsons have sold Edgeworth to a Kentish gentleman for £40,000.

March 30.   I went by 10.10 train to Charfield station and from there took a dog-cart and drove through a lovely country. The road bordered Tortworth (Earl Ducie's beautiful seat) and afterwards Eastwood the residence of Sir George Jenkinson. Then on to Thornbury and Olveston where I inspected two vacant houses (for his Eveleigh cousins). The village is very nice and joins another equally pleasant called Tockington. They seem well looked after by the clergyman and his curate.

April 17.   To Cirencester. Dined at Earl Bathurst's at Oakley Park. Sir Michael and Lady Hicks Beach, Lady Mary Arkwright, Miss Owen, Col. Chesney, Sir Cecil Beadon, Capt. & Mrs Bates, Miss Julia Ponsonby and Miss Gifford daughter of Lord Gifford and niece to Lord Fitzhardinge. We had an exquisitely served dinner of which the entrees were most refined, a profusion of all kinds of new vegetables, potatoes, beans, asparagus. I took in Miss Owen but sat next to Miss Ponsonby at end of the table opposite to Sir Michael Hicks Beach who I found remarkably agreeable. Most of the party amused themselves with cards and others with books from the library especially Atkyns Gloucestershire 1712. Small quantity of nice old china, and very pretty Gobelin tapestry of scene in Don Quixote. The Duke of Rutland has the remainder of the series, and the late brother of Lord Bathurst offered this one to him, but he refused for which the Earl is very thankful.

April 19.   London. City in morning. Horticultural Show in the afternoon very charming. The azalias, roses and Veitch's Stove plants especially the anthuricum Scherzerium with its gorgeous scarlet bloom and spiked centre tongue of rather lighter shade. Evening at Burlington club conversazione. We met Gambier Parry, Millais, Tom Taylor etc. Collection of fayence Urbino ware, Wedgewood, bronzes, Marquis of Westminster's collection of paintings including Turner's sketch and Constable's greatest picture.

April 20.   Called at 90 Great Tower Street and saw S.B. Miller[16] sitting representing A.H. Lushington & Co. The offices are clean and respectable, and he looks all that one could desire. I wished him success and felt rewarded for my labour and expenses on his behalf by seeing him so comfortable. I only hope he will make the business pay.

April 22.   I have had a pleasant week and much enjoyed my visit to Veitch's at Chelsea, the finest horticulturist in England, also Bakers pheasantry where I purchased a pair of pea fowl, Brent and Barnicle geese, Carolina Ducks and call ducks.

April 24.   Heard the nightingale singing gloriously at Bowden.
   Sold Eliza's bay horse to Rev. Jex Blake for £50. He told us a capital story about Oberammergau Passion play. In a fearful thunder-storm Judas Iscariot alarmed knelt down and said 'Oh Lord God forgive me I am not Judas Iscariot but Simon Flick the carpenter'.

April 28.   The nightingales are magnificent here. They are singing incessantly.

April 29.   Meeting of the Stewards of the Festival. It was agreed to hold it on 4 Sept. and the rehearsal to take place on that day. A committee consisting of Gambier Parry, Sir M. Hicks Beach and Price were appointed to confer with Dr. Wesley[17] as to arranging with singers. They were tied down to £1,000 for the principals.

May 7.   Mr Green preached from text "Murder, drunkenness". The apostle joined these two together. The first was the effect of the second. Drunkenness caused nearly half the crime in the country. He alluded in fearful terms to the sin of Benjamin Rodway and warned him he would, if he continued his present course, be the murderer of his mother. The sin was increasing in our village, and all classes should do their duty and endeavour to abate it as he had done by appearing in court against Bolton's public house.
   Mallows opened the pea-fowls' door and the hen ran away and got into a tree and later her feathers were found indicating her death by violence from attack of fox or dog.

May 9.   Gave Mallows notice. The last two days have been frightfully hot, glass at 73°F. and I asked why he did not turn the calf out — a month old. This morning with a bitterly cold wind without sun I found he had turned it out for the first time.

[16] His cousin.
[17] S.S. Wesley, organist of Gloucester Cathedral 1865–1876.

May 14. The nightingales have sung incessantly night and day for the last few weeks.

May 15. Went to call on Mr Hunt staying at Prinknash.

May 16. Mr Hunt lunched with me. He said the small wistaria by the fig at the bottom of the yard he brought home with the large one attached to the house, and they were put in in 1841. The one has never settled or increased but the other has met with a congenial home.

May 21. 14 Pall Mall. Saw the International Exhibition. In afternoon drove to Chiselhurst to see Mrs Janson. She has a small house with 3 acre garden and 5 acres of wood for £310 p.a. From part of her garden we saw the Imperial party in the grounds of Camden House where they are leading a very retired life. The Empress[18] seems sad and weeps half her time.

May 22. Lunched with the Ellicotts, 65 Portland Place. Had a dinner party for seven at the Pall Mall and the bill came to £5 and the dinner was not *à merveille*.

May 27. Bowden. Canon & Mrs Venables and Maud and Winifred came for a week. Canon V. says Gladstone said to him the Queen had a strong will, more she is obstinate. He denies that the Gladstones are Roman Catholic. The Venables girls are most charming specially the eldest.

May 28. Mr Green had rather a scene in church. Two infants with large parties came forward for baptisms. One he apparently rejected and its friends sat down for a few minutes. Then in a most noticeable way during the baptismal prayers, all got up and walked out. With the other, when Mr Green got to the point of baptism he discovered the water had all run out. Mr Green, too impatient to wait while the old clerk Freeman went to the drawer well, continued with the usual evening service, and after a most interesting sermon from Canon Venables, I suppose completed the baptism.

I accompanied Canon Venables to Hereford. We found the Bishop away. Mrs Atlay entertained us with her usual hospitality.

June 3. The Duke of Beaufort was prevented by gout from laying the foundation stone of the new Art Museum in Gloucester. The High Sheriff old Mr. Playne and two Marlings did the whole thing and made an amusing hash of it. Luncheon with Mayor at Tolsey. Walter Jowitt tomorrow concludes a very pleasant visit. He made himself agreeable to the young Venables and delighted Clara by his appreciation of our new Mastiff puppy bitch. I have not attended the Sacrament for two Sundays, feeling too *distrait*.

---

[18] Empress Eugénie.

June 11.   Attended service at the Cathedral. In the afternoon took a long stroll to Painswick Beacon.

June 12.   Edward Parry, Farm bailiff came to me at 20/- a week with house and garden.

June 18.   Miss Somerset is engaged to Mr. Hayward.[19]

June 19.   I dined at Sir John Seymour's. Some ladies came in afterwards, one a Rossetti-like looking creature, very fond of art.

June 22.   Arrived at Enderby. On my arrival I find that Amy[20] has this morning accepted Capt. Cecil Drummond, nephew of the Duke of Rutland. He has five brothers and two sisters, the latter are married to Lord Scarbrough and Baillie Cochrane. Capt. D. is 32 years and in the Rifle Brigade. He has served in Malta, Canada, and other points. His mother, who is a widow, is living in Hampshire and Amy thinks the eldest son is insane. His present and expected fortune consists of a sum of £10,000. The affair has been atrociously managed. They met for a week at Belvoir. Afterwards Amy mentioned the matter to Mr Power who went of his own accord to the Rev. Fred Norman, professedly to preach for him, but really to find out. The Normans confessed to him that their nephew wished to marry Miss Brook, that he was an estimable young man and a good son. After this Capt. D. called at Enderby. Next Mr Brook met Mr Norman at Peterborough and they talked the matter over having laid bare to Mr Norman all the weak points of the family. Mr & Mrs Brook do not profess to like it, and the latter is oppressed with apprehensions.

June 28.   Amy is very happy in her prospects. Capt. Drummond has the hearty congratulations of all his relatives.

July 7.   Came up to town and spent the day inspecting Utrecht velvets and other productions for covering chairs and eventually chose a stupid satin which Marsh and Mr Walters, the maker, pronounced not much more expensive and far more durable than the blue-dyed velvet which was the only kind that I fancied.

July 8.   Crossed to Paris. The train runs through all night. We crossed one bridge constructed of wood. It was erected by the Prussians, the original stone structure having been blown up by the French.

July 9.   Went to Enghien, beautiful lake, good restaurant, whitebait irreproachable. Visited one of the German batteries. I was making a note in my

[19] Rev. Henry Basil Hayward afterwards Rector of Winstone, near Cirencester.
[20] Dearman's sister-in-law.

red book, and an old woman cried out *'Voila un espion'*. We were struck by
the awful and complete downfall of all the good buildings in St. Cloud, and
the frightful destruction in Paris by cannon, chassepot and petroleum.

July 31.   Dined at John Jowitt's (Leeds). They all seem very well.

August 3.   Opening of the Convalescent Home at Meltham Mills. Nearly
everybody came from Huddersfield, the day being kept as a holiday, the
rain fortunately kept off and the proceedings were very interesting. The
festival in the Mill dining rooms where I was an invited guest were most
hearty. The building and land are estimated at about £25,000 but Mr Brook
stated he would not stick at even this, and was prepared to increase the
endowment. Altogether the gift amounts to about £40,000. Mr Freeman
[solicitor] succeeded yesterday in obtaining the Vice Chancellor's
permission for Amy's wedding in October and in arranging the settlements.

August 5.   Garden party at Hardwicke Court. Drove my new pair of cobs
in Eliza's phaeton. They were extremely admired. Received letter from the
Clerk of the Peace that I was put on the Commission.

August 11.   Croquet party. The numerous pug pups were brought out for
the guests to see. One of them on seeing the footman bringing four in his
arms related how at Lady Ramsden's a servant was doing the same and said,
"'ere your ladyship is the pugs but dang 'em they won't sit on the waiter".
He also told of a clergyman who was aroused in the middle of the night by
his wife who said, "John, dear, I am sure there is a robber under the bed, I
heard him moving. Do get up and see". John replied, "Oh its only the
Newfoundland dog. I just put my hand out and he licked it". Next morning
all the jewellery and many other effects had disappeared.

August 14.   We had a fearful storm while in church last night. It was soon
dark and we had not half a dozen candles. The sermon by Mr Green was
"My flesh is meat indeed and my blood is drink indeed". He was calm and
collected. A telegraphic message arrived for Georgie Somerset announcing
sudden illness of Count d'Epineul[21] whose hand she had refused three days
ago. The scene in the vestry was most exciting, disjointed conversation
amidst a blaze of lightning, roar of thunder and torrents of rain. None could
leave the church but all crowded into groups. Carrie tore up the two
telegrams in her excitement after offering to take Georgie to London, 12.40
train. She said to me "He is the best of fellows, I fear I may prove to be his
murderer."

Aug 18.   The nephews [Sophy's boys] left for Weston. They have enjoyed themselves immensely here and done no mischief beyond killing a pig

---

[21] Miss Georgiana Somerset married Count d'Epineul in 1872.

by running it down during the intense heat.

August 20.   I walked to Gloucester to attend the re-opening of the Choir of the Cathedral and afterward luncheoned with the Dean, and met Sir John Seymour, Lysons and his two sons and their wives, a Mr Palmer and his daughter, the Rev and Mrs Bathurst and Mr James. Afternoon service in the Cathedral. I then had a cup of tea with Mrs Ellicott. The Bishop was elaborating a scheme he has had for years for making the Festival [Three Choirs] a religious service, confining it to the choir, and excluding Opera singers, etc. After a walk with Mrs Ellicott, I attended evening service at St. Mary de Crypt where Mr Spence preached a most serious and solemn sermon from the text, "Why stand ye here all the day idle". I then went home with them to supper. Miss Ellicott and Mr James were also with us. I walked home by 10 p.m. after a most interesting and satisfactory day.

August 26.   Attended the Quarter Sessions to take the oath and qualify to act as a Magistrate for the County of Gloucester. Sir Archibald Little sworn at the same time.

Carrie Somerset dined and we discussed Mr Hayward's appointment to the living at Winstone, value including 80 acres of glebe and house, £300 a year, given to him by John Rolt. Parish and church awfully neglected.

August 29.   Attended the Gloucestershire Cattle Show held in the Pittville Gardens at Cheltenham. In itself it was a poor show; but the spirit of the people had provided numerous extraneous attractions, a poultry and flower show, and fine arts gallery, and all the fair part of the population attended to grace the scene, nothing could be more charming, and I was so pleased I decided to send a party next day consisting of Parry, Morris & Hill and their wives, Thomas, Ann, Harris, Jane, Ellen and Wood and the painter who could not get on when he heard of the chance of an outing. I gave them 3/- a piece to spend.

Sept. 2.   Police Court. A man called Norman committed for a week for begging bread. He looked a professional beggar.

Sept. 4.   Guests for the Gloucester Festival. The Newloves, the Brooks, Amy and Capt Drummond, Miss Starkey and Edward [Dearman's brother].

Sept 5.   Te Deum. Handel Jeptha. We filled up the end of the nave with schools and choirs as the tickets went off more slowly for this day than for others. There was a perceptible want of spirit in this morning's performance, but was atoned for by the rich treat of the evening, Haydn's Creation, Handel's Israel in Egypt.

Sept 6.   Elijah. This was the gem of the Festival, a most glorious performance, very well attended. We did not go to the concert in the Shire Hall this evening but Georgie Somerset dined with us.

Sept 7.   Everyone agrees that the Passion music was an immense success. After doing my duty as a steward I stole out and had a chat at the Harveys.

Sept 8.   Messiah. Not equal to the Elijah in execution. Very full. Collection today £180. County Ball. Fortt prepared for 300 and only 140 came by which he loses heavily.

Mr Brook's estimate of his property — real estate £200,000, Mills £100,000. Shares £60,000. Other property £40,000, making a total of £400,000.

I gave Amy and the Captain a good talk on extravagance and its effect. They go abroad for 5 months and afterwards propose settling in England with a regular establishment, housekeeper and cook, 2 housemaids, 2 men, lady's maid. Amy has induced her uncle to promise her a piece of jewellery valued at £900. I pointed out the insanity of such folly.

Sept. 12.   Garden party at the Dickinsons 4–8. Then supper at 7.30, but many had left. The party must have numbered 150 and the place looked very pretty. The sun shone and Croquet and bat and ball were played with the greatest spirit.

Sept 13.   Dined at Dr Ancrum's to meet Count d'Epineul a marvellous fellow reminding one strongly of the Count of Monte Christo, in spite of his recent illness, which had caused him to faint twice today, he was the life of the party and amongst plenty of play and wonderful tricks he caused umbrellas and sticks to stand both perpendicularly and obliquely on the carpet without touching. I never was more surprised in my life.

Sept 16.   I took the Count, Mrs Somerset and Georgie to Birdlip, Lady Cromies. He was very very amusing but had a very serious fit after arriving at the Lodge.

Sept 17.   The Count appeared at church but in the night had a terrible fit during which he was unconscious for two hours. Georgie Somerset gave me a most interesting account of the Count's grandfather who had a post at the French Court with Louis XVI at the outbreak of the revolution. He was aged 24, and offered to get the Count d'Artois out of Paris and seek help from the King of Prussia They both passed as actors a role in which they were especially fitted from acting in the court plays at the Trianon. At Lyons they had to give a play before the police. At a later period Count d'Epineul returned to Paris and was seized by *Les Sans Culottes* and was only saved by one of them who had been his gardener and recognized him. The next day this honest fellow was guillotined for his kindness. The Count escaped and died in 1836 in London.

Sept 19.   In the afternoon I took train to Longhope station to see the Longhope estate belonging to Major Probyn consisting of 687 acres of hilly undulating land intersected by railroad and Gloucester Ross road. In the northerly direction it reaches almost to May Hill which I ascended and thus gained an incomparable view of the country. Price said by Knowles to be £25,000.

Sept 20.   I drove Miss Van and Clara to Cheltenham. Saw in Martin's window an exquisite reliquary of Italian workmanship based on a portion of the arm bone of a saint, and given by Catherine of Braganza to the Comptons of Hartpury from whom it has descended to Mrs Gordon Canning.

Oct 1.   Mr Hayward calling here, said the Count d'Epineul is a regular adventurer. His fits are all sham or hysteria, his fortune is nil, and he is in debt and has duns after him in all directions. He thinks Georgie is bewitched, but not much in love.

Oct 4.   The Bishop of Hereford and Mrs Atlay came to us for three nights. Dinner party and the Bishop of Gloucester and Mrs Ellicott, Mr & Mrs Dickinson and Miss Wemyss, Dr and Mrs Ancrum, Miss Somerset, Capt. & Mrs de Winton, Mr & Mrs Sumner, Mr & Mrs Bathurst, Canon Lysons.[22] We had a lack of flowers but put two begonias and a Japanese grass plant in their stead. We also had strawberries being part of a second crop, we took out of the beds a few days ago and stuck in the hot house.

Oct 5.   Our party went to see the Cathedral, and Mr Gambier Parry's church.

Oct 7.   Accompanied the Atlays to Worcester on their way home via that town. I went on to Enderby (to stay with the Brooks) where I found the Bishop of Ripon. A number of villagers came to present a little silver and china to Amy. She seemed very much pleased.

Oct 9   The Bishop of Ripon preached at Trinity church Leicester. He was very eloquent. Amy had admitted that she has for years been jealous of Lillie's memory and doubted the affection of her uncle and aunt. I think the separation caused by marriage is the best cure and I hope time will work wonders. Came up to town and experienced the immense difficulty of finding jewellery to one's mind. Hancocks, Attenborough, Emanuels, Pyke, the latter supplied Amy's present in the end. Emanuel showed me the Empress's jewels which I understood he had purchased and they are all on sale. Their intense beauty and brilliancy exceeded all else. Returned home by night, and thankfully I trust found all well.

---

[22] Canon Samuel Lysons, 1806–1877. Rector of Hempstead and Canon of Gloucester.

Oct 17. Quarter Sessions. In afternoon I walked with Mr Dickinson to Lunatic Asylum, Barnwood. This is an extensive private establishment with a committee; all pay but there are three grades.

Oct 18. Curtis-Hayward sat in the Crown Court. . . . Mr Dickinson in the other hearing criminal cases. Many pleaded guilty, there was nothing of especial interest. Last night 100 magistrates dined at the Judges Lodgings, tonight about 20.

Oct 19. I left the Sessions for a short time in the middle of the day to lunch at home and entertain the parents of Bishop Ellicott. The trial of members of the firm which swindled shopkeepers at Cheltenham attracted the most attention. Mr Griffiths the Gloucestershire Buz fuz bullied the witnesses almost into fits, frightening them out of their ideas. Some of the barristers were very poor.

Oct 24. Night train to town and found the Brooks at Thomas's Hotel, Berkeley Square, nice, quiet, dull and immensely expensive. We went about shopping. Amy was very calm and collected and looks well. Mrs Brook looks on the whole affair from a gloomy point of view and thinks Capt. Drummond is gay and fond of women. She is wanting facts.

Oct 25. Last thing at night I had a painful scene with Amy and Mrs Brook. Their long estrangement seemed to have come to a point which needed ventilating. All ended more happily than at one time seemed possible.

Oct 26. Amy's wedding at St. James's Piccadilly. Breakfast Thomas's Hotel. Bridesmaids Clara and Miss Drummond, etc. The whole went off extremely well. My partner at breakfast Lady Scarbrough was most lively and agreeable. I never had one I could converse with more freely. All took their departure but myself. The little bill including the breakfast which cost 1 guinea a head and wine £35, came to £246 odd and Mr B paid £8 to the servants. The landlady wished to induce Mr B. to give her 5/- a head more. They would have done it better at Claridges, and it would have cost no more money.

The Morning Post describes the "wedding of Capt. Cecil George Assheton Drummond of the Rifle Brigade (the Prince Consort's Own) the youngest son of Lady Elizabeth Drummond and the late Mr Andrew Drummond of Cadlands, Hampshire and nephew of his Grace the Duke of Rutland with Charlotte Amelia Brook, niece of Mr Charles Brook of Enderby Hall, Leicestershire and of Meltham Mills, the munificent philanthropist, so universally beloved in his own neighbourhood and a liberal contributor to local charities, etc, etc. The Band of the Rifle Brigade played "Good-bye Sweetheart" as the happy couple left the reception. The presents included a diamond and turquoise brooch, ear-rings and ring from Mr J.D. Birchall."

In Nov. Dearman was staying with the Brooks for shooting and on Sunday November 12 he called on the Jowitts at Harehills.

Nov 20.   Back at Bowden. Lord Bathurst, Lord Alfred Harvey, the Bishop of Bath and Wells, Frederick Peel, Miss Ponsonby and Miss Harvey and Mrs Ellicott lunched with us, and after lunch all (except Mrs Ellicott and Lady Alfred) walked to Gloucester under the guidance of Miss Somerset and myself. Lord Bathurst was most nimble in getting over the fences and assured us at dinner it was 5 miles.

Nov 21.   Meet at Frocester; must be 14 miles from here. I left home at 9.10, and trotted briskly most of the way, arriving at 11.10. We had a number of nice bursts. My horse went nobly.

Nov 27.   Birmingham Show. Bought a sow in breeding class from Joseph Smith, Henley-in-Arden, 5 months 3 weeks old farrowed 1st June 1871. The pen of 5 obtained 1st prize for pen of breeding Berkshires and 1st prize as best pen of pigs in the Show.

Nov 28.   Had bad headache for 3 days. Consulted Acton [in London] who recommends abstaining from tea and coffee, living simply and taking plenty of exercise.

Dec 4.   Went to the meeting of the S.P.G. at the Bell Hotel. Sir M. Hicks Beach in the chair. The Bishop of Rupert's Land gave an account of that vast territory 6 times the extent of England. The Indians, who are hunters and mostly dependent on the Hudson's Bay Co. seem peculiarly amenable to Christianity, and life is as safe as in England. The missionaries are great favourites.
     After the meeting Mr Green, having just spoken to Archdeacon Prevost took me aside and with some deprecatory remarks and with much diffidence said that he had heard an excellent account from the Archdeacon of Mr Rawlings; but that the latter could not give up £150 p.a. for £100 though he wished to come here [as curate]. Would I supplement Mr Ackers's gift? I said I had already thought of offering to do so and had written to make some enquiry about Mr R. "Ah" he said "you will hear he is a High Churchman". "Well I think I must refuse assistance if that is the case" I replied. Wednesday morning I received a note declining all assistance.

Dec 22.   Feast at the school. Christmas Tree was covered with salt by Miss Van to represent snow but it sadly spoiled the presents underneath.

Dec 25.   Eliza, Clara and I dined alone. The weather was wet and nasty. Eliza felt much for poor Sophy and William who have lost their little girl from pneumonia and who seem sadly distressed.
     Improvements at Bowden during the winter were an additional grape

house, backed by a raising house with heating water apparatus to supply both old and new house.

The pond showing signs of giving way and leaking heavily in the low or southern side, I set about and had the water let off and the whole fresh puddled to make it more secure, and, to prevent injury from the effects of the swans dashing about, I had it all coated in the south side with a facing of stone.

Dec 31.   Walked home with Col. & Mrs Somerset. They told me Georgie was defiant, praised her as being an angel; but lamented she was going to throw herself away on an adventurer. From Philadelphia they have received news that he is not known as a Count, but as a business man. When he left he was in debt, and writs and warrants have been issued against him during the last month. He is not known in society in England. He assumed the title finding that a card with 'Count' paid amongst the English. Col. Somerset does not think he has any right to the title. Georgie says when they thought he was rich and had a title they urged her to marry him. "I agreed with reluctance. When I find he is poor I stick to him. If I do find he is worthless it will be my mission in life to reform him". So the melancholy sacrifice is to be consumated on Thursday, because no-one can come forward and prevent a steady young lady from throwing herself on a regular scape grace.

1872

Jan 13. Dined at the Palace. The Bishop had a bad cold but was in great force in some ghost stories. One of his rectors was so affected by the repeated appearance of a lady dressed in blue that he begged to resign his living. His Lordship said to him "I am not prepared to doubt that there may be troubled spirits who cannot rest and force themselves on the presence of the living. Have you courage, yes, then I counsel you to meet and address her with words of sympathy and kindness and offer to pray for her." While speaking the thought came into his mind — sympathy is what she wants. "She will not come again" he said. The fact has confirmed the prediction.

Jan 25. Saw George Whitcomb touching Buckholt wood. The agent living at Buckholt tried to make out the worst and reckoned all they had to sell was timber and 3½ acres freehold with cottage. Ecclesiastical Commissioners are Lords of the Manor. He thinks Upton, Brockworth, Brimscombe, Birdlip and Witcombe all have rights of commonage. Whitcomb says these rights have become abrogated by reason of want of usage. There seem only the Freeholders of Cranham, whose rights seem more serious than before. They all pasture cattle, pigs etc. and one dairy man has little other land. The outcry against enclosure would be most serious.

Jan 29. Lunched with the Dean and gave him £100 towards the restoration of the Cathedral. He was very amusing about Mrs Ellicott and said she kissed his mastiff dog more heartily than he guessed she ever kissed the Bishop.

The Doctor says Clara's is almost the mildest attack of measles he has ever seen, and he thinks her about the finest girl he remembers to have met with of her age. She is in capital spirits, and is to go into the morning room tomorrow.

The immense demand for coal in the midlands is raising the price enormously. Boats and waggons are waiting at Cannock Chase where I hear they are raising 8000 tons a week. Coal is said to be 50% dearer than this time last year.

Feb 2. Canon Venables spent an hour with me in Lincoln Cathedral. . . . The Canon does not agree with me in my wish to remove the organ in Gloucester Cathedral. He was heartily amused at the story I told him of Dean Law tossing a letter of Gambier Parry's over the table to (Sir Gilbert) Scott to read, it being full of the most virulent abuse of the latter. They afterwards met at dinner at the Deanery; but they are the reverse of happy in feeling towards one another to this day.

Feb 5. Oxley dined with me at the Junior Carlton. He professed deep and old seated attachment and affection for me and then made a most intemporate attack on me and my proceedings with Carrie Somerset. He also said he considered the Brooks were evangelical snobs; an interview too disagreeable to be described further.

Feb 6.   Rose Tinling's marriage to Mr Henry Sedding in the Cathedral.

Feb 8.   Dined at Major Allen's, Parkfield Lawn, Cheltenham at 7.30. We found it very dull and do not feel encouraged about Cheltenham dinner parties.

Feb 11.   The Cranham Woods are the last possession of a Land Company in liquidation. They had been induced to purchase the property some 6 or 7 years ago for £5,600 on the representation that on payment of certain claims they would have a freehold estate suitable for building purposes. They had found endless difficulties. I wrote and accepted the contract of sale of Cranham Woods 255 acres at £2,750. I left the contract in the hands of George Whitcomb. Spent the morning in walking over the property, very pretty, with an immense variety of view and graceful undulation of surface. It is covered with growing timber which Bruton Knowles value at £2,300. George Whitcomb thinks the Ecclesiastical Commissioners might be induced to part with any rights they may possess on the mines and minerals as Lords of the Manor.

Feb 13.   Mr Hyett says Emeris (to be new vicar at Upton) is an invaluable man, good at business, an admirable parish priest, a scholar, and a gentleman. He was a pupil of Dr Arnold and admires his master's views.

March 30.   Came to Enderby with Eliza and Clara. The Drummonds here. Amy's fortune seems to have totted up to about £90,000. They are going in for a cook-housekeeper, butler, footman, carriage and horses and ladies' maid.

April 5.   Grand Jury at Shire Hall. Dined with the judges. Present: Mr Byles, Sir James Campbell, Hon. Mr Rice, Curtis Hayward, Hon. Mr Talbot, Mr Barnard, Gambier Parry, Dorington,[23] Granville Baker, Barwick Baker,[24] Playne, Mr Marling, Mr Monk, M.P., Major Hartley, Mr Craven.

April 8.   The Drummonds came to stay.

April 9.   Drove Drummond to Highnam. Inspected church and pinetum. Dinner at Prinknash. I took Miss Green in who was in a dashing and amusing state. Amy was a little faint and retired during dinner. I see she is most delicate; but in her condition perhaps one should not be uneasy. We

---

[23] Sir John Dorington of Lypiatt Park, 1832–1911. M.P. for Stroud 1874.
[24] Thomas Barwick Lloyd Baker of Hardwicke, 1807-1886. Social reformer. Granville was his son.

Thomas Barwick Lloyd Baker,
social reformer

Sir John Dorington, M.P. for
Stroud

Thomas Gambier Parry, artist
and philanthropist

Benjamin St John Ackers, M.P.
for West Gloucestershire

are enjoying their visit exceedingly. Henry Jowitt [also staying] is a merry and amusing companion. He is much struck by the bad and careless farming in these parts.

April 14.   Edward [Dearman's architect brother] came to us. He took the measurements of Buckholt manor, Warley's cottage and our stables, all with a view to alteration more or less important.

    Amy's servants are on board wages, the higher ones 16/-, the lower 12/- a week. Her housekeeper has £45 and butler £55.

April 18.   To Ozleworth to visit the Rolts. Charfield station from which it is distant 5 miles on the hills. Mrs & Miss Brown, of Stout's Hill dined in the evening. She is sister to Barwick Baker. The parson Charles Clutterbuck came in for a pipe, a game of whist, and a glass of grog which seem to have no small attractions for this plain-looking but most convivial parson.

April 19.   We took a drive round by Wotton-under-Edge to Stinchcombe which has one of the prettiest views in England, by Dursley and seeing Miss Cornwall, [daughter of the Rev. Alan Gardner Cornwall,[25] rector of Beverstone and Bagpath] up the high hill out of Dursley, and so back to Ozleworth.

April 21.   After 10 days fine sunny but still cold weather with frosts at night it snowed all day which may prove a great misfortune, as Messenger has taken the boiler out of the hothouse and is putting in a new one. I fear we shall have our vines injured. They are in bud but not fully out.

    Had a long talk with Tuffley and agreed to pay him 10/- a week to look after Cranham Woods and to let him garden a croft just for this season for £5. Tuffley is strongly opposed to any enclosure.

April 22.   Brought before us on the Bench, Henry Head and Edwin Brown on a charge of riotous and violent conduct in church at Upton St. Leonards last Sunday. The evidence showed that these two came into the church during service having dogs under their coats. They laughed, knelt down while we were standing and used bad language to the churchwarden. We gave them one month each in prison.

April 24.   John and Deborah Jowitt dined with me in Leeds. They both look exceedingly well and cheerful.

    To explain the following entry for April 27, a paragraph is here quoted from Clara Sinclair's life of her father. "His (Dearman's) place of business was in

---

[25] Rector of Newington-Bagpath, 1827-1871, Chaplain in Ordinary to the Queen. His Recollections printed at the "New" Office, George Street, Stroud, 1872. Restored Bagpath church, now in ruins.

Wellington Street, Leeds. He had several partners of whom the first was Mr Webb, and a little later Mr Archibald Campbell joined the business. His subsequent partners were Mr Warburg, Mr Oswald Birchall,[26] Mr Kafka and Mr Cheetham. His confidential clerk was Mr Fearnside. His prosperous business career began in 1853 and terminated to a certain extent when he moved to Gloucestershire in 1869, but not actually till he sold his share in the concern in 1891. His success was owing, not so much to his knowledge of practical manufacturing, for of that he had little, but firstly to his judgement and skill as a merchant or buyer and seller of goods — and here his artistic temperament came in with effect, for he was fertile in giving ideas to manufacturers, especially in the combination of colours — and to his charming persuasive and diplomatic ways which gained him an always increasing clientele; and not least to his hard work, his energy and perseverance, to his high sense of honour and to the confidence he inspired."

April 27. Mr Webb and Campbell have had a tiff, three weeks ago. Fearnside attributes it to the growing friendship with Stenson Spencer and forebodes evil, without so far as I can see legitimate grounds.

April 29. I was glad this morning to find that Mr Webb had called on Mr Campbell and they had a most agreeable conversation, the result of which was to bring about a better understanding than they had ever had before. I hope my anxieties on this score are now at an end.

May 2. Uncle Harris has succeeded in purchasing Oxton Hall, Tadcaster for £28,000. 167 acres. It belonged to Mr Ramsden. The house is most commodious and handsome. The glass and the gardens are very nice. Timber worth £1,000.

May 7. George Whitcomb dined with me after walking over Cranham Woods. He had no idea previously how lovely they are.

May 10. Dined with Amy to accompany them to the Opera to hear Mlle. Albani. In the evening Amy and Drummond went to a ball at the Marchioness of Bristol's. Amy has cold in her head and looks very delicate. She has been this week to so many balls I fear she must break down; but he does not see it. She comes home early, he stays on. He says people write the most abject notes praying for invitations to any ball or party of notoriety.

May 11. I spent more of yesterday at the sale at Christies of articles *de vertue*, arms, bronzes etc. saved from the communist fire at the Palais Royal. I bought three swords for 58/-. Two bronze cinque cento figures, size of life, fetched £1,760 and £1,010.

---

[26] Oswald was one of the sons of Edwin Birchall, and therefore Dearman's cousin once removed.

May 15.   Went to the Horticultural Show at South Kensington, not much to boast of, and very inferior to the Crystal Palace show. It keeps as cold as winter. Most ladies have not cast their seals. Dined at 77 Queen's Gate; the Duke of Rutland, Lady Elizabeth Drummond etc. After dinner Mrs Tinling and two daughters. Delightful evening. The Duke related a long talk he had had with John Bright. Yesterday I had a box at Covent Garden for *La Favorita*. The spectacle is very pretty and Donizetti's music, never dull. At Christie's I bought two splendid *cloisonné* enamel tableaux for 115 guineas.

May 18.   Invited my partners to stay at Bowden. T.P. Webb, A. Campbell, J.C. Cheetham, M.M. Warburg and Oswald Birchall came. The active and I hope healthy state of business gave them additional cheerfulness, and in this respect made a striking contrast to the state of affairs when they were with me last year. Warburg's recent Spanish tour gave us plenty of conversation, Mr Webb goes for a trip by way of the Rhine to Switzerland on leaving here. He looks well but as usual complains.

Richard Pitt leaves. He has had the impudence to take out a licence to shoot and has been driving the birds away from the estate by firing in all directions in my absence in London. He only admits to two squirrels; Parry told me, and I think behaved well about it. For the future I have told everyone I will have no shooting whatever.

May 19.   Webb, Campbell, Cheetham and I took a most delicious walk to the Cranham woods, alternately fine and dull, ending with an unparalleled sunset of which the fiery golden glows were at their acme of perfection as we entered our garden where the nightingales were sweetly singing. None of us are likely to forget the beauty of the scene or the exquisite gorgeousness of the trees lit up with and bathed in mellow glory.

Winstone proposed to restore the house at Cranham woods for £300 making a pleasant and inhabitable home.

May 22.   Came to town last night, to my capital lodgings, 22 Duke Street, St. James's. Cecil (Drummond) has gone down to join the Leicestershire militia. I took Amy to show at Botanical Gardens, a pretty sight.

Trinity Sunday, May 26.   Called on the Ellicotts and attended Litany at All Saints, Margaret Street. Evening to Pro-Cathedral, Kensington, to hear Mon^r. Capel in a series of sermons on Ritualism. The cathedral was crowded with thousands. He considers the catholic revival in England the greatest work of God. What the Romanists could not do, wanting opportunity in either their churches, publications or the Press, the High Church clergy have done. They have rendered familiar to the English mind the Mass, High and Low, Confession, religious fraternities etc: they have translated into English and spread abroad over the land Roman Catholic books of devotion. The Ritualist and Roman Catholic view of the real presence in the sacrament are absolutely identical. The baptism of dissenters is perfectly valid, and is not repeated on their reception into the Roman Catholic church. Though incidentally endorsing the doctrine of only one church he said that if people only acted conscientiously, God would judge them only by that light that his Spirit had afforded them.

May 29.   Saw Miss Beeston about lessons in painting. She thinks she can teach me in three lessons.

May 30.   To the Crystal Palace with the Ellicotts. Mrs E. took two daughters and self in her open carriage, the others came by train. Nothing could be more agreeable or go more pleasantly. The fireworks were gorgeous. We refreshed ourselves at the 2/8 cold colation room; never will I visit there again — 15/- for two tankards of horrid claret cup, 10/- for ditto cider and nothing nice to eat.

June 1.   Taking alarm at the indefinite accounts from Enderby I determined to go down and left by evening train. I found Dr Shaw who has been spending the night there. He told me Mr Brook's left lung is affected with slight effusion. I returned to town. Mr Brook had a comfortable day and does not know that I have been.

June 4.   Great disappointment to discover no one knows the process of making Nankin — no Englishman can produce it. The balance of opinion at Minton's studio is in favour of its being under glaze; but how put on or how fired they cannot tell.

June 5.   Went to Flower Show at Horticultural. Nothing could be more lovely, the attendance enormous. Waterer of Woking has a superb collection of rhododendrons, just in perfection. I think the private gardeners almost bore the palm away from the professionals in many classes.
    Called on Amy. Cecil was to dine with Rifles to meet the Prince of Wales. Afterwards he proposed going to the Alhambra to see *Le Roi carotte*. He makes use of his latch key. I fear Amy will feel his absence.

June 6.   My fourth painting lesson from Miss Beeston, 63 South Audley Street. Took Eliza and Sophy (his sisters) to hear "My Aunt's Secret" at the gallery of Illustration.

June 7.   I left town 9 p.m. to Gloucester. At Swindon the Inspector had received a telegram advising me to go to Enderby at once. I found it was best to return to town. I had called on Amy in the morning. Cecil had gone to Chatham to cricket match.

June 8.   Caught 6.15 a.m. train from St. Pancras. Mr Brook was rather better, but the doctor says he cannot recover. Mrs Brook is prostrate and waits in a semi-hysterical state. Dr Shaw says his responsibility is more than he can bear. He fears Mrs Brook thinks he has not done his duty. At 3 in the morning we were all present and Mr Brook took each by the hand and addressed the most solemn words of love and blessing. His words seemed from the depths of the tomb and were groaned. His mind never lost its balance for a moment and was continually occupied in thinking of the circumstances of each. Of Amy he said "I feel much for Amy, I dread her getting to love the worldly gaieties of a London life. As we brought her up I don't think she will find happiness in the distractions and vanities of the world".

June 11.   Mr B. took 3 bottles of cognac in 36 hours.

June 12.   Went back to London, and to Bowden on 13th. Appointment with Miss Beeston postponed *sine die*.

June 30.   Mr Emeris read himself in and dined with us. Oswald and Edward staying. Oswald has been staying at Howth in County Wicklow and has there fallen in with a family of Fetherstonhaughs and not unnaturally the result has been an ardent attachment springing up between him and the eldest Miss F. a girl of 16 or 17. He had proposed not only to the girl who accepted him but also to the parents who took time to consider. He thought that if he could take any satisfactory account of his prospects of advancement from me it would probably facilitate matters. I told him that for his age he had done wonders, and we must suppose that the same attention and industry which had carried him thus far would lead in due time to even greater success.

July 11.   Mr Brook died: one of the dearest best and kindest of men.

July 15.   Cecil Drummond and I were the chief mourners at Mr Brook's funeral. The funeral, a walking one, was I think the most solemn and affecting I have ever attended. As we went to and fro hundreds lined the way, many weeping like children, both men and woman seemed equally affected.

July 25.   Yesterday Mrs Brook was very weak but I got her out for 20 minutes in the pony phaeton. She was crying bitterly most of the time, and coming in she saw the hatchment for the first time and got into a most hysterical state. I left her in sad and irrepressible distress. She said she clung to me more than anyone and begged me to come back as soon as possible.

July 30.   Unexampled downpour of rain started at 10 o'clock last night and continued till this morning with occasional claps of thunder. It seems a continuation of the remarkably stormy weather we have experienced during the past two months. The Gloucester Park is flooded. Men and boys have taken headers off the platform erected for tomorrow's show. Morris was driving Thomas to the station early this morning when he left my service and found the post boy walking up to his middle in water near Saintbridge and he thinks without his assistance he would very likely have been drowned.

July 30.   Gloucestershire Agricultural Society Meeting. The Show has been held; but everything was injured by the storm. Stewart got 2nd prize for pen of 3 breeding Berkshire sows. Humphries 1st: this reversed the judgement of the Royal with the same pens. My old sow got reserved prize.

Aug 4.   Mr Emeris handed the cup to 4 or 5 of the last communicants having replenished it from the flagon on the ledge in the wall without a consecration. We cannot tell whether this was done from inadvertence or by design.

Aug 6.   My birthday. 44 years of age this day. We dined at Gambier Parrys and met the Wilsheres of Welwyn, Herts. I took the daughter into dinner. She is a very highly accomplished girl who has passed much of the time abroad and knows Rome well. She seemed rather taken with ritualism and betrayed it by crossing herself. I should like to see more of her which is very unlikely as she leaves the neighbourhood tomorrow.

Aug 7.   Elizabeth Cecil Drummond born. Returned to Enderby and found Mrs Brook looking better. News arrived that Amy was confined and is the mother of a very fine little girl with black eyes and dark hair. Both doing well. I induced Mrs Brook to write a short note, and this gave great satisfaction.

Aug 10.   Constant rain. The county near here is dreadfully flooded and accounts are bad from all parts of the country. Potato disease prevails; foot and mouth amongst cattle. The seven milk cows have had it here, and now the sheep have it in their feet, swollen, mattering and maggoty, with the most disgusting stench. The quantity of keep in the park, and the dreadful wet season seem the natural causes. The sheep are sore, without wool and often bleeding in their breasts from lying in wet grass. It is thought they had better continue in the park in the hope of recovery which I suggest might be accelerated by nursing in a dry barn or what not.

Aug 19.   Ann has a letter giving account of poor Cobb's lamentable suicide in the Barnsley Canal. She had first tried to be run over on the rails. Our cooks have not been fortunate. Mrs Dyson an incurable; Jane died from cancer and now Mrs Cobb committing suicide.

Aug 27.   Miss Somerset was married to Mr Hayward. Georgie came down for it as brilliant as a butterfly, and it is only a fortnight after I received the Colonel's note saying she might be a widow any moment from the fearful fits of her husband. The Brooke-Hunts would not be present at the wedding in consequence of her coming. Nothing could exceed the apparent stolidity of Mr Hayward; perhaps it was more apparent than real. They have bought a piano with my £20.

Aug 31.   Licensing meeting. An anonymous letter received complaining of drink being sold in a butcher's shop connected with the Red Lion, Upton St. Leonards after hours. Though we could not officially notice this the police were warned to be on the alert. The hours on Sunday are now to be from 1 to 3 and from 6 to 10. On week days from 6 in the morning until 11 at night. Under new Act no house can be licensed for a beer house that is worth less than £10 p.a. without land; but existing houses may be continued if worth £8 without land.

Sept 4.   Miss Sumner's marriage, breakfast and ball. Very pretty sight in the new little church at the Edge.

Sept 17.   Meet at Robinswood Hill. Asked Lord Fitzhardinge to come and have a day at Bowden Hall, and mentioned the way we were overrun with foxes.

Sept 19.   Dined at Prinknash. Mary only left there, the Ackers departed to America a week ago, and Miss Ackers was mysteriously united in wedlock to old Mr Shaw aged 75, (brother of the Brooks' doctor at Enderby) at Cranham church. Nothing was known of the time or place until all was over and they gone away.

Sept 23.   I lunched at Lady Wedderburn's, and afterwards we walked to Rudford church, a small structure with Norman arches recently restored by the Prices (of Tibberton).
   Richard Tothill entered my service at salary of £50 per annum.

Sept 25.   I rode to Miserden. Called upon the Elweses; from there to Sheepscombe to see Dr Baylee. Afterwards I sent him £10 for his church rebuilding. He showed me his Infirmary tables executed with immense labour, and they show that when he took the subject up the average period in the hospital was between 90 and 100 days. Then to Painswick and saw Mr Hyett, who is full of his quarrels etc.

Sept. 26.   Went to Longhope and walked over to Huntley and met Colonel and Mrs Hope and Miss L. Hope. I went with them to see the church lately restored from designs by S.S. Teulon. We then turned into their house, Court House, had tea and stayed to dinner. Walked back to train. I pressed the Colonel and his wife to dine with us next Wednesday, bringing Miss H. and spend the night.

Sept 29.   A note arrived from Mrs H. saying they cannot make any engagements next week, and Miss H. is going to the north immediately.

Oct 1.   Amy and Cecil came for a week.

Oct 3.   The Gambier Parrys, etc. came to dinner. Gambier Parry either affected or felt a profound astonishment and delight with the Satsuma (cream-coloured Japanese pottery). He had never previously met with it.

Oct 4.   Mr Bathurst has seen Lady Wedderburn who mentioned my expedition to Huntley. He gathered from her that her niece had no intention of marrying, and that she did not recommend me to take any further steps. She had always herself been much drawn to me, and the knowledge that I admired her niece would increase this feeling. Evidently she would have done her utmost to further it had she not believed that it would be fruitless.

Oct 7.   To Leeds to dine at John Jowitt's. Very pleasant evening.

Oct 8.   Church Congress in Leeds. The Archbishop of Armagh preached to a most enormous congregation in the parish church. I never saw anything like it in my life.

Oct 11.   The conversazione was held this evening and previous to it I dined with Uncle and Aunt Harris at the Great North Hotel where they had been extremely comfortable. On going into the Victoria Hall I found it very crowded. One of the first persons I encountered was Emily Jowitt alone. Following the impulse of the moment I offered her my arm and we spent the evening walking about together. She was very sociable and pleasant and I was much smitten with her. Though very short-sighted her eyes were bright and luminous and worked on my imagination after I had parted from her with regret. She took me up to the refreshment stall where were standing Sir John Pakington and Miss Barran, the latter with her sister being the lions of the evening.

Oct 13.   Edward and I went to Harehills in the evening and accompanied Emily and Flossie to Chapeltown church. The congregation with one or two exceptions seemed composed of faces unknown when I lived at Gledhow. Eight years has worked an eventful change. Emily looked bewitching in church, and was very communicative on her way home of her lamentable want of a mission. Oh that she was a man and had a career. The impulse of Friday night still possessed me, and wandering up and down the Harehills gardens I asked her to accept the mission of living with me and taking charge of Clara.

Astonished and overpowered as she was she pleaded unfitness and repeatedly asked why with all the world to choose from I should have selected one so young (20 last July) and inexperienced. After naming the matter to her parents, I went back to Edward with nothing settled.

Oct 14.   Breakfasted at Harehills[27] and took a walk with Emily. We were both constrained and ill at ease. A long talk with Deborah (Emily's mother) ensued in which she advised its being off unless reflection should make it appear feasible: disparity of age main objection; but she always preferred middle-aged men. Emily has devoted herself to study since leaving school and has passed an almost unique examination in Divinity and other branches of learning under the Oxford examiners. Undecided I left, and went to Canon Venables at Lincoln.

The examination which Emily passed and to which reference was made by Dearman when he got engaged to her, was the Cambridge Examination for Women.
Emily Jowitt obtained first class honours, distinguished in divinity, literature and French.
There were 154 candidates in England, and seven centres where the examination was held of which Leeds was one. Of the 26 ladies who entered at Leeds only two obtained first class honours.

Oct 17.   Returned to Leeds and had an interview with John Jowitt who counselled my consulting with Eliza before coming to any conclusion.

Oct 18.   Came home. Eliza was overpoweringly startled; but the more reflection she gives to the affair the better she likes it. Emily is willing to join the church and has a mind much more formed and cultivated than most girls of 20 years.

Oct 21.   Wrote to Emily renewing my offer and explaining that my hesitation was at an end.

Oct 23.   Emily writes she was happy to receive my letter. She never had any doubt of my being able to make her happy. Her hesitation arose from the fear she had of her own inability to be to me all that I should wish if I am willing to take her just as she is with all her youth and inexperience and imperfections. She will try her very utmost to be worthy of me. She is pleased to learn that Eliza thinks favourably of the matter and kindly of her. Thanks me for sweet photograph of Clara — a nice ladylike modest retiring letter utterly free of vanity or self-assertion. Replied naturally and suggested turning up at dinner on Monday night next.

On Oct 22 1872, Emily wrote to her intimate friend Maida Mirrielees.

---

[27] Now called Potternewton Park, then Harehills Grove, "a neat Neo-classical house with a segmental Ionic porch," Derek Linstrum 'West Yorkshire Architects and Architecture' 1978.

Harehills, near Leeds

Oh my own darling Maida. Now I will tell you all about it as far as I can. I told you how nice Dearman was to me at the Conversazione and that he was coming to tea on Sunday with Edward. Of course I had not the faintest idea of what was coming. They walked with us to Chapeltown church that evening, D and I a long way behind arm in arm. He was being nice and affectionate and pumped me about my pursuits, tastes, etc. Still I had not the slightest suspicion. At church we sat in a square pew. Though I did not notice it, Florence says he hardly took his eyes off me all the time. He squared himself round in the corner so as to have a better view. Even Carrie noticed this and she was several pews behind. After that I did notice that he put on my shawl very carefully and then put my hand in his arm and hurried me right off, *sans attendre*, as the others did to speak to Benson and Carrie. We had a very nice talk about life in general and I felt somehow quite at home with him, and told him some of my inmost thoughts.

When we came to the turn down to Elmhurst the others caught us up, and Benson and Carrie carried Edward and Florence off to supper and pressed D and me too; but he would not. So we were left alone. I cannot help thinking it really was — to use a very country phrase — a providential opening. Well, we walked on, and just as we were going down the carriage drive, he proposed. I could hardly believe my ears, the suddenness of it all took my breath away and I was silent for ever so long. Instead of going in we walked about the lawn and garden talking it all over for half an hour. Then I knew it must be time for the parents to return from chapel and so we went in and were just in time to receive them demurely. I went upstairs to take off my bonnet, and he told my parents. They were of course amazed. When the gong sounded I came down and he took me in to supper and bent down to whisper "I have told them all about it". I never felt to fearfully excited before; but they were all silent and I tried to keep the conversation going on ordinary topics but oh it was hard, and I could not eat any supper which made me feel still more foolish and self conscious. He had no appetite too.

Well, after supper those three retired and by this time Florence had guessed it from our looks, she said. Then prayers, and then all the others marched out one by one and D and I were left alone, only for about ten minutes however, and we parted D going back with Edward. I had not accepted him but neither had I refused him; but I think I meant to accept him all the time, only I felt so dreadfully conscious of my youth and unfitness, etc.

Well, next morning he appeared at breakfast and we again both of us quite lost our appetites in the most idiotic way. He seemed very excited. After breakfast he was again closeted with parents for what seemed ages but I believe it was really less than an hour. I could not sit down or do anything but just pace up and down in a perfect fever of excitement and then suddenly turned quite faint and I was given some port wine. I had no idea I could have been so absurdly excited.

At last Mama came for me and I was alone with D and then instead of accepting him I began like a fool putting all the difficulties in his way telling him he would be disappointed and deceived in me, and all sorts of things. Then Mama came in and suggested our going out, so we did and had a lovely walk and long long talk but came back no more decided than we went out, so I finished up with advising him to give up all thought of it. Why I did so I cannot conceive; but he himself seemed to see all my objections and to dread the responsibility of taking "a bright young girl" to waste her life on an old battered fellow like himself. Then he had a long talk with Mama and I think she also, seeing he had doubts and misgivings, advised its being given up. And so he went away. He had an engagement in Lincoln. Then I felt the reaction from all the excitement, so flat and dreary. Next day came a note to Papa saying how deeply penitent he was, he felt he had made a fool of himself in speaking so suddenly and disturbing me. On Thursday he came to Leeds for a few hours and had an interview with Papa who told him to go quietly home and think it well over.

Last night I sat up ever so late just thinking it all over and at last I obtained peace, for I felt with all my heart that it would come if it were right. I was able really to cast it upon God and to trust it all with Him, and then just when I had learned my lesson and become quite resigned came the joy. I will love him and I will try to help him to be happy and be a good wife to him, God helping me. I am now going to write to him. It is an awfully responsible position for me but somehow I do really believe I shall have strength for it but oh dear how young I feel. I must stop.
Signed   Your Em.

Oct 25.   Went to Enderby. Mrs Brook stronger but still depressed and overpowered with the responsibilities of managing this great estate. She has already lent Tom Hirst (her brother) £10,500 to the surprise of the executors. The Drummonds here. Amy looks thin, pinched and poorly. It is to be feared her constitution is rather suffering. I don't think he looks well but he always has a whitish appearance. They have been at Lord Scarbrough's at Sandbeck. The baby has been here all the time and Mrs Brook seems to have taken to it and is much interested. Mrs B. tells me Amy is again in the family way. What a misfortune!

Oct 28.   Came to Leeds. Had a most exciting interview with my partners regarding Warburg's demand for ⅓ in place of ¼ of foreign profits. I held forth at great length on the benefit that had accrued generally from our association with this man. I think my expressions had weight. My offer was unconditional acceptance of same remuneration for one year longer.

Dined at Harehills. Emily was constrained and timid, but warmed up in conversation during dinner and in the evening we got more sociable and at our ease. We consider ourselves engaged but another day will no doubt settle all matters.

Oct 29.   The Bensons dined with us at Harehills. Emily and I more drawn together than hitherto. She read me some letters from Mary Wakefield, Meg Mirrielees or whatever her name is, and Miss Pope at Stutgarde. They were all loving and serious and enhanced my opinion of the deepness of Emily's heart and convinced me of how little was to be thought of a certain coldness of manner and undemonstrativeness which I feel so markedly in a morning.

On Oct. 29th Emily wrote again to Maida Mirrielees.

I have only time now for a little scrap but I want you to know about it. Dearman came to dinner. I cannot describe my feelings during the day. He did not kiss me when he arrived, only shook hands very warmly. After dinner he and I were alone in the library for an hour till 9 o'clock when we went in for tea. He was very nice but didn't spoon or say anything special then, only talked about Bowden, the people there, his pursuits, and constantly made such remarks as "Oh, you will like her, she will be a nice companion for you". "You must help me to do so and so." Rather embarrassing. He seemed to quite take it for granted that we were engaged. After prayers we had another tête à tête of ¾ hour which was delicious. He kissed me ever so many times and generally spooned a good deal and said "Oh my darling I do love you so", and was altogether most sweet and tender. He kissed me before parents on saying good-night, and again this morning. He has kissed me four times this morning though he went off at 10 o'clock to Leeds. Ever yours, Em.

Oct 30.   I arranged with John Jowitt to settle £6,000 and he £4,000 on Emily. This is what he has done with his other children. His property which amounts to £120,000 after paying annuity to his wife is divisible equally amongst his children. Benson (Emily's only brother) has ⅔rds of the wool business. Last year they turned over nearly half a million, and made a profit of £20,000, but it was the first year they have made anything very handsome for long and the commissions they have to pay, which are a very serious item, amounted last year to £5,000. John would like to go out of business but he has such a lot of capital locked up in it, and in his will he has made arrangements for continuing the business for a certain amount.

Oct 31.   I joined our party at Enderby and was most warmly welcomed by Mrs Brook and my sister.

Nov 1.   Had a most affectionate letter from dear Emily.

Nov. 4   We came down to Brighton; took the whole of 32 Marine Parade for three weeks. Clara's and Miss Van's luggage amounted to 600 lbs.

Nov 9.   Lunched with Amy in London. She looks much stronger and had one of the little Sandfords of the Isle with her and at 2 o'clock they took me off to Cockspur Street where they had a window to see the Lord Mayor's

Show. It was of no interest. All the old medieval pageantry has been eliminated. I hurried off to Kings Cross to meet Emily who is coming to spend a week with us at Brighton.

Nov 22.   I took Mrs Brook to see Jimmy who is staying at St. Leonards. He has his face shaved and looks pale, thin and rather spotty. He smiled pleasantly and aferwards walked about laughing in a most idiotic fashion. He bites his nails, sucks his thumb and spits. His general effect affords no ground for encouragement. He made no observation and declined a more intelligible answer to our enquiries than a grunt.

Nov 27.   It has rained more or less every day during our three weeks in Brighton. I took six lessons at Mahornet's Gymnasium for one guinea.

Nov 28.   Attended the opening of Dr Baylee's church at Sheepscombe. The Bishop gave us a most wonderfully clear and interesting sermon on waiting, the attitude of all true Christians in view of Advent.

Dec 1.   Mr Emeris took all the morning service including Litany and a churching, and during the administration of Holy Communion he refilled the cup without re-consecration.

Dec 2.   I had a little conversation with Mr Emeris. He promised to give up the introduction of churching during divine worship. Also, as regards the omission of re-consecration, he knew it was indefensible, but thought it was only a spoonful, or so.

Dec 5.   Dined at Theodore Howard's [Theodore Howard was married to Emily's sister Susie] at Chiselhurst, to meet John and Deborah Jowitt and Emily. All were very kind and sympathetic for I was only temporarily feeling relieved from a very bad and oppressive headache.

Dec 6.   Amy and Cecil were sitting at home, alone, when I called. The baby is pronounced better. They say it has cried very little during its illness but has looked round with a most piteous expression.

Dec 11.   Party at the Bourne Bakers at Hasfield Court 7 o'clock. We left at 5.30 to be in time but got on to a wrong or the lower road near the Severn. We found the water out and pushed the horses through the first 100 yards when it subsided. A quarter of a mile further on it again was thoroughly flooded and we scarecely liked to venture. Sent Tothill to a cottage to enquire and was informed it was impassable. Turned back, and after numerous enquiries and much hard driving we arrived at Hasfield at 8 p.m., having spent 2½ hours on the road. The party were much relieved as they feared we had met with an accident in the floods. Mr Yorke who was there had had the water in the bottom of his carriage. The bride and bridegroom

Canon and Mrs Lysons were present looking very bright. We had a pleasant evening but came to the conclusion we would avoid visiting the Bourne Bakers in the middle of winter.

Dec 12.   Attended Infirmary Board. Ran to the Cross this frosty morning from Bowden Hall in 34 minutes.

Dec 13.   Attended the meet at Beech Pike near Winstone. Very slippery. No sport and I lunched at the Haywards to meet Elwes. Eliza had also come up in the brougham. They have got their house very nice and cosy; but it is a dull village. We used to pass through it in driving from Cowley to Miserden.

Dec 17.   Went to Harehills. Left Gloucester 11.27. At Derby we were only ½ hour late. The country between Birmingham and Derby is three parts under water. From every quarter we hear of the most distressing floods. Autumn wheats are nowhere sown nor can be now. People are getting uneasy about next year's harvest the present one having turned out very scanty. After leaving Derby the country was covered in snow and the storm last night has destroyed the block system of telegraphs and we dawdled along arriving at Leeds 2¼ hours late. Found the family had left for Prof. Seeley's lecture on the two Pitts, Emily remaining alone to welcome me.

Dec 19.   Dr Heaton's evening party with Emily. A majority present were of a class that object to balls but had no objection to dancing in the absence of any chaperones to see that all was conducted with propriety. Mrs Heaton trembled violently and looked very ill; but I called to pay my respects on the 20th and found her most bright and cheerful.

1873

1873 was the year Dearman married again and went on a honeymoon tour which lasted from January to June. He was also very much occupied with his firm's business.

Jan 1.   Miss Ellicott had a sad fall hunting at Hatherley. In rising her horse struck her head and so injured her ear that it only hung by the skin. She was taken to the Palace in a spring cart. It took the doctor 20 minutes to sew up the ear.

I had an interview with the Bishop about Cranham. He concurred entirely in what I said about the inefficiency of the present spiritual assistance. Mr Moore is old, feeble and miserably poor. He cannot be induced to resign; but if I can get the churchwardens to write a letter to the Bishop complaining he will take it into consideration, and provided we are prepared to find the income he thinks he could get a resident curate appointed and he would insist on having three services at Brimpsfield and Cranham — two each Sunday alternately at one end and the other.

The magistrates entertained the Barristers. It was rather slow than otherwise.

Jan 6.   Dined at the Palace. I had a game of billiards with the Bishop . . . and beat him. The table is not only very small but easy. Mrs Ellicott told me about her daughter's engagement. Poor girl the accident has laid her low. Mr Travers saw the occurrence and came and proposed the same day.

Jan 13.   Took Eliza to Liverpool to see Mr Bowes's collection of old Japanese *cloisonné* enamels. The delicacy, refinement and exquisite beauty of these unique works is beyond all description. The enamels are much decorated with the Kiri crest being trefoil of drooping leaves with three blossoms erect: Kiku crest being the back view of a chrysanthemum flower: the celestial bird the Hoho, which only descends when any event happens to the Imperial family: the Paulownia Imperialis or Imperial tree. It is a marvellous treat. Sassuma also very fine. Went on to Leeds. Dinner at Harehills. Found Emily very well and cheerful, and all gave me a warm welcome.

Jan 20.   After a week of indescribable consultation, propositions and counter-propositions we have at last all shaken hands and arranged the terms of a new partnership for Birchall, Webb & Co.

Jan 22.   At ¼ past 11 Emily and I appeared for the last time as units before the altar, and were joined in the bands of Holy Matrimony by Canon Woodford. The morning was snowy, the roads wet and muddy, the air thick, and such light as penetrated through the stained windows was solemn enough but scarcely sufficiently brilliant to display the beauty of the bride and bridesmaids' dresses. So far as I could see there never was a prettier wedding. All was soon ended and we started for Harehills. Flossie [Emily's younger sister Florence], Amy Wakefield, Maida Mirrielees, Helen Heaton, Dora Howard [Emily's niece], and Clara were bridesmaids.

To London by the 4.46 train. We put up at Brown's Hotel, Dover Street where we had excellent accommodation.

Jan 23.   We spent this afternoon at the Bethnell Green museum of which it is impossible to speak too highly. Sir Richard Wallace's collection of pictures, and inimitable and exhaustive display of Sèvres china are worth travelling any distance to inspect.

Jan 24.   Cantini who was engaged two months ago to spend 3 months with us, came in tonight to say he had got rooms for us at the Grand Hotel in Paris and had obtained a passport; but that urgent private business over which he had no control would not permit him to leave town. He therefore brought a friend Mr Perini whom he could sincerely recommend as a conscientious courier to take his place. He showed us testimonials from Lady Herbert, etc.

On 25 January they arrived in Paris and the tour began. Marseilles, Cannes, Nice. They walked from Nice to Mentone — 18 miles. "The most delightful walk I ever did. Poor Perini seemed to think us mad and went by train." Monaco, San Remo, Genoa. Perini said "I would rather be dead in England than alive in Italy. I have spent my savings in buying a freehold property at Brompton. I pay no taxes on it and it is in the cemetary."

Emily wrote to her sister Lily Crewdson

Rome 15th February 1873

My darling Lily
Today is the first day of Carnival; we have taken a balcony for the whole time (it goes on till Shrove Tuesday) price 400 fr. or £16. They are now asking 1000 fr. for the same accommodation. Ours is a very good situation indeed nearly opposite the King's balcony and very near Prince Arthur's. We spent the whole afternoon on our balcony engaging vigorously in the fray, both of us protected by wire masks and throwing vast quantities of confetti, and also bouquets. Lots of real sweetmeats and jolly crackers were thrown at me, all of which I took care to pocket. The bouquets I threw again; but the bon-bons were too precious. The Corso was crammed and the fun ran high, the battle of confetti being kept up with unremitting fierceness. We spent a nice quiet evening in our salon winding up with a game of bezique.

Feb 17.   Rome. My cold and head very bad. Fearing to have the week spoiled I sent Perini to enquire if there was a Turkish bath. He found one and ordered it to be heated for 12 o'clock. It consisted of a cell lighted by one pane of glass and containing a large iron stove with open front. I stripped and sat down but soon found it was not hot enough. I put on some bits of wood and then discovered the chimney pipe was closed. I contrived to bring the attendant by shouting and he opened the flue. The cell was so full of smoke I was almost choked. He then piled charcoal and sticks on the fire and pulled down the door. When it had sufficiently burnt up he opened it wide again and left me. I now perspired freely for 20 minutes but at the end of that time felt a faintness creeping on me. I pushed the door open and rushed out. The man ran for some warm water and stood on a tin platform and turned a tap of cold water on to myself. In a few minutes I felt better, wiped myself and put on a flannel waistcoat and shirt. They neither understand Turkish baths nor have the necessary appliances for giving them with success.

At present we are taking the Roman & Tiber Times, Swiss Times, Daily News, the Gloucestershire Chronicle and the Leeds Mercury. The latter has the proud distinction of being printed on the worst paper and having the most shabby look and the commonest type and filthiest ink of any of them.

March 3. Naples, till March 18.

Extracts from Emily's Journal

Tuesday March 11th. Naples. Although we have made an appointment with Miss Le Jeune to be photographed on Friday, we heard so glowing an account yesterday from the Marchese Palmieri of another photographer, Ferretti by name; and Dearman was, moreover, so charmed by some he had seen of his, that we decided to try him also. So this morning we had a long séance with him and were taken, Dearman and I together in cabinet size, I alone ditto, and both of us twice in *cartes de visite.* The jolly old man Signor Raffaello Ferretti (these Italians have such high sounding names) seemed to take a great deal of pains, so we hope the photographs will be successful.

Friday March 14th. This morning at noon we went to Miss Le Jeune's by appointment (E. Le Jeune, 47 Strada Cavallerizza) to have our photographs taken. She is a most original person, very short and abrupt in manner, wasting no words and ordering her clients about like children but she gives the impression of being a true artist, and is certainly the most painstaking photographer I ever saw. She was an hour and a quarter at work on me and only took two portraits, the rest of the time being spent in posing me. Her first proceeding was to pull down all my back hair, in order to fix the rest against my very skull: her second to cover up the white lace on my dress with some little strips of black, and her third to powder my face. She did not bestow so much time on Dearman, though he says he felt like a small child with its school-mistress when meekly obeying her directions. She would not allow either of us to be present while the other was being done and she had no assistant whatever.

Naples

Emily
by E. Le Jeune
14 March 1873

Dearman
by E. Le Jeune
14 March 1873

"Together in cabinet size"
by Raffaello Ferretti

Sunday March 16th.   To church morning and afternoon, hearing the Archbishop of Dublin in the morning. Our photographs have come from Ferretti, and we are much pleased with them. As photographs they are perfect. (Emily was obviously a very animated person but she never smiles in her photographs. It was not fashionable then to say "cheese" at the right moment.)

Messina, Taormina, Sorento, Capri, Positano, Amalfi, Paestum, Caserta.

Letter from Dearman to Emily's mother.

Sorrento March 30, 1873.

My dear Mother
Here it is so exquisitely pure and wholesome, I cannot imagine anything more health giving than the view from our window over the bay of Naples like a huge and placid lake, the long line of coast dotted with houses and villas to the base of Vesuvius. Professor Palmieri prophesies an eruption. Oh that we may not have taken our departure before it begins. Nearer on the other side are the Sorrento hills amid a delicious mixture of foliage, equally composed of grey olive trees, orange trees full of thousands of fruit which give a golden tinge and the opening leaves of vine and fig, with a goodly show of peach and nectarine trees in full bloom.

The people here are always singing or playing or laughing, occasionally moved by deep but evanescent passion. I saw two children, little boys fighting and soon the youngest pulled out of his pocket a skewer which he endeavoured to rip up his adversary's neck; and two cabmen who took to knives and would have killed one another but for the interference of others, and in ten minutes were the best of friends.

The people are intensely courteous to us and offer us unexpected attention; my wife receives flowers always when walking in the country, and at Catania last Sunday we were driving out in the afternoon when I pulled up and alighted to see the most extraordinary *bougainvillaea* in full bloom it has ever been my fortune to behold. It almost covered the side of a house and was so gorgeous with crimson bloom that the leaves which were there were almost invisible. The gentleman being in his garden came out and invited us in, and while we were inspecting it more narrowly sent off his gardener to cull some oranges and lemons for our benefit.

Having given Emily a bad character in my last to you in the matter of early rising I must in justice to the dear child tell you she is becoming quite a reformed character and I hope ere long to find her a model mistress of a house in this respect. The improvement was first inaugurated by rising at four on board the ship to see Stromboli and she paced the deck during all that storm until 2 in the afternoon, her long hair entirely loose floating in the wind, her face gradually encrusted with salt and her dress saturated with sea water. I was, in her emphatic language, rather "took" and had retired to my berth. Since this she has broken the habit of oversleeping, I fear at Harehills, with no-one to look after her at night, she sat up reading till all hours and nothing could be more likely to quench the desire of going out in a morning.

We had a most amusing evening in Naples on Friday. We had met a gentleman with the Pyemont Smiths named Aurelio Cedroni whom Emily called a sweet youth (there are so many of these I am not jealous), and his brother and sister the Marchese and Marchesa invited us to spend the evening with them — everybody has a title here. Emily was in a painful state of excitement because she found it impossible to decide what to wear. She was eventually got up as well as could be effected in a black silk dress and we set off. Our driver went everywhere but to the right house; Marqueses abounded in every house. Eventually to our surprise we had to walk to the bottom of a court-yard string of stables and up some dirty stairs in common to the families inhabiting every landing. *Au premier*, Count — *au second*, Marquese —, but not ours. *Au troisième* we were ushered in by an old coachman on his last legs with improvised black suit and his huge paws enveloped in white cotton gloves. The Italian gentlemen were all so alike I never could tell which was which, all had black moustaches, but was not one a duke. It commenced very slow. The women could not sing, the men could not because they could not find anyone capable of accompanying them. At last when all became stiff and constrained the Marchese adopted the Italian expedient of sending to a chemist where professional musicians can be heard of in case of parties failing to turn out as convivial as the host and hostess expected. Two were found and ran across in a trice and all began to improve, and shortly we danced a quadrille and *Sir Roger de Coverley*, and came away about midnight. Nobody was dressed except in the plainest style and coming out we could not control a hearty burst of laughter, the whole thing was so unlike what we expected.

Dear Emily gets on most fluently with the various languages; she talks German and French like a native and Italian exceedingly well. I named her the Polyglot and my appreciation of her powers was shared by a German professor we met in Sicily far more capable of exercising a sound judgement in this matter and to my surprise I heard him apply the very same epithet to her. She enjoys such robust health she has no thought of taking care of herself and without the slightest encouragement would have attempted Etna covered in snow, or anything requiring pluck and endurance. We both unite in dearest love.

Yours most affectionately. J. Dearman Birchall

P.S. Our plans are to occupy this week with Capri, Amalfi, Salerno, Paestum, to Naples about Friday and Rome again on Saturday. The Empress of Russia telegraphs to her husband from her hotel a stones throw from us and fully in the sight of our bedroom window. Thank you for sending me to this earthly paradise. We are at a great height above the lovely blue sea and throw pennies wrapped up in paper to make them visible, down as far (out) as we can to induce the numerous amphibious half-naked boys to dive for the treasure, which they do with intense delight.

Back to Rome on *April 6th* where "we had our photographs taken for Sanlini's cameos, then to Sanlini to arrange for them to be carved on one shell mentioning we should want four".

Writing from Rome on April 6th to her mother Emily says "Don't you think letter-writing is rather Dearman's 4 te (A word)".

Letter-writing was certainly Emily's *forte* and the letters written by her on her six month honeymoon would make a travel book on their own. In the same letter she wrote. "We both felt quite pathetic about leaving Naples for we have both grown quite fond of the beautiful, lively place and whatever Dearman may feel it his duty to say about dirtiness and the cruelty to animals and laziness (for he has a great idea of giving both sides of a question — I don't see the good of it) he is really just as attached to it as I am, and we both agree it is out and out the most beautiful city we ever saw, from whatever point seen it is always lovely and there is a warmth and glow about its colouring seen nowhere else".

Emily nearly always ended her letters by writing across the first sheet and so the date of the letter very often has to be disentangled from the cross-writing with a magnifying glass. In this same letter (April 6th) she writes across the first page "The Matthew Arnolds are staying at the same hotel as the Pymont Smiths. I should like to see them; but I don't see that I can do anything. I couldn't call, could I? You see Dearman doesn't know them, and they would never remember this babe".

In a letter she complains mockingly that Dearman calls her "babe", even sometimes in public. And she did succeed in making friends with the Matthew Arnolds again. On April 14th she wrote. "I sort of reintroduced myself to Mr Arnold and he remembered me at once and was most pleasant and talked about my exams which they seemed to know all about, "but we have heard you are no longer Miss Jowitt". So I then introduced Dearman. We have very nice rooms in this bright, new, nicely conducted little hotel; it is close to the Piazza Barbarini and our windows look into the Palace gardens. This morning we went to the Capitol and ascended the tower and enjoyed the most magnificent view of the whole beautiful grand old city. Mr Arnold so revels in the view that he goes up the 270 steps there nearly every day".

In 1869 Matthew Arnold had published *Culture and Anarchy* in which he urged the middle classes not to remain satisfied with the Puritan virtues of energy, determination, concentration and self-control, which he admitted that they possessed, but to cultivate the Hellenic Virtues. He summed up what he saw as the essence of Hellenism in a phrase that became famous, 'sweetness and light'. Sweetness meant the creation and enjoyment of beauty in all its forms; light was the result of intellectual curiousity, the desire 'to see and learn the truth and make it prevail'. The mutual admiration of Matthew Arnold and this enthusiastic and intellectual girl was recalled after her death eleven years later, by Aldam Heaton who sent Dearman a water-colour of some autumn crocuses entitled 'Sweetness and Light; a memory.'

On April 19 Perini was recalled to London, and on April 26 they went to

Venice without a courier and stayed at Danieli's, and on to Vienna on 30th for the Exhibition. "Oswald is here but can do nothing as the stands have never arrived from London. The English department looks miserably unfinished beside the Japanese."

May 1.   Opening of the Exhibition. The Dome in which the ceremony was held is of prodigious dimensions, raised by Scott Russell it is a credit to English engineering. Everything is incomplete. Inspected the cloths so far as ready, Germany and Portugal, the latter deeply uninteresting. We lunched at an American bar, an experiment not worth repetition.

May 5.   Our stand has arrived. The sameness of our patterns strikes me and I feel most disappointed that not a single thing has been made for it or anything done but sending a nice assortment of the plain everyday things we are usually selling.

   Called on Frank West. He travels 2,300 miles a year for Hoopers of the West (Stonehouse). They are excellent people and have always treated him as a gentleman and increased his salary and made him presents beyond what he ever thought was right. Old Mr Hooper takes the lead in everything, knows all that is going on, buys every bag of wool and passes every piece going out.

May 7.   I spent the day almost exclusively with Oswald hanging the cloth; the worsted, twist, check, wiesbaden, and other coatings are exceedingly good and I hope will secure us a medal. We put all the choicest in the best side where the light is incomparable, leaving all the poor dull stuff for the back. Having praised the coatings I am bound to say I never was so disappointed as I am that not one piece, pattern or idea has been brought out for the Exhibition. Neither Beavers, Witneys, elysian, naps or cloth of any finished goods are represented, and with space at our command to exhibit for half Leeds we have shown nothing that could not be done by the smallest manufacturer.

May 8.   News from London of Amy being prematurely confined of a little boy who lived about a couple of hours, and was baptized Charles Brook Assheton Drummond. I wrote to Cecil, and also to Eliza, the latter on the subject of Barnwood Court which is for sale; £6,000 is asked for house, outbuildings and 22 acres of land. I think if Eliza could rent it at a moderate price she would not hesitate.

On May 12, Emily wrote amusingly from Vienna to her sister Anna Dora Howard — Beloved Anna your charming letter was most welcome particularly as we have had very few letters of any kind lately. We feel rather injured and neglected and we think we are somewhat out of sight out of mind, for whereas a few months ago all our affectionate relatives were beseeching us to return speedily, now *on a changé tout cela*. Our only letter from Bowden is from Mrs Brook who is staying there and she says "Miss

Birchall seems very much pleased that she will have more time here as you are not coming home so soon as she expected", and not one word of regret, and Coz Eliza herself says "I can occupy myself very well here, indeed I am glad to have a little more time. . ." As for my home people they take the news with the most philosophical calmness not to say cool indifference and do not make even a polite feint of regret or longing. Dearman thinks it behoves us to hasten home before we are clean forgot. I think 'twer rather well to prolong our absence *ad infinitum* as we are so very little missed.

We like this hotel but it is not cheap; our bill for one week came to £27. Our dinners *à la carte* are first rate but come to 12/- or 13/- a head every day. Even Oswald's tiny room on the third floor is 12/- a night. The washing is awful, 2/6 each for my petticoats and 2½d for each pocket handkerchief. Still we are very comfortable and don't feel inclined to change.

We have very good accounts of Amy but the baby died. Mama will say it is a great mercy because the other you know is only nine months old. Amy sent for the curate at once when she heard it would not live and had it christened. Lady Elizabeth (her mother-in-law) was there; but Capt. Drummond did not get home till after the babe was dead. Ever Yours in bonds. E.

On May 17 Dearman and Emily left Vienna for Budapest, by steamer, and were surprised to find such luxurious accommodation in Hungary as the Grand Hotel where they stayed. They were back in Vienna on the 29th, and left for Lintz, and then London on June 3rd. "On the 24th January I weighed 12 stone 4 lbs. and on 5 June 11 stone 2½ lbs. in the same clothes.'

June 12.   Having written home last night we should be arriving at 2.50 we were disappointed not to find any carriage to meet us and on going up in hansom cab we found all unprepared. Four triumphal arches were in course of formation, very handsomely decorated by Mr Eshelby. Outside Bowden Hall gates they were erecting a beautiful arch covered with flowers. It was a miserable day raining in torrents at intervals. We made a progress through the village at 6 p.m. in open carriage, the rain falling in torrents we were met with much enthusiasm, firing of guns, shouts of boys; nothing could have been heartier and the church bells were pealed.

June 15.   The Dean of Gloucester called and made some pretty speeches to Emily and to me. "Your motto should be 'My cup runneth over'."

June 19.   Engaged Henry Knight as groom at 16/- a week and to live with Morris. Very good character from Henry Clifford of Frampton Court.

June 23.   Luncheon at the Deanery. Canon James took us round the Cathedral and to see the new reredos erected by the Freemasons which is singularly beautiful. Called on our way home on Emeris who said the Dean was very morbid in his fancies and had been under care for many years. He fancied he could not stand, and had other delusions.

June 24.   Emily, Florence (her sister) and I went to Bath for the Royal Horticultural Show by express 11.17. The day was wet and dull but the show was excellent. Cranstone roses magnificent, ferns, cut hothouse plants beautiful. There was a new rose, crimson bud with white leaves [*sic.*] and some very decorative geraniums with fine edges. Jackman exhibited his clematis but only two were striking, *Jackmanni* and *Languinosa*. They were in large pots trained round like azalias.

June 28.   John and Deborah Jowitt, [Emily's parents] came to us to stay until July 2nd.

July 11.   David and Dora Howard,[28] Theodore and Lily Crewdson[29] [Emily's married sisters] came to stay.

July 19.   Emily's 21st birthday. Benson Jowitt [her brother] came to stay.

July 23.   Potter's garden party.[30] No amusement but patrolling a small portion of lawn, little play or food or beverage could be obtained and people got away as soon as possible.

July 25.   Met Rev. C.B. Trye of Leckhampton at the Gaol. We saw all the prisoners. We had Capt. Wilson with us and were much interested (as visiting magistrates). We had no complaints but two men were anxious to be sent to sea. There seemed nothing more likely, and as the expense of a similar case had proved almost nominal it was granted. One also asked for some money and as he has been ill in the infirmary during his incarceraton and he goes in 14 days, we allowed him 5/-.

Aug 2.   Heavy day at the Petty Sessions. A number of cases of drinking and disorderly conduct at Ashleworth Quay. The people concerned pretty respectable and paid the heavy fines we imposed on them say from 5/- to 10/- and expenses amounting to 7/- and 8/-, each in addition. Serjeant Child very active in apprehending them.

Aug 6.   I spent the day in London seeing Dent about the clock which Mrs Brook is about to present to Enderby church,[31] and Norman Shaw about the tomb and brass, to commemorate poor Mr Brook.

---

[28] The Howards were grandparents of the Labour politician and diarist Richard Crossman.
[29] The Crewdsons were grandparents of Professor Frederick Sanger, the Nobel prize winner.
[30] Richard Potter of Standish House was a successful speculator. He had nine daughters, one of whom Beatrice (afterwards Mrs Sidney Webb) was 15 in September 1873 when she began her diary, published by Virago in October 1982.
[31] Enderby church Leicestershire was designed by Edward Birchall, in 1868.

Aug 7.   From Enderby Em and I went with Joseph Hirst (Mrs Brook's nephew) to Belvoir Castle, by train to Melton Mowbray, thence 12 miles by road. It was well worth the trouble. The castle is a noble and majestic object overlooking the rich vale of Belvoir and from which Lincoln cathedral is visible.

No china or works of art of much interest. Some good Poussins in the picture gallery and capital Teniers representing all the best known proverbs as current in England as Holland.

Aug 9.   Bought a plot of land belonging to the late Henry Jones for £1,450.

Aug 16.   Warburg came back after 5 weeks of continual travelling from Hamburg, Berlin, Vienna and Rome. He has only passed 12 nights in bed. He came here this afternoon and agrees to sign the agreement, and wrote a note stating this to be his intention. On 28th he takes his departure for the States.

Aug 18.   Mr & Mrs William Benson [Deborah Jowitt's brother] came here with their son and daughter last Friday. They live near Montreal. He is an ardent admirer of shorthorns and enjoys a country life.

Aug 23.   On going to the Gaol I was stopped at the police office and asked to remand Edward Butt who was taken up at Abergavenny for the murder of his sweetheart. I signed the remand and he is to be brought up at Whitminster next Tuesday morning. It is supposed that the evidence is very conclusive. He looks a respectable young man, very short, and he is connected with a very large number of the best Gloucestershire farmers.

Aug 25.   My partners, Webb, Campbell, Cheetham, Oswald and Warburg came to stay. We had a long discussion today. Warburg expects to be nearly 4 months in America and his winter patterns are to follow him. He does not believe in showing any in Canada. In the afternoon we drove over to Stroud and inspected the Mills of Marlings and Strachan. The advantages of the best machinery were obvious in every direction. Coal costs only half per horse power what it did before. Marling's Ebley Mills are very old fashioned and uninteresting.

Aug 27.   Engaged William Keen as head gardener at £80 per annum.[32] Called today and saw Mr Sowery who recommended him as the best man he has ever turned out. I much regret parting with Hill but want a man who is more up to all the novelties introduced of late years.

Aug 30.   Went to stay with the Sandfords of the Isle, at Shrewsbury, where we found George Armitage. It is a pretty peninsular of the Severn called the

---

[32] He stayed for about 50 years.

Isle of Rossal. The children are much left to their own natural development. The youngest called Ba, 12 yeas old, is a regular tomboy, and rows and fishes, rides or scampers about only doing lessons when her mother has no other occupation, and from the number of guests their hospitality induces them to entertain, this may be very occasionally.

Sept 1.   George Armitage, Sandford and his son Humphrey and self spent our day shooting. The standing corn prevented us doing much good with the birds. We only got 6 brace of partridges, 5 or 6 hares and a few rabbits. Caught a pike, 3 lbs, from Sandford's pool. The Isle of Rossal came into possession of the Sandford family in the time of Queen Elizabeth.

Sept 6.   Went to the Prison. Saw Edward Butt who seems calm and collected and we were told behaved with the utmost propriety. He has had no less than four visits from the Dean and is fully alive to the awful position in which he is placed. Capt. Wilson is away but the prison is in beautiful order.

On Sept 13th Emily again wrote teasingly to her sister Anna Dora from Bowden. — Friend Dora, Yes indeed you have treated me ill, and why didn't you ask Susie and Lily to forward me some of the volumes you wrote to them? Thou dids't not well to cut me off entirely from communication with my family, to ignore me thus totally, and I feel "grieved" as Sally Ross [their mother's maid] would say with tears. Your note this morning was to a certain extent balm to my wounded spirit, oil to my stricken soul, a precious ointment to my sore heart; but I am not yet appeased utterly. I shed a tiny drop as I read thy cruel mandate that I am to be deprived of thy delectable society during my sojourn in t'north. However least said soonest mended and 'tis an ill wind that blows nobody any good so I hope thy "poor husband" will appreciate the bliss of basking in thy presence since I am excluded from it.

We have a very nice party staying here. Amy and Cecil are most agreeable, Amy so sweet and pretty and utterly unspoilt by all these grand friends remembering the ostriches at Harehills and playing in the hall curtains with Florence and me 12 years ago. Cecil is particularly nice and so handy and useful, always quietly amusing himself and other people and never hanging about in the way like so many gentlemen at large. He can turn his hand to anything and if nothing else offered would be content and happy sitting twiddling his thumbs all day long. I like him, he is so extremely gentlemanly and pleasant and easy to do with. He brought his footman to valet him.

Then we have the Beavington Atkinsons, he up in his room (the oak chamber) busy writing his new book all the morning and she is busy with the index, and looking over the first proof sheets. He is deeply blue-looking, with long lion-like hair and huge head and spectacled eyes and talking much like a book. She is gawky and long-chinned and medievally dressed and talks most cleverly and originally but rather like a book too, and plays and sings at sight and improvises and is very good company altogether.

The Drummonds go from this lowly cot to Lord De la Warre's and thence to the Baillie Cochranes, thence to Lord Zetland and then to Lord Scarbrough's, and where after that deponent knoweth not. We had heaps of music in the evenings. To-day we have a garden party of 120 if fine, if wet probably only the odd 20 will come, and I am sorry to say it is at present by no means fine. Yesterday we played Badminton and croquet in the morning and after lunch most of them went for a drive, and Cecil and I for a walk. Yours ever Em.

Sept 17.   Came to Harehills, to attend the meeting of the British Association. We had to run to catch the 6.30 train to Bradford. The inaugural address on the *Atomic theory and establishment of scientific education by government* was utterly devoid of interest and about as dull, dry a performance as I have ever had the pain and weariness of listening to.[33]

A later discussion in which Lord Houghton took part was very good. He said if all the property in England was equally divided today by far the largest number would have got rid of their share by the end of the week.

J. Head of Fox & Head, Middlesborough, said they had working men who earned as much as £800 last year, more £600 and others £400 and £500. Trades Union discussed on both sides.

Sept 18.   In Leeds I saw Cheetham and discussed the Mill.

Sept 27.   Agreed to buy the Hill (at Bowden) 10½ acres, and Handgrove 17½ acres for lump sum of £6,000. It will enhance the value of the property.

Oct 4.   Called at the Infirmary and Gaol in consequence of the death of the laundry officer from typhoid fever occasioned, rumour said, by infection taken from the infirmary linen.

Oct 14.   Quarter Sessions. Much discussion of the clothes question. Statement prepared by Capt. Wilson showing the marvellous decrease in the typhoid fever cases since July 1869 at which time the new drainage was just completed and coincident with this the practise was started of taking the Infirmary linen in to wash.

Oct 16.   Theodore and Susan Howard came to stay.[34]

Marnock[35] spent the day here. He is very much pleased with the estate and has taken a few particulars to think over. He recommends the removal of trees so as to clump them, and the planting of Scotch and Austrian firs at the

---

[33] Presidential address by A.W. Williamson (1824–1904) Professor of Chemistry at University College, London.

[34] She was Emily's eldest sister. Two of her sisters married Howard brothers. These were the grandparents of Raymond Sturge, Chairman of Lloyds, in 1958.

[35] Robert Marnock 1800–1889, landscape gardener; laid out Botanical Gardens, Regent's Park, London, becoming curator.

extremity of Handgrove for a background.

Oct 18.   I visited the county Prison alone and authorized the Governor to introduce gas into the carpenter's and brush shops, the expense not to exceed 10/-, the cost of necessary piping, and the work to be done by the prisoners; also purchase of new carpet for the bedroom of new laundry maid which has been papered and painted since the death of Miss Higgs from typhoid fever.
   I saw Butt who has a cold, and Cole who has nearly murdered his wife with a hot poker.

Oct 24.   Meeting of visiting Justices at County Prison. We settled to have estimates for supplying the prisoners cells with town water in place of that pumped up from the well which is known to be contaminated by organic matter. The prisoners are now cautioned against drinking this; but it has been disregarded until lately when the taste of tar from the newly pitched tanks has caused them to desist.

Oct 25.   Dr and Mrs Ancrum, Mr & Mrs Emeris, and Miss Stewart dined. I had a consuming headache, mostly nervous, by taking a copious draft of hot brandy and water and keeping quiet all the evening, never seeing my guests, I recovered pretty well before bedtime and Sunday morning was able to go to church.

Oct 28.   Joined the Berkeley hounds at Hare and Hounds, Cheltenham Road. A very large field, many from Cheltenham. We killed at Chosen Hill, tried Hatherley and Barrow coverts, got a fox at Norton. More spills than I have almost ever seen in the second field. Dr Ancrum had a heavy fall. Jupiter pecked but recovered himself without my losing my seat. I was not so fortunate shortly afterwards for at full gallop in a grass field he came down and I was precipitated many yards ahead of him which was a mercy. Hat smashed, rather shaken but no more thank God.

Nov 4.   Long day with the Berkeley hounds. Meet at Hardwicke. Found at Elmore church covert and ran to canal very fast. Hardwicke covert fox killed in gorse after short run on scent of hare. Afternoon found in Netherhall covert, ran through Frampton park at great pace to Eastington, Stanley, home through Stonehouse and Standish.

Nov 22.   Ordered new segmental Brougham with basket drag chain, cane seat, square lamps, Morocco lining, complete with no extras to be delivered 3 months £185 nett. Peters & Sons.

Dec 4.   Dined at Bourne Bakers; again lost our way and drove to the very brink of the Severn. Two hours on the road and mentally resolved it should be the last winter dinner we would take there unless we could spend the night.

Dec 10.   Our dinner party. The Bakers never arrived at all but sent a note of apology on account of the fog in Gloucester.

Dec 13.   Invited to the Drummonds. Leaving Gloucester at 8.40 a.m. we arrived at Fawley via Reading, Basingstoke, Southampton and Hythe where Cecil's carriage met us at 4 p.m. We found it dull, dark and inexpressibly cold. Bourne Hill Cottage is opposite the Isle of Wight, Cadlands opposite Southampton Water; near the cottage is another very pretty place Eagle Hurst. All these belong to Edgar Drummond who has about 8,000 acres mostly of Forest lands covered with Scotch firs, brambles, gorse and heather. It is wild picturesque country undulating and well wooded.

Dec 14.   Attended Fawley church containing many traces of Norman times. A most eloquent sermon on the text 'Prepare to meet Thy God'.

Dec 15.   We went to Cadlands (designed by Capability Brown) for a days covert shooting. All was conducted in the finest order Cecil taking the lead as Edgar does not care much for shooting. The rain came on so furiously that at lunch time I retired and joined the party in the Hall, Lady Elizabeth, Amy, Em, and Mrs Drummond. Spent an agreeable afternoon inspecting the splendid engravings, Wedgewood and Dresden china, and autographs of Marie Antoinette, Napoleon, etc.

Dec 22.   Attend the trial in Gloucester of William Bailey and Anne Barry for wilful murder. It lasted for 2 days and resulted in verdict of wilful murder in each case but with recommendations to mercy. The case against the man could have been very weak but for the positive statement of Chabot, the expert, that the envelope containing the poison was undoubtedly written by the same person as the numerous letters and bills sworn to be in the handwriting of the prisoner.[36]

Dec 24.   I was in court all day for the hearing of the trial of Edward Butt for the muder of his sweetheart Selina Phipps resulting in conviction and sentence of death.

---

[36] They were afterwards hanged with Edward Butt.

1874

Jan 8.   Emily, Flossie, Capt. Hood and I attended the meet at Hardwicke. We had a short run to Elmore church covert, lost our fox and came home drenched to the skin.

Jan 13.   Went to Leeds. Had conversations with my partners and Fearnside on the subject of the present and prospective position of Warburg. With the exception of Oswald they all with the utmost courtesy stated that full reflexion had not only failed to convince them of the advantages of taking Warburg into partnership but had confirmed them in their original conviction that we should have done wisely never to have entered into a discussion of such a position with him. Treated with greater confidence and allowed more latitude he has become far more exacting, with an iron will he has opposed the views of the majority with such pertinacity as to induce them to give way against their judgement. I am determined not to force him down their throats.

Emily and I took a ride on horseback through Bramham Park to Scarcroft. It was bitterly cold and we were insufficiently clad.

Jan 29.   Attended meeting of stewards of the Festival (Three Choirs). It is proposed to make the gatherings this year more exclusively of a religious character omitting both Ball and miscellaneous concerts. Sir Michael Hicks-Beach declines to serve as steward unless this is carried out. Date proposed 7th Sept.

Feb 16.   Davies gives 3 months notice. He and his wife are about to emigrate to New Zealand. E. Parry gives 3 months notice. Stephen Winn applies for my situation in Davies' place.

March 21.   Shire Hall. Four boys were charged with stealing sweets from the shop of Mrs Brown of Wotton. Previous convictions were proved against all except one who was dismissed with a caution. The others were sentenced to 5 years in a reformatory and a whipping each.

March 23.   Barnwood House. There are 20 servants and 90 patients all paying according to their means. We saw all the patients. Miss Wood is a very violent lady who gives much trouble. Mr Preston very urgent to be released and appeared absolutely sane. Application from General Money of Cheltenham for admission of Col. Donovan who is a poor knight of Windsor.

April 7.   Invited 180 school children to tea and an entertainment in the grounds. Nothing could have been more successful. We obtained the services of the Cranham Band and had incalculable quantities of cake and bread and butter.

April 14.   We have taken 15 Rutland Gate for 3 months from today at the weekly rental of 20 guineas. The drawing room furniture to be covered with fresh cretonne. We came up to town with Mrs Gittins, and maid Margaret and under-maid, Tothill and George. Morris to follow tomorrow. Found 15 Rutland Gate looking very plain but clean — the furniture neat but not gaudy. Tothill says beer allowance is 6d. a day for men and 4d. for women. Declined to entertain the subject on those terms. At Gloucester Infirmary we gave the men attendants £4 per annum and I have been told that for maids 1/- a week was usual and 1/6 was enough for butlers.

Agreed with Wimbush & Co. of Halking Street to take a pair of horses for 3 months and put up 3 carriages at their place and I have the assistance of their groom for £100.

Wimbush sent up 3 pairs on approval. I selected some bays, 16 hands, both seasoned horses and to go in a single or double harness.

April 22.   Oswald lunched with us. He wished to consult me on his love affair. Mr. Fetherstonhaugh seems now to wish the marriage to take place and has offered to give Oswald £400 to furnish with. He also thinks that his father will do something. I expressed most strongly my dissent, he being 24 and Miss F. only 18 and not having yet made anything in business and his father being in poverty with nothing to look to in case of illness or unforeseen trouble.

April 25.   Emily and I left for Withyham at 7.45 and arrived at Highfields Park in time for breakfast. Clara and Miss Van have had a delicious visit. Lady Elizabeth and Amy have been kindness itself. Amy is expecting to be confined end of May when Cecil should be doing duty at Leicester. We all came home by 6.15 train.

May 21.   I spent most of the day in the City with Mr Webb. He dined with us last night. In afternoon wrote a very long letter to Edwin about Oswald, praising his moral and personal qualities and assuring him of my affection but explaining my deep disappointment at his limited success in town and explaining in detail the failure of Whitworths' ladies costume cloth as explained by Mr Webb. There has been no rain here or at home for six weeks.

Letter from Eliza written in Florence, which says she is enjoying herself and can give no idea when she is coming home.

June 5.   The Bishop of Hereford's[37] little boy was baptized by his father in a most impressive manner during the afternoon service in the Cathedral. The procession from the choir to the font was very imposing, singing "The Church's one foundation". After signing the child with the Cross and naming him Harold Trevelyan, he implanted a solemn kiss on his forehead.

---

[37] James Atlay (1817–94); Vicar of Leeds, 1859–68, Bishop of Hereford, 1868–94.

The Godfathers were General Atlay, Dr Benson and myself; Godmother, Miss Wallace.

I came home and my gouty foot feeling better I walked about the gardens. The windows are in, but painting proceeds very slowly.

June 7. Attended church, going down in the pony phaeton owing to my lame foot which is much swollen today.

June 9. Sale of Cowley estate. Sold to Mr Gardner the Member for Windsor. £76,000 and £4,000 for timber, it seems very cheap.

June 24. Oswald Birchall married Miss Fetherstonhaugh in Dublin.

Sunday June 28. Morning to Eaton Square chapel. A Mr Scott an embryo missionary occupied Mr Wilkinson's pulpit; the latter always preaches at 4 o'clock afternoon service. At 3 to Westminster; it was anniversary of Coronation of the Queen and Dean Stanley gracefully touched upon the thoughts such an anniversary evokes. He spoke very beautifully. Evening to Pro-Cathedral and heard a splendid exposition of Catholic doctrine and dogma from Archbishop Manning, 1¼ hours without fatigue.

June 30. Excursion with the Lloyds to Richmond. During the course of the afternoon Dearman Janson proposed to Louisa Lloyd and later we heard he had succeeded in his suit.

July 4. We went to Withyham where I stood sponsor to Muriel Constance, Amy's second little girl. Amy looked very nicely. Lady de la Warr and Mrs Blomfield were the godmothers. Emily had to stand as proxy for the latter as she was ill. Lord and Lady John Manners were staying there. Eliza returned to town after having been abroad since August 1873. She called at 15 Rutland Gate in our absence at the Drummonds.

July 6. Eliza dined with us. She is looking in good spirits but very thin indeed.

July 11. Tenancy of 15 Rutland Gate terminated. Emily went to Harehills. The servants came to Bowden in the afternoon and I followed by the night train, sleeping at Bell Hotel because Morris came too late.

July 13. Meeting at Barnwood Asylum to appoint successor to Dr Wood. We appointed Mr Dickinson our chairman. Meeting at Prison to select Governor.

July 15. To Cheltenham to meet Eliza and continue the search for a house for her. Eventually took a villa on the Evesham road just beyond Saxham Villas for one year at £100 per annum. It is not quite finished and is very much enquired after. Eliza and I left Cheltenham about 1 in the night and went by train to Midland Hotel, Leeds.

July 19. Emily's 22nd birthday. Garden party at Harehills. We quite enjoyed the afternoon.

July 28. To Alderley Edge to stay with Theodore and Lily Crewdson [Emily's sister]. We had a charming drive with our most hospitable host and hostess.

Tewkesbury Show. My prizes for Channel Island cattle were very well competed for and Ackers presses me to continue the same encouragement for future shows. I was very sorry to be unable to attend.

Aug 13. Garden party at the Gambier Parrys. Our movements were much circumscribed by the rain which never entirely ceased. We dressed at the Bell and dined at the Palace to meet the Judges and High Sheriff. Mr Justice Lush took Emily in to dinner and was interested on hearing she had been at Miss Taylor's school as they were old friends of his.

Aug 15. Bought a grey cob, 13 hands, sound and not over 9 years. £35.

Aug 22. Engaged Thomas Williams, aged 18, as groom. 17/- a week. Advance if he pleased after being one year in my service and I said I would not engage him unless he meant to remain at least that time. He is to come as soon as he can get liberty.

Sept 15. Meeting at County Prison. Some talk about the prisoners' relief fund. Mr Leighton, the parson, gave an account of about 78 cases discharged during the last two months in which he had only found it necessary to give anything to 6 to help them on their way. Women he sends to Miss Sessions' home at 1/- a night; but they generally go wrong. Boys he often sends to Cardiff where they are kept for a week or two at 1/4 a day and then apprenticed on board some ship, and these generally do well.

Sept 18. Clara and Miss Van returned home from Enderby after two weeks. Clara looks very tall. Mrs Brook told Miss Van she thinks Clara much improved and was especially pleased with her manners and music.

Sept 28. Barnwood. I brought forward the case of J.W. Preston who came to Barnwood Dec. 1873 and has been confined since 1856, at Dr Newington's at Ticehurst. In conversation with myself and Mr Curtis Hayward he seemed perfectly sane; but the doctors says he has delusions. He explained his delusion about the horse, which was the one the doctors named, and urged us to permit him to have an interview with a solicitor without consulting his brother who committed him. I later received a letter from Mr Preston, very clever, containing an amusing account of Dr Newington who considers Ticehurst a paradise on earth and wonders everybody does not rush in to be confined.

Oct 14.   Aldam has agreed to make the Delf case and 2 pendants for sides of the dining room for £100.

Oct 26.   Mr Preston has been more unruly and having cut the putty from part of his window had to have his pocket knife taken away.

Oct 27.   Eliza took up her abode in her new house in Cheltenham.

Oct 29.   We have had a very charming visit to [the Bishop of] Hereford and Emily seemed so much appreciated.

Nov 7.   Came to Enderby. Mrs Brook has sent £3,000 to the Huddersfield church schools, also bought a piece of land at Leicester and is erecting schools to cost £3,000. She was given £500 to another school, and a number of other heavy donations and seems sadly overdone with applications of all kinds.

Cecil and Amy have bought a house in Princes Gardens for £8,800, a 64 year lease. They estimate the expense of furnishing by Atkinson & Co. in the Westminster Road will cost about £1,500. They leave for the Mediterranean next week.

Edward Brook, Carlile, Julius Hirst and Mr Fisher shot smaller covers; 22 pheasants, 47 hares, 10 rabbits.

Nov 12.   Two nights at Hatherop Castle. Lovely place close to Williamstrip Park, Sir M. Hicks-Beach's place. Both are fine estates and are divided by an iron fence. Mr Bazley, the son of Sir Thomas Bazley, the member for Manchester, bought the place of Dulheep Singh, the Maharajah. It belonged to Lord de Mauley who rebuilt the castle in grand and palatial style. Other guests include Lord Sherborne and Mr Witts. Mr Bazley showed us his hand organ, and his telescope. Shot 44 pheasants, 3 hares and 20 rabbits. I did not shoot either here or at Enderby, not having a licence this year. Mr Bazley is 44 years of age and married the daughter of his father's partner Mr Gardiner. They retired from cotton spinning with very great accumulated wealth 13 years ago. The wife's fortune has enabled them during the life of his father to live in this magnificent fashion. Mr Bazley is an M.A. and very clever. He has a lathe which cost £1,000. He plays the organ well, and knows the Latin name of every plant and tree his immense garden produces.

Nov 30.   Birmingham Cattle Show. As regards animals there it was only a moderate show with many owners withholding their stock for Smithfield club, because owing to present regulations nothing can be shown at both. I bought some Brahmas and a turkey. Coming home we found a train laden with coals off the line and were delayed nearly an hour. I was riding back from the station on my chestnut cob and unfortunately charged a spring cart coming into the city between bar and railway arch. I was violently thrown, and my horse galloped back along Barton Street and was stopped near the Greyhound. The cartman picked me up and drove me back till I recovered my horse.

Dec 1. Dined at the Grays at Parklands. The night was so dark we much feared a capsize. We came back via Gloucester, a longer but better road — quite a pleasant party but much too far for a winter's night.

Dec 3. After the Infirmary meeting Mr Marling and I visited the whole of the prison during the dinner hour and thus inspected all the prisoners in their cells. Several were in the Infirmary suffering from various causes. One had a swollen stomach from swallowing earrings and a brooch which he had stolen.

Dec 19. Attended school of Art and then on to see Eliza, who has this day dismissed her cook on the spot. She has been feeding her husband day by day with Eliza's meat, etc. though she had previously assured her he had gone to Australia.

Dec 25. Christmas Day. We have a very sharp frost and the ground covered in snow which has now lasted some 10 days. Clara and the boys (her Atkinson cousins) enjoyed skating in the afternoon.

Dec 26. Most brilliant day. We had the Cranham band to enliven us while we skated. In the evening the Brockworth bell ringers gave us a concert in the hall during our dinner.

1875

Jan 1.   We have had intense frost for a fortnight. There are immense drifts of snow at Cranham, and on the Painswick road there is an impassable bank from the east wind. Edward, Wayland (Ancrum) the Atkinson boys and I ascended Brotheredge and saw a drift probably 10 feet deep.

Our pond has not been smooth; but it has afforded the neighbourhood much enjoyment in skating. Acme skates are at a premium and not to be had.

Jan 2.   Marling and I wrote the prison report to the Quarter Sessions. All that was proposed was eventually agreed to. We had a very pleasant concert at the Palace after dining with the magistrates.

Jan 9.   Edward Leatham bid £85,600 at the Sale for Miserden. It was bought in for £90,000, so as he has bought it since the figure is presumably between these two. The timber is valued at £15,000.

We came to Harehills.

Jan 14.   We dined with Benson Jowitt (Emily's brother). No one to meet us. We passed a very pleasant evening. He told me that R. Jowitt & Sons had turned over £480,000 — nearly half a million — in 1874 and nett profit £11,000.

Jan 18.   I went to Hull [from Leeds] and bought a horse of John Robinson alias Gipsy Jack for £150 subject to vet passing him.

Called on Barrett & Duveen, 49 Waterwork Street, Hull and saw remains of his sale. Nothing worth buying; but he said, on receipt of some novelties he was expecting from Holland, he would send a box on approbation.

Jan 20.   With John Jowitt [his father-in-law] I visited the Green Lane Board Schools [Leeds] with accommodation for 800 children, divided into 5 classes, infants, young boys, older boys, young girls and older ones. All seemed working admirably. The buildings and land cost £12,000.

We then visited Armley Jail which has room for 500 prisoners. The men and women both make mats, the latter only those made in a frame and not in a loom. There are also 5 sewing machines and they pay well in making mechanics' cotton jackets. They have a Nelson machine for baking clothes to prevent infection. Prisoners grind all the corn required. The crank goes into two cells and the two prisoners who have handles grind about 9 or 10 stone a day which is baked whole as it comes from the mill in loaves for rations, 8 and 10 ozs. each. No tread-mill but cranks in the cells which show the number of revolutions outside. They weave sacking for hammocks, woollen mats in two qualities and also with patterns in maroon and black. Only 3 or 4 men in hospital. Health very good. 20 exercise yards round a centre where a warder with eye-hole to each keeps watch.

Feb 9.   Mrs Brook came to stay at Bowden for a week. She has a rather poor account from Amy written at Thebes 26 Jan. When she went home I travelled as far as Cheltenham with her in company with Mr Addison who most strongly urged our taking James William away from Ticehurst thinking that as he had derived no benefit from Dr Newington's treatment it was time to try some other. I said I had not the slightest opinion that any treatment we might advance would cure him but that as the cost was about £1,200 per annum I thought he was entitled to greater attention, better apartments and more luxury. I promised to see if Needham could recommend any better place.

March 1.   Tothill gave notice to leave. He has nothing against the place but finds the country dull and thinks a young man should move about. He has no wish to marry at present. He does not wish to inconvenience us; but would look to leaving in about six weeks.

March 13.   We dined at the Heatons [in Leeds] only meeting Prof. Martin Duncan[38] who is lecturing to the Gilchrist Charity on antediluvian animals. Prof Rucher and Miss Heaton were also present. They all say Leeds is sadly overlectured and none of these are too well attended. Unversity extension is promoted by men who cannot hold their own at either university and therefore go starring it about the country. Duncan says ladies might as well learn about old armour as political economy — it's a solemn farce, Huxley[39] has been giving some lectures to ladies and said to a friend, "if I did not discontinue these lectures I should die from a new disease — suppressed laughter."

April 3.   Clara's birthday, and we had a capital school feast for 197 children. The weather after being very beautiful for a week was lowering and threatened a storm. This however did not come on until after they had left.

April 4.   We have a magnificent show in the conservatory, gesnerias, amantophyllum, begenia fuchsoides, hyacinths, tulips, camellias, cinerarias, primulas, brooms, roses, azallias, tropeolium, cyclamen, daffodils, geraniums. We have been excessively gay ever since our return from Leeds.
   The spring bedding is lovely, white arabis, violets, primroses, single and double pansies, tulips, hyacinths, myosotis, scillas etc.

April 5.   Wrote to Warburg at Grand Hotel Turin, pointing out the state of the stock, failure of efforts at Mill, and general discontent and informing him I saw no chance of the opposition formerly manifested to making him a partner being removed, or the consent of the majority of partners being obtained. I reminded him of his precipitate retreat from America as an instance of hasty judgement.

---

[38] (1821–91) geologist, FRS etc.
[39] Thomas Henry Huxley (1825–95) biologist, FRS and Darwin's champion.

April 6.   Tidal waves on the Severn, 6th–9th. Arrives at Gloucester ¼ to 10 and an hour later each day.

Applied for space in Philadelphia Exhibition for 1876. Goods must be in by 31 March '76.

April 15.   John and Deborah and Flossie came to us for 10 days. Gave dinner party and all passed off very pleasantly; but the uncertainty of who would and who would not come kept Emily, who was not very well, in some agitation.

April 29.   Oswald came down from London. He thinks when Warburg finds out he has no chance of a partnership he will settle down on the old terms. Webb vibrates between likening Warburg to Judas Iscariott . . . and the worst insult calling him a damned Christ killer. How the notion of his Jewish origin has spread I know not.

Dearman and Emily with Clara and Miss Van and Margaret a maid went to London and then abroad. Watering places were tried for Dearman's gout.

July 4.   Homburg. Church very crowded, must have been nearly 600 present. We had a terrible thunder storm which beginning at the Litany lasted until the conclusion of the Communion office. Homburg gets fuller every day. We were sketching yesterday in the Schloss gardens which are very pretty and much drier than the neighbourhood of the *Mineral Guellen*.

Back in Gloucestershire the gossip continues.

Aug 6.   Baker told me Capt. Curtis Hayward was left in very moderate circumstances. He has let Quedgeley to Mr Robinson for 5 years at about £300 per annum. Mrs Curtis Hayward and daughters will probably go to reside in London. The Cliffords find they cannot afford to keep hunters and live at their house so have departed to Munich for a year or two and have let Frampton Court for 5 years. I did not hear who was their tenant.

Aug 16.   I was at an adjourned Petty Session with Mr Hallewell and we convicted two boys from Norton under the Juvenile Offenders Act of stealing two rabbits value 1/-. We sentenced one to receive eight and the other ten strokes of a birch rod.

Sept 24.   Mrs Jowitt [Emily's mother] came to us yesterday. She looks wonderfully young and handsome and seems to have derived great advantage from her visit to the continent this summer. No sketching lesson today, the fury of the elements rendering it impossible. We have previously had a month of superb weather. Poor Mr Jones of Whitley Court was knocked down by a heavy bough this morning — his forehead frightfully bruised and his leg broken just below the knee.

Sept 26.   Emily taken ill at 3.30 a.m. We sent for Mr Graves and nurse at 5.30 a.m. Both arrived at about 8 a.m. At 12.40 p.m. Mother (Mrs Jowitt) rushed down and announced the joyful news of the birth of a fine boy 7 lb. 11 oz. 1 ft. 7 inches.[40]

Dr Crichton Browne visited James William Brook on 5 Aug and reports he finds him moody and dull looking, unhappy with no morbid appetites but with intense restlessness of body and mind, memory mostly gone, affection blunted and occasionally has fits of violence, which represent epileptic seizures. He should therefore reside in an asylum and be under constant medical supervision, and that at Ticehurst he commands advantages as regards accommodation, comfort, and medical skill unobtainable in any other private asylum in the country.

Sept 29.   Engaged Charles Bertie at £60 per annum as butler. He has been with the Dowager Countess Beauchamp who says she considers him to be a butler thoroughly to be depended upon, very sober and steady and trustworthy.

Sept 30.   Mr Marnock spent yesterday with me advising about planting in the garden and on the hill behind.

Oct 2.   Refused to grant a licence to Wintour Phelps of Elmore to sell cider on the premises. He already has his licence to sell off. Refused licence to Henry O. Hopton of Hucclecote, he being rated at £23; but his orchard was worth the money.

Oct 6.   Clara and Miss Van go to Clarefield [Eliza's house in Cheltenham] and Clara begins her music lessons with Von Holst[41] 8/6 per lesson, and dancing with Mrs Webster and French with Mlle. Thiercy. I went to Hereford and lunched with the Bishop and Mrs Atlay and saw Anna Harris [his cousin] who is staying having come there to stand sponsor to their 3rd daughter and 10th child.

Oct 7.   Meeting at the Tolsey; most enthusiastic, Bishop in the chair, Earls Ducie and Bathurst, Sir J. Campbell, Lord Fitzhardinge, Col. Kingscote, the Dean, etc.

Oct 11.   Keen [the head gardener] says he would like to have beds robbed of their flowers today to allow time for spring bedding. I mentioned Nov 1st as first time we could think of it. We discussed making plantation at the corner of the pleasure ground, putting soil to feed the Cedar Atlantica, also taking roses away from front and replacing with clematis and smaller round

---

[40] This baby, known as Jack, was to become Sir John Birchall M.P. for N.E. Leeds for many years.
[41] Gustav Holst's father.

beds and planting roses along the wall.

Oct 14.   Gave Bertie a month's notice.

Nov 11.   Thomas Powell came as butler at £50 per annum.
Attended Professor Morley's[42] lecture on Wordsworth.
The floods are out again as far as the eye can reach west of Gloucester.

Dec 9.   Prof. Morley's last lecture on Literature of the 19th century. He spoke eulogistically of Emily's paper on *In Memoriam*, saying it was a privilege to read such a carefully written and most interesting analysis — gave her very highest mark.

Engaged Thomas Webb of Lydney as footman at £20 per annum, livery and morning suit — all found — except washing.

Meat ordered for men, half from Davis and half from Co-operative who each bought one of my oxen. Keen 10 lbs, Morris 10 lbs. Davis 12 lbs, Warley 10 lbs, Barnes 10 lbs, Tower 10 lbs, Betteridge 8 lbs = 70 lbs.

Dec 22.   Yesterday I lost my diamond ring between home and the Asylum after attending meeting of school managers. It was picked up in Barton Street by an old woman and obtained for me.

Dec 23.   Lunched with the Bishop and talked over Cranham. Both the Horfield and Warneford trusts could be applied to for assistance. The former has for president Mr Monk, M.P. the son of the founder. The Warneford could give temporary assistance so as to supply a preacher.

---

[42] Henry Morley (1822–94), man of letters and professor at University College, London.

1876

Jan 24. Harehills. Emily began her instruction in cookery. 3 weeks, 2 lessons a day, 3 days a week.

Jan 26. Florence's 21st birthday. We had all the married sisters and brothers-in-law and brother and sister-in-law at dinner and no others except one old friend Mr Jackson. We had a singularly happy evening. They are all so loving and united. Mr Jackson took occasion to offer up a most touching prayer enumerating the blessings showered down on Mr and Mrs Jowitt and contrasting their happy life surrounded by their beloved ones and their descendants with the bereaved and desolate condition of so many families.

Jan 31. We had a quiet evening at Harehills and I note this down being about the only one during our long visit.

Feb 7. Lunched and dined with the Drummonds at Princes Gate. Clara and Miss Van are here. Went with them to the Admiralty to see the Queen pass on her way to open Parliament in person; though drawn by the well known 8 cream coloured horses, she was not in a State carriage, nor in the House of Lords did she wear her robes. Rumour says her crown almost slipped off which is not thought a good omen.

Feb 19. Clara frets sadly about Miss Van leaving.[43] Miss Brown came instead, at £120 per annum, and to pay for her own washing.

March 12. We had a tremendous fall of snow accompanied by terrific gales. In the hedge bottoms there was about 12 ft of snow between here and Upton Church. The Scotch firs lost some of their boughs and a weeping willow was blown down by the pond.

March 14. Operations at General Infirmary. Stone extracted from a boy's bladder by Cole I thought clumsy — must have taken half an hour from first to last. One or two minor things. We tried alternately ether and chloroform.

March 17. I went down with Mr Lucy (Chairman) to see the new docks at Sharpness Point and the new entrance into the Berkeley canal. A vessel had just unloaded at Mr Lucy's new warehouse — 9,000 quarters (sic) of corn from Odessa probably the growth of 4,000 acres. There is every preparation for an immense business.

---

[43] Clara's daughter Diana Ross-Ross afterwards said her mother had told her that Miss Van's removal by her stepmother was the unhappiest moment of her life; but Emily evidently thought she should have a more intellectual governess.

March 24.   Cecil and Amy have a son born yesterday making their fifth child. The poor little fellow died this day.

March 25.   Edwards gives up my farm today. He says he has been making nothing from it for long.

March 28.   Emily has very bad cough with shivering at night. She caught cold out drawing with me at the end of the week.

March 31.   Emily's temperature 103. She had two mustard leaves on last evening and bore them well. I ran over to see Eliza instead of attending the Bench.

April 4.   We had a very disturbed night. Emily had delirium. Mr Graves said intellectual people with active brains always suffered from delirium when they have fever.

April 7.   Attended the Assizes and dined with the Judges. I sat between Mr Price and the Revd. Mr Wilmot who is chaplain to the High Sheriff, Edmund Waller of Farmington. We passed a very pleasant evening.

April 9.   The last week has been remarkable in temperature night and day. It has been so very warm we have been compelled to give up our fires and the house has stood at over 50°.

The horse chestnuts are bursting into leaf, plum in blossom, even the wild ones in the hedges. Our spring beds are gorgeous with bulbs and everything looks more cheerful.

April 12.   Maida Mirrielees came for a fortnight. Emily tired herself by walking about the house too much (in preparation for the visit of her great friend).

April 15.   Ten persons have with difficulty been caught elvering and they were brought up before Sir William Guise, de Winton, Marling and myself. Cases were fully proved. They had taken boats with watch dogs and threatened the police and waterbailiffs. We fined them each 10/- or with the option of going to prison for a week.

April 17.   Dr Evans and Graves examined dear Emily. She has had bronchitis, pleurisy and some little inflamation of lower part of the left lung. They have ordered a blister between the shoulders.

April 20.   Went up to town. Warburg dined with me at the Burlington Hotel. He looks flourishing and gives a good account of himself. He has found Austria in a deplorable state, Prussia a little better and Italy the most flourishing country in Europe at present. George Salt told him that at their last stock taking, on July 1st. 1875, they had made a better profit than at any former period.

Called at Lord Chamberlain's office and presented my cards receiving 2 in return to be filled up when I go to Levée.

April 22.   Returned and found Emily looking decidedly better; by Graves' orders she still remains in bed.

April 27.   Went up to town. Business is very depressed and I hear that one effect of the general curtailment is that horses have fallen very much in price and there are hundreds of coachmen seeking situations without success.

April 28.   I was introduced at the Levée at St. James's Palace by Lord Ducie.[44] All went off without a hitch. It was not very fully attended.

May 3.   I took Emily a drive in the fields in pony trap.

May 5.   Sam Bowly called and went all over the place and was much pleased with the conservatory flowers. He strongly recommends stone rocking a terrace walk and the cultivation of irises, peonies, delphiniums which he advised us to purchase from Robert Parker of Upper Tooting.

May 6.   Pleasant letter from Mr Webb in Philadelphia. He describes his voyage with the iceberg and fog episodes, New York and its marble mansions and wooden huts, bad paving and sumptuous cemetery with monuments of white marble valued at thousands sterling.

May 7.   The fox has taken two more lambs that were only dropped a few days before. The bells on the ewes necks seem to have no terror for Reynard. Last week he took a hen from her nest where she set 15 eggs.

May 8.   Emily and I came up to town leaving Clara, Miss Brown and Jack at home. We have apartments on second floor at the Burlington Hotel, Cork Street.

May 10.   Attended Drawing Room. The weather was tolerably sunny but piercingly cold with north east wind but in Cecil's warm and comfortable brougham we did not suffer in the least. We left the Burlington at 1.30 and returned 5.15. The progress through the numerous suites of apartments was slow but we found much to interest us in them, and the company, the beauty of the English race was never more conspicuous. The ladies' dresses were rich and exquisite in colour, the jewels were plentiful as blackberries and singularly lovely. We had no inconvenience from overcrowding and Emily escaped without catching the least cold. We had a capital view of the

---

[44] Henry John Moreton, 3rd Earl of Ducie, Lord Lieutenant of Gloucestershire 1857–1911.

Prince and Princess of Wales. Amy was presented by Lady Scarbrough.

May 13.   We dined at the Drummonds. They have had a scare about scarlet fever. The under nurse was taken ill on Thursday and yesterday the doctor recognized it as a mild case of scarlet fever so she was sent to the fever hospital. Nobody was there except Lady Elizabeth. Cecil has heard this afternoon that the Government have very bad news from Turkey and that war is imminent. The outbreak at Salonika is likely to be repeated elsewhere and the mussulman blood is rising; with 7 million soldiers in Europe desiring war, as much as a spark could set such inflammable material on fire.

May 23.   Mr Warburg came for one night. Looks well and is in good spirits. He describes the general business as being well managed beyond former precedent (the absence of Mr Webb in America as beneficial). We stand well everywhere abroad. He says the waters of Carlsbad are very efficacious in the cure of severe forms of gout [Dearman's chief weakness] and that the Grosvenors and Bedfords are never absent. He describes Bohemian scenery in the neighbourhood of Carlsbad as very lovely.

May 27.   Margaret left us today (the faithful maid). She was much depressed. We gave her £10 and hope her marriage may prove a happy one.

June 2.   Visited Hawthornden the seat of the Drummond family. At Dalkeith we saw the Duke of Buccleugh drilling a handsom regiment of militia in his park. He has a collection of most beautiful china. Blue and other oriental especially some very large vases of famille rose, also Sèvre, Dresden, Capo di Monte, Chelsea, Worcester, Vienna and Berlin. It is a very grand place.

June 10.   Had long conversations with partners. Mr Webb in particular who gave us a most interesting description of his American experiences. No improvement at the Mill. Average this year 86 pieces a week, 2230 pieces value £18,900. Trade getting much flatter. Today we had separate interviews with Cheetham. He first privately told me of his sorrows, father dead, sister insane, brother wretched, uncle unkind, wife ill at Scarborough — fears for her brain. I suggested Oswald spend half his days at the Mill till the end of the year, as a support to Cheetham to make more sympathy between the departments. Webb, Campbell and Oswald agreed to do away with cheviots and confine themselves to certain specified makes — at present with all their patterns they are getting few orders.

July 13.   Heat at Bowden 94° in the shade. Since the spring rains this has been a very dry season. Keen says that for two months they have had but one rain to do any good. Grass not half cut but what is carried is in splendid condition of excellent quality.

Emily Birchall aged 25. Portrait by F.G. Cotman, exhibited in the Royal Academy 1878

Bowden Hall and terrace with Gloucester Cathedral seen in the distance.
Watercolour by Dearman Birchall

Emily's grave in Upton Churchyard. Monasterboyce Cross carved by
Farmer and Brindley under Aldam Heaton's directions in Parian marble.
Watercolour by Dearman Birchall

July 26.   Emily, Eliza and I went up to the encampment on Minchinhampton Common. It took 2¾ hours with the Barouche and was very fatiguing to the horses. We lunched with the officers of the North Gloucestershire Militia by invitation of Sir David Wedderburn. There are the North and South Gloucesters' the Bucks and Berks, and 2 Tower Hamlet Militia Regiments' in all about 5000 men.

Williams was sent to Gloucester on some errand on foot. He disobediently went on horseback and leaving home at 12.30 he did not return until 7. He expressed his sorrow. Morris is savage.

July 28.   We went to tea in the Cranham woods and met Eliza and Miss Venables and Ruth, Winifred and Maude. The two former accompanied us home.
Finding that Williams' cob had gone to the Bell at 4, I taxed Williams with disingenuity and he explained that he started on foot and walked as far as Chequers, then found he had bunglingly left his instructions at home, returned and rode down, admitting he had partaken of several glasses of drink with friends in Gloucester. I gave him a good talking to and he appeared repentent.

July 30. Resolution (to last till Dec. 31. 1876).
To abstain from all wine or spirits except of course medicinally. Diet. Rise at 7. Devotional reading until breakfast. At least one hour per day to be devoted to some solid reading. Exercise at least 5 miles a day walking or equivalent in riding or working in garden or otherwise. No smoking in any form.

Aug 1.   Canon Venables joins his daughters here today.

Aug 5.   The Venables (7) all left for home.

Aug 7.   Heard trial for rape by 10 men. 5 got 15 years penal servitude, 3 for 10 years, 2 got off. It was a Forest of Dean case, very brutal, but the girl a poor miserable creature scarcely seemed of a character to enlist one's sympathy.

Aug 11.   Called on Mr Turner and paid him £3 for damage done to his field by my Scotch oxen. Saw Mr Jones and agreed with him to take Gransome Close as soon as he can get rid of Turner. He will give him notice at Michaelmas and he can either leave then or Lady Day.

Aug 13.   Heat in shade in garden 97°.

Aug 14.   Garden party James Stanton. Took us 2 hours to return. The heat for last fortnight has been intense, never less than 88° in the shade in the afternoon. All the numerous garden parties have been favoured with the most gorgeous weather. We have had no rain for weeks.

Aug 19.   Mrs Newsholme leaves us today, the best cook we ever had. She complains of nursery and dairy. We have twice advertised in the Guardian, applied to Mrs Pope, Mrs Massey, Mrs French, and now in Times and Daily Telegraph, so far without success. Mrs N. has agreed to stay another fortnight.

Aug 22.   Bowden Hall garden party — about 88 to 95. We had the Militia band as the Artillery Band was engaged for a flower show at Sudely Castle. There are scarcely enough men in Gloucester.

Aug 23.   Bristol and Gloucestershire Archaeological Society meeting in Gloucester with excursion to Tewkesbury. Admirable address by Sir William Guise, the President. About 400 members; a great success.

Aug 29.   Davis has been down to the Bill of Portland and purchased of the principal breeder there two thoroughbred rams at £3 each. His expenses were £3.8.4. One of these is for Mr Ackers.

Sept 1.   At Enderby for shooting. 14 brace partridges; 16 hares; 4 rabbits. Next day 13½ brace partridges; 21 hares; 2 rabbits. I shot a nightjar or goat sucker and gave it to young Wood to stuff.
   Mrs Brook in consequence of solicitation has sold The Mount and six cottages to Arthur Armitage for £4,100. Edward Brook first asked her and offered £3,200 which was tinker's valuation. Arthur is about to build himself a house — he had been looking to Healey House but there was no prospect at present Mrs Brook appearing as likely for life as ever. She joins Eliza and Mary [Sam Birchall's widow] at Exeter next Monday for 3 weeks tour in Devonshire.

Sept 11.   Stayed with the Atlays for Hereford Festival.

Sept 16.   J.H. Wright the tenant of Reservoir Inn, Matson convicted of keeping open house on Sunday and having company drinking during prohibited hours. A policeman dressed in a smock frock cleverly got in, both back and front doors open. The three men who were drinking all appeared as witnesses and this being the third conviction he was condemned to the heaviest penalty £20 and expenses. This involves closing house for 2 years; but we had previously refused a fresh licence for this ill-conducted house which belongs to the Corporation.

Sept 21.   School feast which has been postponed now owing to various complaints having been rife amongst the children. 235 and the Sunday and weekday teachers making over 250. Miss Maria Rice, the Ancrums, Emerises etc. We had superb weather and everything went off well. We gave books on this occasion for good attendance to the number of 44.

Amy very ill with asthma caused by the extraction of a tooth. We have had daily bulletins from Cecil.

Warburg came for two nights on his way back from Italy. He considers our worsteds as excellent and cannot be bettered. Slaters coatings fulfil more the idea of what he as been asking for for years than any he has previously had. Our own Mill goods are the only ones for which he has not a word of praise. He has been very successful in getting money that is due to us in Austria. Trade bad and depressed in every country he has visited. He crosses to New York in the Germanian on the 5th prox.

Oct 1.   Jack is now a year old. He cannot say a word but he runs about and plays, shuts the doors and can drag his pet lamb round the nursery and even take up and walk away with my waste paper basket. He never fails to point to the right person when asked where is Papa, Mama, Sissy or Miss Brown and knows buttons, tops, pictures and bells when attention is called to them.

Benson and Carry postponed their visit owing to severe accident. Father (Emily's) had fallen from his horse yesterday.

Oct 10.   James Webb gave me notice for the third time. He says that Sandy only sleeps in the house occasionally and in his absence he has to sleep in the pantry, and last night after a week's absence he suddenly came back and Webb had to go into his own room and found his sheets damp from the weather. He could not get on with Sandy any longer. Sandy having betrayed the trust I repose in him and violated his word on above matter which he does not deny, I gave him notice to leave. Sandy on enquiry at Mrs French's for situation gave her to understand that he did not expect to work much but to overlook others and see that they did the work. With me he has failed even in this, and glass, silver, windows have all been neglected.

Oct 15.   Emily accompanied Benson and Carry to Leeds. I walked up Painswick Beacon with Clara and Miss Brown, and leaving them called on Mr Hyett who was very nicely.

Oct 16.   Considered the servant problem. Mrs Newsholm had said that Sandy having left she would not mind coming back. Margaret said Mrs Newsholm was conscientious and well disposed but prejudiced and inclined to listen to tales. Mrs N. said that Sandy's language was shameful and unfit for young girl's to hear and he neither could, nor did work, leaving all to the footmen to do. Ann said for long servants had set one another against the place. Even Keen was unsettled the first year he was here, and told her he had heard tales enough to induce him to leave ten times. Tothill, although a good worker, had never been a friend of the family and never lost an opportunity of saying and hinting and insinuating things against us, and there was no love lost between Tothill and me. He was very ungrateful, Mrs Newsholm did not think Emily exactly put her in her right place in reference to under-lings, and especially the housemaid whom she sometimes took into the storeroom.

Dined at Quarter sessions, a very large party, Lord Ducie and Sir Michael Hicks-Beach. At 8.52 I caught the express to Leeds.

Oct 21.   Went to Oxton by way of Wetherby. The country looks exceed-ingly pretty, the tints in their variety and richness were very marked in the woods near Thorner. The bridges are said to be sinking a little, and the trains are run at a very slow rate; the embankments are scarcely settled down as yet. Found my aunt (Harris) looking nicely and pretty cheerful. Robert Steele staying here which is very pleasant. Benjamin Brooksbank dined with us and did not whistle.

Sunday afternoon I walked down to Healaugh [the Brooksbanks'] to see the collection of china, formed by their ancestor. The old man is a very amusing specimen for 86 years and told some capital stories; but the old lady would not lend us the key to examine her treasures.

Oct 22.   Left Oxton. Supper with Edward in Leeds and caught the 10.5 mail for Gloucester.

Oct 23.   Met Tothill at The Bell at 12. He has left Mr Craven and intends to marry in the spring. Engaged him to come back on Nov. 10th. Mrs Smith, the cook, to stay three months longer.

Oct 30.   We dined at the Rectory. Emeris does not think of having a mission here. I urged it strongly and pointed out the lethargy of Upton, the neglect of church and sacraments, the frequency of cases brought before the magistrates, the saying that his interests were in Gloucester. He was most amiable, and authorized what I proposed that I should write and ask Mr Edward Jackson to come for the mission.

Mr Bazely [rector of Matson] told a story about William Jowitt who on taking a service for a friend was told by the clerk he must not preach above 15 minutes or the squire would hold out his watch. William's sermon was arranged for the identical period so he lengthened it, and when the squire opened his watch and held it out at arms length, he suddenly stopped, and stared at the watch until the squire was abashed and withdrew it.

Nov 6.   Visited the Prison with Capt. de Winton. Saw a man who had suspended himself from his loom by a rope and was only just cut down in time to save his life. He said that starvation had driven him to self destruc-tion. His diet was reduced when he was convicted, and he had been 2½ months before trial.

James Dandy left my service. Richard Tothill came today, at £55 per annum.

Dec 12. Stayed with Lord Ducie at Tortworth till the 15th. [The house looked so forbidding Lord Ducie had the word WELCOME inscribed over the entrance to encourage his guests. When the house subsequently became a prison the inscription was removed.]

Dec 13. I walked with the shooting party. 133 pheasants, 26 hares, 14 rabbits.

Dec 14. Walked out to see the Shorthorns. Lord Moreton is endeavouring to get up a herd like his grandfather and he has got a beautiful bull and some fine cows — a very large breeder of white small pigs.

At the Maharaja Duleep Singh's at Elvedon the Prince of Wales and party shot about 6,000 head in three days.

Dec 15. We left Tortworth this morning after a pleasant visit. Yesterday a telegram informed Lord Ducie of the sudden death of his eldest nephew Mr Oakley from diptheria in the Navy. It was kept strictly a secret, even from the Oakleys, until after we left that the party might not be broken up. The maids knew but were charged not to inform their mistresses.

Dec 18. Aunt Harris died at Oxton Hall at 2.30 this afternoon. After a week of unusual good health she fell down in a fit of apoplexy and never rallied.

Dec 23. Aunt Harris's funeral at Bolton Percy, was very plainly conducted; the church decorated for Christmas looked very pretty. After lunch we started for Leeds in a fly at 2 p.m. Caught 4.30 train and were in Gloucester at 11.30. Edward returned home with me and we found Eliza at Bowden. John Rolt of Ozleworth killed by a fall in the hunting field.

Dec 25. We have a prodigious quantity of rain and the country is flooded. We passed a very happy day but without any event worth notice.

Dec 28. The Ancrums had a great party at which we hoped to have been present, but had to decline owing to dear Aunt's death.

1877

Jan 8.   Made an expedition to Hull to call on Duveen where I bought some blue china.

Returned to Leeds. Bought some china which has been submerged 131 years.

Agnews showed me proof of Cousins's engraving of Uncle Alfred Harris's picture by Leighton of the Greek girl. It has come out singularly beautiful and is selling at 12 guineas, that is twice the cost. Uncle told me he only obtained £50 for according the liberty to have it engraved by Cousins.

Sent back one vase to Duveen to be sold.

Feb 22.   I have agreed to give £94.10/- (Knowles valuation) for 2 cottages adjoining Joseph Bettridges' which I have previously bought for £58.

Bought bottom field of Arthur Rodway (over 2 acres) for £400 with £20 for timber. There are about 30 trees.

At lunch Anna N. said: "Should the Philadephia Bonds go down to nothing you will see that I don't lose?". I said, "Well that's cheeky"; but afterwards agreed to take the £600 at 94. the price she paid for them. They are now at 50½–£267 loss; but I shall then have no reproaches, and shall give the young lady a wide berth and certainly beware of advice in future.

March 7.   Emily safely delivered at ¼ before 5 this morning of a fine boy. Weighs 8 lb. 8 oz. 21 inches. [Called Percy by the family.]

March 15.   Emily still keeps her bed but is remarkably well and very cheerful. Baby thrives.

March 17.   I attended the funeral of Mr Hyett at Painswick cemetery. The day was bitterly cold and while there we had a snow storm. Much delay was caused by the immense size and ponderous weight of the coffin. It was very largely attended and much sympathy with the family and regret at the loss of so great a man.

April 10.   Arthur Percival Dearman Birchall christened by Mr Emeris. Canon Venables, Benson Jowitt [Emily's brother] and Amy Drummond sponsors.

May 1.   Engaged apartments at Brown's Hotel for a month.

May 6.   We called at Burne Jones's The Grange, North Road, Fulham and by merely leaving our cards were admitted to his studio and saw many classic works of lovely execution and superb colour. His female faces are surpassingly beautiful. Of Christian sentiment there is an entire absence.

May 7.   Levée. Prince of Wales — very well attended. I talked to Mr Price and a number of other Gloucestershire people. The Prince looked well though he only arrived from Paris at 7 a.m. this morning.

Maida Mirrielees lunched and we called on Mr Muir in Holland Park — furnished by Collinson & Locke, and the Alexanders at Aubrey House, their guiding spirit being Whistler, the tone is eccentric and they have some very pretty Japanese things.

May 13.   To call on Norman Shaw, no great distance behind Hampstead church. We were delighted with his surroundings and charmed with rooms and Persian pots.

In the morning we had attended the Grosvenor Chapel and heard the Archbishop of Canterbury, most ponderous and anything but eloquent, and in the afternoon St. James's Piccadilly to hear the Archbishop of York, who compared the annual expenditure on Missions as half a million and on drink as one hundred and forty eight million. Returned to Gloucester by 9 p.m. mail.

May 14.   Visited the County Asylum with Chairman. Spent 4 hours there and very fatiguing to the mind to see so many distressed persons without their wits. At home found Clara and the boys all very well, and servants all going on well. I had a very hearty reception and was overjoyed to see my young folks.

May 23.   Had interview with Herman Weber, 11 Grosvenor Street, for medical examination. My height 6′ 1″ and weight 12 stone 2 lb. Regular exercise in open air. Never drink beer or champagne.

June 2.   Returned to Gloucester.

June 6.   Emily, Clara and I had a charming drive with the cobs to Cirencester lunching at the College. We took Birdlip going and returned through Oakley Park 5 miles, then Miserden. It took us 2¼ hours going and 2½ returning. The country was lovely.

On July 4 they left for Switzerland, (St. Moritz) taking Clara and Florence, returning on August 16th.

Aug 17.   Came home and found all well. Jack looks a little pale and delicate but Percival has improved wonderfully and is a very fine looking boy for 5 months. Keen [the head gardener] has sent fruit continually to the Infirmary, Eye Institution, to Dr. Ancrum and my sister Eliza.

Meeting at Barnwood. Dr Needham reported Miss Allen had escaped and spent two days in Cranham woods living on sorrel and water.

My pair of horses sold at Swindon for 37½ guineas.

They then entertained a house party for the Three Choirs Festival. Afterwards Mrs Venables wrote that Emily was "so surpassingly delightful to look at and listen to". By Sept 14 Dearman was at Enderby and on the 18th at Leeds staying with his brother Edward where he was ill with gout. Emily's Father and Mother and sister Lily dined with them.

Sept 25.   Went to Spofforth and saw a number of horses at Godfrey Long's. He asks 220 guineas a pair for most of them. Selected a pair of blacks rising 5 and 6.

Sept 26.   Met Mr Hartley at Godfrey Long's. He likes the blacks. Bought them for 220 guineas.

Oct 8.   Mr Hicks-Beach lunched with us and I signed an appointment of Hayward for Cranham appointing him to receive certain fines from those trespassers who send cattle into the common without right.

Oct 23.   Drove Emily to Miserden Park and called on Mrs Leatham in their new house built by Alfred Waterhouse. He was in Huddersfield. Evening, I drove Keen down to Gloucester to attend a meeting of the Church of England Temperance Society at Shire Hall.
   Dr Ancrum has given up keeping any drink for his servants of any kind. He allows his butler £5, cook £3.15 and women servants £3 and £2 per annum. Tothill agrees to sleep in the house whenever we are away and take the responsibility of the place. I told him he should have his cottage rent free, and same wages viz. £55 p.a. and I would give him a wedding present of £5. He is to be married on Tuesday.

Nov 7.   I lunched with Ackers and met the professor of agriculture at Cirencester College. We afterwards inspected the Prinknash herd including the champion cow Queen of the Georgians, 1st prize Royal this year and Lord Bective's champion cup for the best shorthorn in the yard; bred by Ackers, born Jan. 1872. There has not been a champion prize since 1862, so he was very lucky to succeed this year. She is not of his best blood. He will not fat any of them for showing.
   The best bull I saw was second, Lord Prinknash of what he calls the Christian blood; the Georgian's inferior because it has a strain of Bates — he would refuse £2000 for this bull not yet two years old. Dark roans are the favourite — reds are called roans if they have ever so little white hair mixed. Bulls of Georgian blood have sold this year as low as £50; but a Christian blood bull would let for £220 for the season. He charges 10/6 for covering a common cow.

Nov 10.   Emily and I drove over to Cheltenham to spend Sunday at Eliza's. We were out in a tremendous storm, sun shining behind us, hail and rain all around and a double rainbow. Some difficulty in controlling the horses. Sunday. It rained all day without ceasing. Heard Mr Wilkinson of Eaton Square preach most beautifully at Eliza's church, and in the evening we went to All Saints.

Nov 19. Cecil and Amy Drummond came to us for the night. Amy looked very well and happy. (They had a dinner party for 18 including Sir William Guise, Sir David Wedderburn, just back from California and travelling round the world, Canon and Mrs Harvey, Mr and Mrs Edward Leatham, Mr & Mrs Nisbet etc.). All passed off well but we were unusually short of flowers. We had the *Farleyense* in the drawing room but it was much too large.

Richard Morgan came as footman from the Bakers at Hardwicke; left on account of ill temper of butler.

Nov 20. Went to Enderby to shoot. Edward Brook and his son Edward, Julius Hirst and Rev. Mr Hoskyns shot with us, and we had a pleasant day though it rained almost incessantly. Game shot — 58 pheasants, 53 hares, 141 rabbits, 7 partridges.

Nov 29. Prison. We took evidence on oath of an insolent speech of John Day's to the governor and awarded him 10 days confinement with bread and water.

Dec 1. Wrote to F.G. Cotman,[45] 10 Boscobal Place, Alpha Road N.W. giving him commission to paint portraits of Emily and myself, saying we would have preferred not to exceed £150 for the pair but as we were anxious to secure pleasing pictures we would not limit him below 200 guineas. He is to come on the 11th and to write confirming the engagement.

Dec 11. Mr F.G. Cotman came to paint our portraits. Kitcats at 100 guineas each.

McDonald a prisoner who had had a month hard labour, was to have left the prison on Saturday when he fell foul of all he could find in his cell including the window, all of which he smashed to atoms. Brought before us, Sir William Guise gave him a month more, he protesting he had not done the damage and that he was annoyed at some people trying to make an entrance into his room. This was an impossible delusion as he was on the 3rd floor. I heard today that the poor fellow had committed suicide by hanging himself from the iron bar of the window by the web used to confine his bed.

Dec 24. Eliza and Edward arrived for Christmas, also Oswald and his wife, Lisa, who is very pretty.

Dec 26. The Ancrums and Emerises spent the evening here. We had a fine spectacular play. Emily also performed show woman to collection of fancy pictures most efficiently. The party was a great success, Oswald showing his menagerie which excited great laughter and Emily's show was excessively amusing.

---

[45] Frederick George Cotman of Ipswich. His portrait of Emily was exhibited in the Royal Academy in 1878.

Dec 31.   Servants' Supper — about 30. Fiddler never turned up. I gave 2 bottles sherry, 2 port, 2 claret. All very pleasant and successful from what I heard.

Emily's Diary for December fills in some of the gaps.

Dec 10.   Exquisite day. Lunched at the Palace; all most pleasant. Then saw over the Cathedral and stayed for service which was very nice indeed.

Dec 11.   I had a nice walk with Clara. Mr Cotman came to paint our portraits.

Dec. 12.   I had a long sitting, 3 hours, and before that busy arranging things.

Dec 13.   A 3 hour sitting. Clara and Miss B. had a narrow escape driving. Snowball fell, both were thrown out but happily not hurt.

Dec 14.   Dearman had 3½ hour sitting. I read 'Prince Consort' to him one hour.

Dec 15.   I sat 2½ hours. Sir D. Wedderburn and his brother came unexpectedly to lunch.

Sunday Dec 16.   Nice day. Mr Cotman spent it with Mr Waller. I took Jack out in afternoon. Dearman walked to Gloucester. [Then there is an entry in code, a method she used frequently for matters which probably only concerned herself.]

Dec 17.   I had a good long sitting.

Dec 19.   Mr F. Waller and Mr Kemp [the artist] dined here. Dull foggy damp day. I sat for 3½ hours.

Dec 21.   I sat one hour.

Dec 22.   I took presents to old women, Clara and I busy arranging Fairy scene. I sat for 3½ hours to Mr Cotman.

Sunday Dec 23.   Most lovely day. All to church. In afternoon I took Jack a long walk. Mr C & Dearman walked to Buckholt.

Dec 24.   Mr Cotman left. [Emily had sat for 17 to 18 hours for her portrait].

Dec 25.   Christmas Day. Lovely day, clear frosty and bright. All to church in the morning. Jack came in for dinner to see blazing pudding.

1878

Jan 2.   Mr, Mrs & Miss Bazley [of Hatherop] came this afternoon and we took them to the Ball at Highnam, which was very pleasant though a little crowded with 280 visitors. We had post horses as Morris remains unable to drive with his arm which he put out a fortnight ago, besides which he has a terrific cough. The charge for post horses was 31/- and man 5/-.

Jan 6.   Emily wrote, "Dearman and I quite alone, first time one day without visitors for more than six weeks".

At the Highnam Ball she danced with two Wedderburns. On Jan 4th they went to the County Ball, and she talked and danced with the same people as at Highnam. "Sir David lectured me about Radical views". On the 5th they dined at the Palace meeting Lady G. Codrington and Sir D.W. again. On Jan 7 she writes "Translated some of Mr Baker's book; began to do so on Saturday." On the 9th they were away to the north "D and I went to Moor Hall to stay with the Lloyds." The house is not unlike Harehills but smaller. There is a very large park here [Sutton Coldfield] which had induced a great many residents from Birmingham. On the 10th they danced till 3 o'clock in the morning and next day went on to Leeds. "Padre [Emily's father] met us." On Jan. 12th Emily says "Padre, Florence and I had most delicious ride in afternoon, gallop". On Sunday 13th they went to St. John's Church; but in the evening "D, F, and I went to Friends Meeting!!" [two exclamation marks]. "We were recognized and all welcomed us on the conclusion of the meeting," says Dearman, and Dan Pickard renewed his "overbounding love and the wellings over of affection." Emily says, "D. Pickard most comic."

On January 16 Dearman temporarily returned to Bowden; but Emily remained at Harehills, riding with her father and sister every day. On 18th there was a dinner party for 22. On January 26 Dearman and Emily stayed with his uncle Harris at Oxton. "We inspected the new Board Schools and the new church, both monuments of Edwards." By this he presumably means his brother Edward Birchall had designed them.

On January 31st they both returned home arriving at Gloucester at 4.42, only to go out again to a "well appointed theatrical entertainment at Lorenzo Lyson's at Hempsted. Dancing kept up till a late hour". They found Clara and the boys well. "Thankful they have not got the measles. There are about 40 cases in the village."

Sunday February 3 was a fine warm day. Emily took Jack out with his hoop which amused him much. "Lunched at Prinknash, walked back."

Feb 12. Emily reports "Delicious day. Famous walk with Dearman and Clara by fields to Hucclecote and Barnwood and visited Asylum seeing lady patients."

Feb 14.   We had a long discussion at the Infirmary respecting Convalescent Homes. There seems to be strong feeling in favour of doing something. I mentioned that my tenant was leaving Buckholt and it would be at liberty at Michaelmas. Dr Ancrum wrote to the Cheltenham Hospital to know if they would join in any scheme or support it by engaging beds. Dr Ancrum thinks our Infirmary might agree to take three beds or guarantee the expenses to the extent of £150 p.a. I rather hinted if they paid me rent I might contribute £50 p.a. towards expenses.

Feb 16.   We went to London. Emily lunched at her club and went to stay with the David Howards and I to lodgings at 6 St. James's Place. We attended a Concert and saw George Eliot, and Mr Lewes. We went to all the Exhibitions and attended family dinner parties, till February 23.

Feb 25.   Mr Cotman came to finish portraits. Pictures look very well.

Feb 26.   I went to Quakers' Yard near Cardiff, (8 a.m. till 11 p.m.) to inspect the colliery opening out by Harris Navigation Co. It has been in progress since June 1872 and it has cost already nearly £200,000 and £50,000 has been nearly subscribed to complete it. They expect to win the best steam coal at 650 yards in about 18 months. They have an immense area at small royalty of 9d more or less per ton. The Harrises are all largely interested.

Feb 28.   Sat for last time for our portraits. Mr Cotman and I attended Fancy Dress Ball at Barnwood. I went in Court Dress. Emily stayed at home with Fred. Harris (on his way back from Quakers' Yard) who read poetry to Miss Brown. Saw Eliza at the station en route for her travels abroad with Mrs Brook. Perrini to accompany them.

March 30.   Meeting of Visiting Justices at the Prison. We appointed committee to visit under the new law.

April 13.   Emily's Father and Mother and Florence went with us in the omnibus to Clara's confirmation at Christchurch, Cheltenham.

May 5.   Magnificent day. Everything looks lovely. Trees all out, even oaks, horse-chestnuts in full flower and lilacs, laburnum, wisteria. Went to Leeds by night train. Arrived at 3 a.m. Took a stroll round Harehills at 4 a.m. More backward than Bowden but still all looked very beautiful.
   They then stayed with Lily Crewdson at Alderly Edge, and went to Brown's Hotel, Dover Street for the season in London.

May 12.   I went down with Aldam to see the Bedford Park Estate at Turnham Green. Norman Shaw has designed the houses and Aldam[46] decorates papers and paints them. Each gets £5 per house. The cost of each

---

[46] There is a good description of John Aldam Heaton in Andrew Saint's biography of Norman Shaw, Yale University Press, 1976. By 1878 Aldam Heaton had set up as a decorator in London.

house is from 7 to 11 hundred including everything. They are about to build a church and club. The houses are very neat picturesque buildings.

May 15.   Aldam Heaton's Reception, an amazing sight; so many medieval and picturesque costumes it reminded me of the historical costume balls.

June 9.   We left Brown's and came down to Gloucester 9 p.m. train. Aldam Heaton accompanied us and we slept at the Bell Hotel.

On June 14 they went to Paris for the Exhibition.

On July 1st they went on to Munich and Salzburg. On the)th Dearman wrote to Bruton that he could not attend the sale of Bubb's property but he would like to buy Cooper's Hill if it is offered very cheap. He would accept their judgement in the matter. Dearman took the baths at Gastein for three weeks. They returned via Nuremburg and were back at Bowden on August 2nd and back to the usual routine, "thankful to be safe at home".

Aug 3.   Summoned to attend the Grand Jury if required. I made the 23rd. Dr Ancrum slipped out of the box when he saw there were just enough. Dined at the palace to meet the Japanese minister and his lady . . . sat next the interesting Jap lady.

Later Dearman was in Leeds. He had met his partner Webb in Paris and there begun preliminary talks with a view to excluding Webb from the partnership. The battle was now rejoined.

Aug 9.   Long conversation with Webb alternately pleading and violent. Altercation regarding value of services and want of consideration turning him off. The law was clearly against me and he would fight to the utmost even if it blackened my name in Gloucestershire, Yorkshire and everywhere. I had been deceived and I should suffer for it to the end of my life. Fearnside tells me he warned Webb if he did not change his mind about Warburg he would be the worse for it. Webb has alienated everybody by speaking ill behind our backs. I urged Campbell, Oswald and Warburg to go into the question of evidence with all their might, sift it, test it and put nothing in black and white that cannot be made good before a jury. The whole house are unanimous in their relief at Webb's going.

Aug 12.   Aldam Heaton went off to London via Bath, having completed hanging the pictures in the Hall.

Aug 14.   Quedgeley garden party very slow.[47]

---

[47] Laurie Lee's mother's father was a groom at Quedgeley.

Aug 19.   Fearnside and three other employees go to Paris exhibition for a week. I paid under £26 for four tickets to include hotel and food and gave them 50/- each for extra expenses. Wrote very long and serious letter to Oswald asking for full particulars of expenditure of £48 in 14 days or less at opening of exhibition.

Aug 23.   Poor Mr Sebastian Dickinson, Chairman of the Quarter Sessions, expired this evening. He has had a suffering illness, inflamation of the bladder, for some weeks.

Aug 25.   Talked over the choir with Mr Eshelby. He says the old ones are rapidly falling out and thinks new members could be found if there was some little inducement held out. I will give him an honorarium of £5 for himself and £5 for a trip to Sharpness or elsewhere next summer. He will then practise them during the winter.

Aug 26.   Our garden party. 152 people. Weather all that could be hoped for. The band played well and everybody seemed pleased and stayed very late. The new hall [redecorated by Aldam Heaton][48] afforded much interest.

Sept 8.   The International Jury [in Paris] have awarded us a silver medal.

On Sept 29th 1878 Dearman wrote to his daughter, concerning the Severn bore.

My darling Clara,
    Yesterday morning Maida and I set off in the dogcart and driving the sprightly cobs at a goodly pace through our pretty lanes we made our appearance at Stonebench on the Severn bank at 5 minutes before 9 a.m. The river looked low and was running rapidly down stream as was evinced by the bits of weeds and wood which floated past us. The road had all been under water during the night's tide and was covered with tenacious mud. In ten minutes we saw the crested wave coming round the bend and striking the banks sending spray into the air. It seemed a miracle; but after it had passed us on its way to Gloucester the whole appearance changed and the whole volume of water ran up-stream more rapidly than it had descended. In an hour it would rise 15 or 20 feet and flood the road. The bore itself might be 5 feet but that was the forerunner of the flow. We were most gratified to see it so successfully.
    We were much occupied with apple stealers at the Shire Hall, and when I walked home I met Emily and Jack carrying a large cross covered with flowers for the Church followed by Dyer and Percy with donkey almost hidden in a mass of flowers, clematis, barley and berries.
    Your most devoted Father.

---

[48] All that remains today are a few panes of Pre-Raphaelite-looking stained glass.

The hall at Bowden redecorated by Aldam Heaton. Summer arrangement

Winter arrangement

Oct 1.   Total cost of altering hall and housekeepers room.

J.A. Heaton	£634.	16.	10
Carpets etc.	34.	18.	0
Clutterbuck	484.	2.	8
Burdock	12.	2.	4
Ed. Birchall	20.	0.	0
	£1185.	19.	10

Oct 2.   12.35 this morning Emily was safely confined of a daughter. Mr Graves came at 11.30 p.m. He gave her chloroform at once and it was soon over. The after pains were very severe and she had considerable haemorrhage which made her excessively faint. Graves gave her two or three glasses of brandy and a sleeping draught. She was so nervous with the faintness that he stayed all night. Little girl (Violet) weighs 8 lbs.

Oct 8.   Amy was confined yesterday. Her fifth little girl.

All this time Emily, recovering from her confinement, reports her sister Florence reading to her, Philochristus and Alton Locke, and Mill on the Floss in the mornings. It is superb hot summer weather, and Florence sits out under the chestnut tree to write letters, always wears only a cotton dress. "I long to go out."

Another letter was sent to Clara on Oct 11.

My darling Clara.
Thank Miss Brown for her kind note. We were most interested in the perusal of your moonstruck poetry. Yours contains some romantic and pleasing ideas and was poetical in thought but a little wanting in proper numbers.
Miss Brown's was a higher flight of genius and sounded most musical but perhaps my want of appreciation for German culture prevented my exactly understanding what she was driving at. It speaks well for the air and sea at Tenby that it should have inspired you in this fashion.
Your names for the infant have unfortunate contractions in daily life, Conny, Milly, Maggy. We are thinking of Violet Maida Dearman or Violet Emily Dearman. After much consideration we have determined to ask you in conjunction with Auntie Bia to be godmother to your little sister. It will make an extra tie between you though the age is so different. Do not think it necessary to accept because I ask unless you feel that it would be consonant with your own feelings. Believe me your devoted Father.

Oct 23.   Had a long conversation with Mrs Smith because Taylor had said not half the stores put out were honestly used in the house. I did not wish her to incriminate any person unless she could substantiate an accusation. "Well" she said "I have seen a box of candles with large pieces of candles many inches long and I know far too many are put out. There is immense waste in coal and candles by this 5 o'clock rising. They get up, light a fire, make tea and get an hour over doing next to nothing. In the afternoon Harris has a fire in her room and lies on her bed. Harris is not pleasant with the young servants. They cannot bear her." Mrs Smith recommends my having coals locked up. They have been stolen regularly in the early morning. I said "Morris I suppose" and she said "Yes".

I praised Harris for her attention to my guests and for her success with the china; but I told her no fires in any of the servants' bedrooms except in case of illness. I think she will adhere to these directions.

Nov 1. Our little girl was baptized Violet Emily Dearman. The sponsors were William Jowitt,[49] Anna Harris and Clara.

Dec 22. The frost and snow very severe but the Bishop walked out and preached to us both morning and evening.

Dec 31. Emily and I sat up to see the new year in full of thankfulness for the mercies we have received and much impressed with the calamities by death and losses and war and accident which have fallen upon the world during this sad year now past.

---

[49] The father of Earl Jowitt, the Lord Chancellor.

1879

Jan 18.   Sent for Webb and after a final struggle he signed a paper renouncing any claim to compensation for leaving firm of J.D. Birchall & Co. I then presented him with £300 on releasing his two sons, the one from an engagement and the other from his apprenticeship articles. After very warm debates they all three withdrew with mutual expressions of good will.

Jan 29.   Emily and Clara skated on the pond. Ice very good.

Jan 31.   Mrs Brook's funeral. Nothing transpired openly about the Will in the absence of one. Left Enderby with Cecil by train and dined with him at Prince's Gardens.

Feb 18.   Gambier Parry said yesterday, "My garden costs me £600 p.a. 1 head man, 3 foremen and 5 men".

March 19.   Cecil writes that the Heirs at Law of Mrs Brook have behaved handsomely to him. They have left the bulk of the furniture intact, 40 doz of wine, the Brougham, Dog Cart and waggonette, etc.

April 2.   The depression in Leeds is fearful. Warburg and Oswald are urging our obtaining a large number of pattern looms, a designer, and going into the fancy trade with great vigour. Their notions are most extensive and if carried out I fear would land us in irretrievable anxiety.
    We have two pattern looms in bad order. We agreed to have these repaired, two more purchased, and a designer engaged.

April 12.   Easter. This morning we have the heaviest fall of snow I have ever seen at Bowden. We were out after breakfast relieving the conifers. It is very serious for the holiday people and the railway which must be choked.

April 21.   Mrs Kerr and her two daughters lunched here and played lawn tennis with Clara and Fanny Emeris. The larches are beginning to look a little green, the horse-chestnut buds are opening. The hedges are little more out than they were a month ago. It is cold at night. Yesterday we heard for the first time, cuckoo, nightingales and woodpeckers.

April 23.   Swallows first appeared.

April 30.   Having suffered from nightmares, flatulency, and feelings of oppression about the heart for a week since I ran from Eliza's to the station in 9½ minutes, I today consulted Dr Evans. He stripped and examined me carefully, said there was nothing really seriously wrong, he considered my blood was rather poor at present, had no doubt whatever that a tonic would quite cure me. He gave me iron magnesia.

May 1.   We saw Toole's performance Artful cards and *Ici on parle Français* and Serjeant Buz Fuz at Gloucester Theatre. A regular bumper.

Emily writes "Took all babes in open carriage; called at Hardwicke and on Curtis-Haywards. All at home. Heavy shower as returning." On May 2 "Miss B., Clara and I read *L'avare* together. Jolly ride in woods with Dearman and Clara, down perfect precipices!" On May 4th "Lovely day, hot sun, all out in afternoon gathering cowslips. Put Jack to bed".

May 13.   Invited to Grays of Parklands to shoot rooks. Postponed for a week owing to the cold weather so had to decline on account of our being in London though we had previously accepted. Mrs Waller and the two Miss Huxleys[50] came to lunch and were charming.

On the next day they went to London, and dined with the Bishop. Frequent visits to the theatre, rides in Hyde Park, the levée, business meetings, society gatherings and church.

May 25.   Canon Farrer at St. Margaret's Westminster confesses with St. Augustine he cannot explain everything; but "act, act in the living present and then it will be right with us whether the call comes sooner or later".

May 27.   Horticultural Show. We enjoyed the splendid collection all under cover, roses, clematises intermingled with Japanese maples, especially in Veitche's stand. I wrote asking Keen to come up and see it but he thought he could not get away at present.

They returned home on 5th June.

June 7.   Engaged Evan Morris as footman, 23 years 5′ 10″. Good references.
    Wrote to Aldam Heaton, "I am glad to feel that the small loan I made of £1,000 has been of considerable benefit to you in starting your most successful business and I am sure you will make no obstacle to the notice I now give you that I wish it to be repaid this year either by instalments or in a lump sum at the end of 1879 as may be most convenient to you".

On June 9 Emily was back in London, attending a concert at Grosvenor House, on her way to Leeds to see her mother who had been ill, and on the 18th the whole Birchall family moved into lodgings at Ilkley, Yorkshire.

June 18.   I with Miss Brown, Clara, Dyer, Annie with two boys and Violet arrived at Leeds at 5.30 and were met by Oswald, Edward and Emily and while I went with Emily to Harehills, Oswald took charge of the party to Ilkley.

---

[50] Mrs Frederick William Waller and her sisters were daughters of Professor T.H. Huxley. F.W. Waller was the son of F.S. Waller, both architects to the Cathedral.

From Ilkley they went to see Mr Fawkes's Turners at Farnley Hall, the church at Studley Royal, and Fountains Abbey. Dearman thought Burges's church was excessively rich but a little wanting in good taste.

July 21.   Gambier Parry says his farm tenants are bankrupt and he can see no light for agriculture in any direction. We talked of Sir Francis Goldsmith who has let Rendcomb estate at 5/- per acre rent. Mr Elwes has taken 7/6 per acre for some of his unlet farms.

Aug 11.   Garden Party. Dawes Band engaged. It turned out a very dull warm dry afternoon and our party was a great success. Flowers were scarce, bedding scarcely ready for exhibition, roses all picked, strawberries just about at an end. I had to buy peaches 1/- each and melon. Without our house party we made out 176, and there were some no doubt omitted in the counting.

Aug 19.   Alice Ancrum married to Patrick Evans. We all went to see it. Very sad [her brother Arthur had just died in India] but nice. Went to stay with the Bazleys at Hatherop.

Aug 21.   Went a perfect cavalcade (in 4 carriages) to Cirencester to see the Flower Show and Dog Show at the Abbey grounds (the Chester Masters). An unusual number of pretty women there. I bought 1st prize Pug bitch, £8. 13 months old.
    Bazley has had 13 miles of continuous fencing and he paid 2/- a yard, an unparallelled price. Expects before 12 months to have 3,000 acres in his own hands.

Sept 3.   Emily went to stay with her sister Lily Crewdson at Alderley Edge for a week.

They then went to the Hereford Festival.

Sept 12.   Returned in the special train after the Messiah.

Sept 16.   In Leeds. A long talk with Warburg. While impressed with the gloom of everything at present he has such innate confidence in his own department that he reckons on a revival of demand for our spring productions later in the autumn.
    In afternoon went to Tadcaster to see the Harrises. Uncle Harris in coming from church last Sunday, peeped into the pond seeing a fish. He thought he could kick him down with a poke from his staff; but unfortunately he toppled in, and as there was 4 feet of water he was pulled out by his daughters with some difficulty, his hat soaked and wig left floating in the pond.

Sept 20.   I went to Scarborough to spend Sunday with Benson & Carry. Went to see George Alderson Smith who is building a house and employing J.D. Sedding.[51] Brilliant morning. Attended St. Martin's church [Bodley's Pre-Raphaelite painted church of 1869]. Alderson told me of the return of Archie Smith from Zululand, disgraced and dismissed owing to some lark.

Sept 26.   Leeds. Archibald Forbes lectured on the Zulu war, a narration of events so far as Forbes took part in them as correspondent of the Daily News. Rode to Harewood with Father and Florence.

Oct 29.   Tricycled down to Bell yard in 30 mins. Return to Bowden took 31 mins. Roads awfully muddy and stony.

On Nov. 30 1879 Emily wrote to her sister Florence

Bowden Hall

Dearest F.

I was so very sorry to bring my most delightful visit to Harehills to a conclusion. I have so enjoyed the nice quiet time. Well, Padre would tell you that Mr McCheane effusively introduced me at the station to his musical cousin, who says he met me once at the Ellicotts. He was smoking so I saw no more of him afterwards. Mr Campbell and Oswald came to see me off. I had a very nice journey. The Pullman was not running having had a slight accident getting on fire or something the day before so I was glad of your bountiful provisions and at Peterbro' I got a bun. Dearman met me at King's Cross and I was soon esconced in our own homelike rooms at Brown's with warm greetings and kind enquiries from housekeeper, waiter and nice hall porters. Then D and I went to see about my new Ulster — then to the Burlington to see some etchings. Then D went to the City and I did shopping and went to the Hunt and Prout exhibition, lovely drawings. I didn't have much time for the Hunts. I care so much more for the Prouts, don't you? I bought a beaver [hat] for myself. In evening we went to the Lyceum and were perfectly entranced with the Merchant of Venice. The Portia was lovely in the extreme and as for Irving's Shylock it is the finest thing I have ever seen, and even Dearman thinks it altogether the finest he remembers, tho' his memory includes Macready, C. Kean, etc. And who do you think sat within a yard of us on the row behind — Ruskin. I recognized him at once and it was most interesting to see his enjoyment of the magnificent acting and to hear some of his remarks. A lady next us knew him and told us that the worshipping youth he had with him, who gazed adoringly at him and seemed to hang on his lips, and talked himself in a very "intense" way, was

---

[51] John Dando Sedding 1838–91.

young Wilde who wrote a prize poem at Oxford. Ruskin smiled most kindly often and looked quite well and less sad than I expected, and so delightful. I did wish I had been the worshipping youth.

Yesterday I went to Chislehurst and found it still snowy. Susie met me and we drove to the Chapel to see the flower-covered granite tomb of Napoleon III and then the great banks of wreaths and garlands that almost hid the velvet hung coffin of Napoleon IV. I am glad I went being a great Bonapartist; did I not get a lot into my 24 hours in London. All well here. Violet walks so old-fashionedly, very very fast and so erect and prim it is quite amusing to watch her.

Ever your Em.

Dec 30.   My horse fell with me in Barton Street, not having been out much because of the frost he was very scared at every tram car and wagon. I was none the worse, thank God.

1880

Jan 28.   We heard today that Lily Crewdson had been confined of a little girl. [Cicely, the mother of Fred Sanger, O.M.]. We came up to town this afternoon where we found an almost inpenetrable fog. Oswald dined with us at the Hotel Continental and we afterwards came down to Dover by the mail. On our arrival at the Lord Warden Hotel we received a telegram from Father announcing Lily's death. The shock upset Emily terribly and I feared she would become hysterical. We did not know what would be the best course to adopt and had much telegraphing with Benson. I did not like to leave Emily in her present condition (to go to the funeral) and Mother had urged her not to lose a day in our journey to Spain.

Jan 30. et seq.   We left by Calais boat with a smooth sea. We arrived in Paris at 6.10 and left Catarozzi to pass the luggage and drove to the Orleans Station where we dined at the buffet getting away by the 7.15 p.m. train for Toulouse. We had a luxurious 1st class carriage. The hot-water tins were long enough for two of them to go the whole width of the carriage. They were changed every hour and a half all night. Two lamps with silk shades. The trimmings of the carriage all in beautiful order. The line is very smooth and we slept well. The appointments shame our English railways. It was a beautiful moonlight night but the frost was not intense.

From Toulouse we visited the scene of the last battle of the Peninsular War of 1814, and we drove to the Garonne and saw the damage done by the floods of 1875, leaving for Barcelona by night train. 4 a.m. at the Spanish frontier — a vigorous examination of luggage. Pretty mountainous forests of picturesque stone pines standing with their noble tops against the skyline, olives, box trees, aloe hedges, walls, dry streams, green corn, ruined villages rather Italian-looking. The natives seem full of life, songs and music, rejoicing in bright colours, wearing sandals, velveteen, patterns like carriage rugs and revolutionary scarlet caps like the Parisian Cap of liberty. Our hotel [in Barcelona] is placed on the scene of incessant promenande of well-conducted people. We were very struck with the solemnity of the cathedral and saw a wholesale baptism of about a dozen black-haired babies. Barcelona looks like an Eastern city, the whole scene more like what one fancies the Holy Land than anything else. There is also a feeling of immense prosperity and buildings of a sumptuous and colossal character are rising in all directions. At St. George's chapel we saw a set of priests' vestments bought in London after Henry VIII's reign. Capital cuisine at Hotel Madrid, snipe, sole, partridge, and all meat excellent, much better cooked than in Italy; sweets rather wanting but fruit first rate.

Dearman was obviously enjoying himself.

Feb 4.   Leaving Emily at the hotel [she was pregnant] I took the courier and went for the day to Montserrat, a most exquisite excursion. Train, and then

diligence with six miles on splendidly engineered road which leads to the
Convent, the most romantic spot in Europe.

They went on to Tarragona, Valencia and to Granada, Dearman describing
every detail with enthusiasm; but on Feb 15 he had an attack of gout. "I have
not drunk a pint of wine since leaving England. I am certainly thinner, taking
little or no butter and feeling unusually well in all respects. I kept to the house
today. We are close to the walls of the Alhambra.

Next day they admired the Alhambra, the Generalife and the Sierra Nevada
and the tombs of Ferdinand and Isabella in the cathedral just as every tourist
has done before and since.

In spite of pages of description Dearman still has space to write — Received a
letter from William Hicks-Beach saying on a more careful examination of
wood [at Cranham] he must own he somewhat undervalued the property as
regards the timber; but he cannot agree with price I put on land — £10 per acre.
Asks the lowest price I intend to sell at, and adds it is still possible we might
come to terms, but he cannot afford a fancy price. I replied thanking him for
his letter; but saying I did not think another offer was worth consideration as
our views were so very divergent. I could have sold my purchase at £1,000
profit at once.

Extracts from Emily's letters.

Hotel Alameda, Malaga, Feb. 18. 1880.

My dearest People
    The travellers we have met this time have been most . . . I don't think even
Florence would have felt drawn to make their acquaintance; one set less
attractive than the last till at Granada the climax was reached in a party of 6
hideous American women with a small ugly sickly boy — the son of one, a
widow. They never seemed to speak to one another and were dull and
common to a degree. There were also there two ladies of masculine and
forbidding exterior, but they looked like ladies, though very eccentric and
ugly. They had with them two Italian maids, a French manservant, a pet
lapdog, a vast pile of huge boxes and a lovely silver tea-equipage, urn,
teapot, cups and tea, which all went into an oak case and from which they
took tea at lunch yesterday. We found they were a Lady A. de Rothschild
and a Lady Somebody Peel. They have been to Tangiers and talked to one
another alternately French, English and German to show off we thought,
Italian to their maids and Spanish to the waiters.

    In Granada Dearman went over the Lunatic Asylum, one of the oldest in
the world having been founded and this handsome building erected, by
Ferdinand and Isabella. Then we went to the Cartuja Convent, with a
wonderfully fine church full of superb marbles and in the cloisters a series of
horrible pictures representing the alleged tortures and martyrdoms suffered
by Carthusian monks in London under Henry VIII. The most unique part

of our afternoon's work was a visit to the gipsy quarter. From the hill there is the finest view, the Alhambra just in front, across a deep ravine with the river at the bottom (in which we saw men washing for gold using the cradle we so often read of in the Australian gold-diggings) then the Generalife Palace and hill to the left, and behind, the glorious glittering range of the snowy Sierra Nevada. Below on our right lay Granada with all its towers and domes and picturesque outlines. The gipsies are the most startling specimens of their strange race. . . .

From Malaga they went by boat to Gibraltar on Feb 20, arriving at the Europa Hotel at 3 p.m.

We were roused before 5 and hurried off to the Gib. steamer, a little paltry boat. Eventually we got away after seeing a most exquisite sunrise. The views of Mount Atlas in Africa and of the Rock were quite grand most of the way. The Europa is a small but comfortable hotel, very full.

Dearman complains of sickness, gout and depression. Emily called on Col. Lemprière and asked his advice and he wrote a note to the Staff Surgeon who visited and recommended a blue pill.

Feb. 21. Europa Hotel, Gibraltar

My dearest People
    We had a delicious voyage from Malaga of seven hours. The day was superb, sea quite smooth and the air delightful. We kept quite near the Spanish coast all the time and soon descried the African coast, and the grand mass of the Rock of Gibraltar. As we approached it grew more and more striking; it is a magnificent rock, a possession one cannot but feel very proud of and it is fortified almost every inch of it, galleries quarried all through the interior besides all the exterior and visible forts. It is a most curious experience to be suddenly in England again, surrounded by one's own country-men, English money, English names on the shops and at the street corners, and English talked on all hands. And yet it is un-English too, with its Spanish elements and large infusion of Arabs and Turks one sees about in the streets. The military character of the whole place is an additional peculiarity; sentries everywhere, bodies of soldiers to be met every few minutes, cannon to the right of us, cannon to the left of us; guns fired at 6 a.m. and 6 p.m. (when the gates are closed,) and again at 9.30 p.m.
    We are very thankful we got here before Dearman was laid up with his gout as it is far the best place for him with English doctors and chemists, a clean airy hotel and healthy situation.
    I went to call on Colonel Lemprière this morning. He is a great swell here, military secretary, and a charming man. We have met him twice at Hatherop as he is a relation of the Bazleys. I consulted him about a doctor. Both he and his wife were most kind, and he recommended his staff-surgeon, who

came to see Dearman about noon. Catarozzi is most attentive and kind. I take him on the box when I make these calls, etc. and he is very useful. The people staying in the hotel are all very kind, only about a dozen but that fills the hotel. Colonel and Mrs Walker and two daughters, a clergyman and his mother and two sisters, Colonels Wellesley and Thynne and a young officer, name unknown, and then our two selves. Gibraltar is full to overflowing. I went this afternoon to see the weekly review which was interesting and pretty. Dearman urged me to go, so I had a little carriage and found myself in the midst of our hotel people and Col. Wellesley was very kind in explaining things, and pointing out celebrities. The lion here just now is Bromhead of Rorke's Drift. I saw him very well. With dearest love from us both.

Ever your loving Em.

Feb 23.   We drove on to the neutral ground and saw heaps of peasants of all ages and both sex sitting on the ground and hiding about their persons little parcels of tobacco and other things to be smuggled into Spain. Many are professional smugglers. The Rock is most galleried towards Spain, that being the weakest side and there are a thousand guns in position. We heard the Rifle Brigade Band play on the Alameda; the gardens are very beautiful with exquisite views.

Feb 24.   This morning opened with a storm. The *Hercules* did not go to Tangiers and our plans all at sea.

Gibraltar. Feb. 24

My dearest People
    Dearman has continued to improve; but the foot is by no means well yet. I am delighted with Gibraltar. The Rock is wooded on this side, with splendid stone pines, olives and a few planes. The gardens are perfectly exquisite, both some of the private ones, and above all the lovely public gardens where an extensive slice of the mountainside has been laid out in lovely terraces luxuriantly planted with charming walks, drives, little shady footpaths and bosky dells, with lots of seats. The chief flowers now in bloom are the scarlet ixias, aloes, fragrant cytisus, bougainvillias, bignonias, and splendid white daturas and arums. I never saw nicer public gardens anywhere. At the bottom there is a promenade where the band plays and Lady Napier drives in her carriage, and lots of people are on horseback. One can walk everywhere amid the batteries and fortifications, through the barrack yards and past the numerous sentries.
    Colonel Lemprière called yesterday and was most kind and pleasant, so is Colonel Wellesley, the heir to the dukedom, and a particularly friendly simple sort of man. We drove yesterday across the neutral ground, a bare strip ¼ of a mile wide, between the English and Spanish lines, to the Spanish sentries beyond.

As we are delayed here we think it best to make a few alterations to our later addresses.

With dearest love, ever yours Em.

Feb 25.   This afternoon we took a carriage and I had my hair cut and called at one or two shops. Emily only alighted once. On returning Emily reclined on the bed but just before dinner she got down with a scared expression saying something felt wrong and she has been uncomfortable for an hour. Hastily disembarrassed her of stays etc during which she became excessively faint, I sent Catarozzi at once for a doctor who being ill sent another doctor and after two attempts a nurse. Uncertain whether it will pass away or come to a seven month birth. The pains continued all night. I spent the night in my clothes in the drawing room and Catarozzi in the passage.

Feb 26.   Emily slept very comfortably, and on the 28th she was better, and this continued so that I went to Tangiers, in spite of my gout.

March 2.   The scene on landing was picturesque with extreme numbers of boats manned with men in flowing robes, handsome black slaves from Soudan, and Moors tall and well proportioned and full of shouts and gesticulation. The Revd. Mr Sandford accompanied me and we both took donkeys and a native guide, and rode round the town. We saw a crowd of camels from the interior, the Mosque with lively music, a story-teller and his mass of entranced listeners, the hemp smokers, the market and ten men brought from the country today to prison, all chained together. The climate is absolutely the most perfect in the world.

When I came in on the 3rd I found Emily looking well and moving about but she complained of uncomfortable sensations; towards evening she was very ill. Secured the attendance of doctor with some difficulty and afterwards Mrs Searle, and at 12.45, March 4, Emily was delivered of a little girl, very small and delicate, weighs 4½ lbs. What a coincidence the same night 17 years ago within a couple of hours I lost my beloved Clara at Bonchurch.

Dearman writes to his daughter:–

Gibraltar. March 4. 1880

My darling Clara

I have indeed a surprise for you. After writing you yesterday afternoon dearest Mama was taken ill and at ¼ before 1 o'clock this morning she was the mother of a little girl. This startling and unexpected event will completely alter our arrangements. We have now the best room in the hotel, looking out on the loveliest view of Algeciras, the bay with shipping and especially H.M. ship *Inconstant*, 16 guns, moored close to us. Catarozzi has been most attentive. He sprained his foot in the night and my exertions have brought up my swollen foot again to large proportion so we are a crippled

party. I feel how inadequately I am able to write to you but assure you of
our intense love and how much we feel drawn to home and our dear ones
there. Goodbye my sweet Clara.

I am your most affectionate father J. Dearman Birchall.

The same day Dearman filled in the time by writing a long letter to his
brother-in-law Benson Jowitt.

Europa Hotel, Gibraltar
March 4th 1880.

My dear Benson
You will hear the news from Harehills of the unexpected arrival and so I
will not dilate on that topic; but confine myself to telling you of a little
expedition I made to Tangiers at Emily's urgent request, not being fit for it
herself, she most generously wishes that I should not leave this neighbourhood without spending at least a day there. The voyage takes 3 hours under
favourable circumstances; but in an east wind even of moderate force the
surf makes it difficult to land.

It is strange, nay almost like a dream to go from England and the ideas of
the 19th century as seen at Gibraltar to Africa and visit one of the oldest
cities in the world where everything I saw has the air of a thousand years
ago. The town is lively as a beehive, the inhabitants always swarming up and
down; men, women and children, donkeys, pigs, goats all fight for passage.
The natives show the naked leg, yellow slipper, barnoose, fez and turban, all
that is flowing; the women absolutely concealed, the men often extremely
handsom. One of our guides was over 6 foot tall. The Jews are very distin-
guishable. Irving as Shylock we saw hundreds of times, and they meet and
talk just as we have seen at the Lyceum. The Jewesses are very good looking
full of laughter with dark sparkling eyes. The real Moors are not very dark
coloured, and their horsemanship is superb, darting about on their little
barbs, necessitating a very firm seat and pretty good grip. There are many
slaves, mostly large men from the Soudan. Another race, but in a great
minority, are the Riffs said to be descended from ancient Romans and
known by their tremendous masses of hair over eyes and face, often huge
curls. They look savage vagabonds. . . . In the whole empire of Morocco
there is no newspaper, or carriage, or cart, or wheeled vehicle. They smoke
Indian Hemp which is very intoxicating and they take it in little pipes like
opium smokers.

Today March 5th it is like midsummer in Gibraltar, the sky cloudless, the
air brisk, the sea blue as azure. The *Himalaya* is opposite our window. It
arrived last night with over 1500 souls on board, 670 of the 46th Regiment
from Bermuda, a number of returned invalids from the Zulu war one with
the Victoria Cross, and no end of women and children. I have been on board
talking to many of the soldiers. They say she rolls terrifically in a sea.

Emily is getting on remarkably well.

I am your affectionate brother J.D.B.

March 5. Emily is doing well and we have secured some cows milk morning and evening and baby is taking to it.

March 6. I registered our little girl in the name of Constance Lindaraja Dearman.[52]

Dearman wrote to Emily's mother.

Gibraltar. March 6th.

My dearest Mother
   It is a great pleasure to be able to send you a very favourable report. Emily is as nicely as can be and has suffered no drawback whatever. The little specimen of humanity is apparently doing well. The colour is changing from Moorish to Spanish. We have secured a gill of genuine cows milk morning and evening. She appreciates the quality. We ourselves never taste anything more noble than the product of the Rock goats. The child is very wee but may thrive yet. We have a sort of idea that the least risk would be to send her home by the Peninsular and Oriental Steamer with a good soldier's wife if one the doctor approves can be found, and to have her met at Southampton. Our advisers here say that this would be much safer than taking her over 2000 miles of land. We have tried to secure a wet nurse but have entirely failed and Emily is not encouraged to attempt to nurse the child herself. The weather is superb, such skies and lovely sea. The middle of the day is tremendously hot and the nights warm and dry. I wish you could see the sunset I am looking on, it would amaze and delight you. My foot remains very bad. I am a complete cripple.
   Your most affectionate Son J.D.B.

Letter written by Emily on March 7 to her great friend Maida Mirrielees.

Europa Hotel Gibraltar.

"On the 4th inst. at Gibraltar the wife of J. Dearman Birchall of a daughter." You may see the above in the Times ere you receive this letter but I think you will be glad to hear a few particulars from myself and Dearman kindly allows me to write a little bit. I am almost as much surprised as you can be by this unexpected event. It is two months before I thought it could possibly be and I cannot account for it in the least. There has certainly been no physical cause for matters being thus precipitated. I had been extra quiet for the last fortnight owing to Dearman's gout and to our forced detention here by it, and by the weather which prevented all ships from leaving Gibraltar and kept us weather-bound otherwise we would have gone to Tangiers and thence to Cadiz. I am thankful we had not as things have turned out for I am

---

[52] There is a garden of Lindaraja in the Alhambra.

more comfortable here than I could have been anywhere else short of England. The doctor and nurse both think it was the shock and mental strain caused by Lily's death that made this affair of mine come off at the seventh month. I was at first awfully dismayed and rather ashamed; but on the whole I am glad it is over and now we shall have nothing to hurry home for and no hindrance to our enjoying the return part of our tour in peace (Holy Week in Seville).

I was awfully bad at the time — more so than ever before — because I did not have chloroform soon enough, but I had a little at last, and got on very well, and am now as well as possible with Dearman to nurse me and keep me company, and a beautiful sunny airy room with a lovely sea view. We thought at first the baby would not live, but it seems to be doing very well and we now think it may live long and prosper. It is very tiny but quite well formed and in proportion and not skinny. The longest fingers I ever saw and perfect nails. It's name Lindaraja is a Moorish one and associated with Granada and the Alhambra. We thought it a nice reminiscence of our tour. In case you don't know how to pronounce it I may remark the j formerly written x is just the German ch in sound.

Your ever most loving Em."

Gibraltar. March 9.

Dearest Mother

We had a very exciting day here yesterday. In the morning the 71st Highlanders were paraded before going on board the *Himalaya* just opposite our window, military bands playing them off. Then there was a great auction of their horses which were sold with bridle and saddle and cloth just as they stood. The bidding was very apathetic and some good looking horses only fetched £9 to £15. One hunter went up to £30.

We were then told to have our windows open while a 38 ton gun in a battery a couple of hundred yards away was let off, firing an enormous iron shot which struck the sea 2½ miles out. Each time it is fired it costs £25. Emily was as brave as a lion, and Lindaraja never woke, but Emily felt her bed violently shake.

Our landlord is encouraged in his shameful extortionate prices for our board by the press of visitors. Yesterday he had to turn away the Earl & Countess of Breadalbain. We dare not expostulate for fear of being turned adrift out of the best room in any hotel in Gibraltar.

Your affectionate Son J.D.B.

March 11.   Baby has improved this week and takes her milk well and sleeps comfortably. Lungs seem capacious and her cries compel attention when she desires food.

March 16.   I took Emily for an hour's drive this afternoon, the 13th day since her accouchement. She looks very well and has never had any drawback.

March 17.   Rev. George Sandford baptized our little girl privately. The godparents who have accepted the office are M.K. Birchall [Mary the widow of Dearman's brother Sam], Helen Heaton and David Howard.

March 18.   Emily and I went to Tangiers. An awful erection was put on a donkey for Emily's benefit and it required two natives whole attention to prevent her landing on the ground. We had a pleasant ride in lovely country lanes, visiting the Belgian Consul's garden etc.

March 20.   Much upset by letters from Father, Benson and Susie who seem much surprised at our plan of sending baby home by P & O with Mrs Macnamara. They express great disapproval. We wrote expressing our views and explaining that it was a pity that they had not telegraphed us to await their letters before acting, as now all was arranged for her to go home in the *Indus*.

Emily wrote to Maida Mirrielees on March 22nd.

My dearest Maid

I am in a whirl. We are intending to leave Gibraltar either tomorrow or Wednesday for Cadiz and Seville. After much thought we decided to send the baby home by sea to Southampton and for her to travel in the charge of a most excellent, kind, nice superior woman whom we have been most fortunate in securing. We were dismayed to get letters from Harehillls strongly disapproving this course and urging our going ourselves straight home by sea. It was intensely trying. On the one hand it is so painful not to have their approval, on the other it was too late to altar all the arrangements. I am not up to home cares and worries and excitements yet, and I long to have the change and refreshment of the quiet homeward journey through Spain. It is impossible to explain everything at such a distance. We have acted for the best and those who are not on the spot cannot judge of all the circumstances; but Padre wrote so strongly that it upset and distressed me dreadfully. He seemed to think it a risk to send the baby with only one woman to take care of her so we have suddenly resolved to send our courier with them. Of-course it is rather awkward to give him up at such short notice and to go on without him, but I daresay we shall get on all right and it is certainly a great extra precaution and safeguard for the baby so I hope my people will be satisfied. We have every cause to bless Gibraltar, having been so comfortable here under such trying circumstances. I have regained my strength more quickly than usual and Dearman's gout too is wonderfully better. We propose to spend Easter in Seville. I never saw anything to equal the slowness of the post between here and Moscow. To England it is bad enough and very irregular. There is such a bustle going on I cannot write any more.

Ever your loving Em.

March 23.   We passed a day of the utmost perplexity being supplied with the greatest diversity of intelligence at the Steamboat offices. They only let me have tickets for Mrs Macnamara, her boy and our baby on condition we would pay the supplement of 1st class fare if 2nd class all full on arrival from Malta. At 5 p.m. the *Indus* appeared and we had a most exciting leave taking and went on board. The purser, a most courteous man, a strange contrast to the Gib. representative immediately appointed me an excellent berth for Mrs Macnamara, our baby and her boy. Nothing could look more clean and pleasant. Returned to our boat sailing to Cadiz; our berth is far inferior to Mrs Macnamara's. We telegraphed Clara that Tothill and Dyer should go down on Friday to be ready to meet Linda on Saturday morning.

Dearman wrote to his sister-in-law

Cadiz. March 24th. 1880

My dearest Florence
      You will be glad to hear that all is going well. We had almost an affecting departure yesterday. Unexpectedly the *Indus* was rather late and the *Lisbon* left at the same time. So we all left the Europa at once in three carriages, all the guests, all the servants, landlord and many loafers being congregated at the door. Mrs Macnamara and her little boy had arrived; but our nurse would not part with the baby until we arrived at the waters edge. We had such a wagging of paws, such a leave taking, so many God speeds I have seldom heard. Ballesterion our favourite boatman and Catevis our chief driver led the way and we embarked at the Ragged Staff stairs, a rather private place, first visiting the *Indus*, a noble and extraordinarily well-appointed steamer. I went on board and selected a most beautiful berth amidships. Catarozzi's feelings in parting overpowered him and he swore fidelity to the little Rockite under his charge. Our stay was very short, and then under the guidance of a new courier we have engaged, Wylie by name, we embarked on the *Lisbon*. Emily admires Wylie awfully and says that he resembles me only his dress is so much better that he looks more distinguished. Our two vessels started near together but we were soon left in the distance by the P. & O. and our berth had none of the luxury enjoyed by our little one.
      Cadiz is a beautifully clean town looking brilliant from the sea. The fish market is one of the most interesting. I saw about a dozen young sharks. They are much esteemed, and scores of octupi and many very beautiful fishes unknown in the Mediterranean. A considerable part of the population appear to spend their whole time on top of a sea wall with colossal rods fishing with worms. I hope Mother is nicely and Father consoled. I am your most loving brother.

J.D.B.

The hall at Bowden as decorated by Aldam Heaton. Watercolour by Dearman Birchall

The Library, Bowden; decorated by Aldam Heaton. Watercolour by Dearman Birchall

Watercolours by Dearman Birchall from the illustrated catalogue of his china collection. (*Left*) Late Ming bowl, as described by Emily, No 229. 'A fine large bowl, in the centre geese and flowers. Outside the surface is graven in geometrical patterns (semi-perforated) and there are six medallions with dragons, birds, etc.'

Emily's sister Dora was moved to write verses for the occasion.

I've come across the sea
I've braved every danger
For a home unknown to me
A poor little stranger.

Born on Gibraltar's Rock
In sight of Afric's shore
I slumbered through the shock
Of loudest cannon's roar.

My garments small were lent
By charity's kind hand
And messengers were sent
For milk to scour the land.

An ancient name I bear
Of Moorish origin
And yet I claim my share
Of English kith and kin.

I needs must brave the storms
Alone of dread Biscay
My soul felt no alarms
My fears begged no delay.

Four weary nights and days
I'm sailing o'er the deep
Good Macnamara's lays
Lulling my infant sleep.

Such courage rare must claim
All praise from one and all
Of those who share my name
In far off Bowden Hall.

Tothill and Dyer will meet
With pride this heroine small
And a welcome still more sweet
From brothers and sisters all.

After Lindaraja's unexpected birth at Gibraltar and her prompt despatch to England aged three weeks, her parents continued on their continental holiday. Emily wrote afterwards to say that the whole tour had gone without *contretemps* except for Dearman's attack of gout at Gibraltar. They subsequently visited Cadiz, Seville, Cordova, Madrid, Burgos, San Sebastian and Bordeaux a round trip of 4,382 miles taking 240 hours' travelling time. However, when they were at San Sebastian they heard that Dearman's uncle Harris had died, so that on Tuesday 13th April Dearman determined to get home to attend the funeral on Friday at Bolton Percy. By the 15th they got to Brown's Hotel in London and Emily went back to Bowden, while Dearman travelled on to Yorkshire. Dearman was the executor of his uncle who had left about £300,000 between his three daughters equally. Probate duty £6,875. After the funeral Dearman returned to London.

April 18th   Oswald and Warburg in town. Campbell complains of want of consideration on their part. He feels cornered. They do things without consulting him; they go everywhere together, the Mill, London, always the pair are seen in close companionship. He has had to put up with more than he ever did with Webb and thinks he has made a mistake in agreeing to Webb's departure. He cannot look to the future with equanimity.

Fearnside complains very much of Oswald's manner to him of late, fault finding without reason and a manner indicative of hostility. Fearnside predicts that unless I mind what I am about Warburg will break up the business, and he pities Campbell who is dreadfully sat upon.

Returned to Bowden. Dyer still looking poorly, Miss Brown very feeble and looking worn. Children all hearty and full of fun. Linda has much improved since we saw her at Gibraltar and Mr Graves reports her a very healthy child.

April 27.   Leeds. Long conversation with Oswald who takes a very hopeful view. He thinks the Mill doing much better now we have 16 looms on double worsteds . . . and thinks the American trade an unmixed gain — it has come at a time when things were unusualy difficult. Benson says the constant advance in wool, amounting to 50 per cent in a few months, is mostly caused by American and Continental demand — the French alone can take more than half the sale.

April 30   Dined at John William Atkinson's [Aldam Heaton's brother-in-law] at Ilkley. Norman Shaw's house [St John's, 1878–9] is very nice and interesting; but I don't like the lattice windows or the ugly tiles of the entrance. Mrs Heaton and Helen were staying there. They allowed me to read some interesting letters from the Archbishop of York and many professors, full of feeling and admiration of Dr Heaton who was to have been made a F.R.S.

Dearman now had typhoid fever but was sufficiently recovered to go to London on June 28.

Emily wrote to her parents on 8 July 1880 from Llandudno.

Dearest Birds

I think this place perfectly Elysianic, an ideal seaside and we are all enjoying ourselve most awfully. The boys amuse me much. They are so thoroughly up in everything. They know all the movements of the steamers, and are in ecstasies with the "pifforming" dogs as they call them on the Pier, and the singing at the children's services on the sands. They know all the walks and the best places for flowers.

Yesterday Clara and I had an enchanting bathe. I dipped right over, head backwards seven times, and it renewed my youth. It was many years since I had a bathe, then a long walk while our hair was drying. This morning Percival and I bathed. I bathed him myself, dipping him in four times, and he was very brave. Then I sent him in, staying 20 minutes in the water myself and being all the time up to my chin. I do love bathing. I then took both boys on the pier to see the steamer come in. "Oh! what splendid fun", Jack said, and Percival "Oh! Mother let us dance for joy".

Dearman does all the shopping here. I mean all connected with provisions. I only go to the toy shops and the Post Office.

Ever yours Em.

July 11.   Instructed Aldam to lay aside tiles and grates for billiard room and blue room, to be put up at my convenience.

July 31.   I bought a grey and roan pair of cobs from Mr Harvey, former he asked £40, the latter £60. I gave him £90. The roan obtained 2nd prize at Gloucester for trotting.

Aug 7.   Dr Moore, phrenologist, said Dyer was passionately fond of children but would spoil them and could not say 'no'.

Aug 24.   Meeting at Cathedral Library at 1.30 p.m. to elect 7th lay member of Diocesan Conference. I could not go but went off to London by early train. Long conversation with Holroyd who showed how impossible it was to sell our goods. We are out of favour and not liked; Webb's departure deplored in some quarters. We are out of the race. Holroyd complains of our poor patterns, nothing in them, shabby, genteel, too tame, dear and poor. He cannot offer them at all and hopes we shall not continue his agency if we think anyone could do better.

Sept 2.   We went to Quaker's Yard, Cardiff to meet some members of the British Association now sitting at Swansea, by invitation of Harris' Navigation Coal Co. Some agents of the French Government and other French and English ladies and gentlemen were there . . . and we had a very lively time. By Emily's desire I accompanied her and half a dozen others to the bottom of the mine, 750 yards. The shafts are 17 feet diameter and there are two. 450 gallons of water a minute are pumped out by a vast Cornish engine, 100 inch cylinder. Coal is raised by Fowler's great and unique engine with immense drum cylinder 54 inches — draws 15 tons at a time.

Letter from Emily to her family.

"The lunch was very gorgeous, no end of champagne, claret cup, salmon, etc: and there were speeches, about seven or eight, one a neat French one from my neighbour. I was under the impression that all or most of the party would go down the mine as that seemed to be the *raison d'être* of the whole thing. I had told Mr Harris I was most anxious to go down and he said "Oh certainly'; but I was surprised after lunch to find everybody shirking it and declining. The ladies all came and warned me not to go, and the old director was most solemn in his exposition of all the awful dangers incurred in going down. It ultimately transpired no one wished to go excepting two of the French, two other gentlemen, Mr Harris, Dearman and myself. So we set off and walked ankle deep in black dust to the pit's mouth where we were ushered into the pay office to change our dress. I took my dress off and clad myself in a great long mackintosh coat down to my feet with a miner's waterproof hat which one of the French gentlemen kindly arranged so as to cover my *natte* behind. He also turned up the too long sleeves for me and was most helpful and assiduous in his kind attentions. The gentlemen were all in hats like mine and either long jerseys or mackintoshes so we looked a strange party.

    We went down in the cage, all coaly and grimy, just as it had brought its load of coals up the moment before. This mine is the deepest in South Wales, very nearly ½ a mile. It was pitch dark except for the little safety lamps each of us carried. We all felt a sort of singing in the ears but this went off when we stopped at the bottom. It was a strange sight, gnome-like figures with black faces appearing and disappearing all around us, water dripping everywhere like rain. It is so wonderfully ventilated there seemed always a fresh current of air. We were down about ¾ hour penetrating gallery after gallery many of them small and low, here and there passing a poor horse or a laden wagon. The coal glistening under our lamplight looked very pretty. I would not have missed it for worlds."

Sept 10.   The [Three Choirs] Festival came to an end this evening — many of our visitors attended the concluding services coming home at 8.45 and we all dined at 9 p.m. Our party has been a great success in spite of the death of Mrs Clayton which necessitated Mrs Hayward's departure for London. [Mr Hayward was vicar of Winstone.]

Sept 13.   Left Mr Hayward in a semi-conscious condition. Called in Graves who told Emily he was suffering from Alcohol. Came down to Leeds and put up at Edward's. Campbell, Warburg and myself discussed matters in a friendly spirit. Oswald writes attributing blame to other manufacturers. Samuel Jagger went round the Mill with Campbell and Warburg and was much pleased and says it is cut out for making cheap goods.

On Sept 24 Dearman engaged one William Sykes and his son as managers in his business in place of Turnbull. "Sykes is not a man knowing only one department; but he has had entire management with men as unpracticable as ourselves and can make cheap stuff better than an educated gentleman."

Sept. 26.   Emily arrived in Gloucester from Dinan at 6 p.m. where she had left Clara who is settling nicely.

Emily had enjoyed this jaunt to Dinan where she seems to have been in command of a party of ladies. In a letter to her mother she writes —

"We seven females put off on board the Guernsey, a very nice, clean pretty little boat. We were 12½ hours to S. Malo, a very good passage in the Captain's opinion, an enchantingly delicious one in mine, and a horrible one, an awful time, terrifically rough in those of Clara, etc. At 7 we all had some tea, and I partook of some ham in addition! Very unlike me but I am always preter-naturally hungry on board a steamer and it was very good smoked ham and decent tea. The others retired to our private cabin at 7.30 I paid frequent visits to it to take them salts, eau de cologne, fans, or to convey them one at a time to it as they none of them seemed able to walk, the ship rolling a fairish amount by this time. I love walking on a rolling deck and I gave them all in turn my arm and saw them safe to their berths. I had a delicious time pacing the decks, or rather staggering rapidly along them but never falling as I saw several gentlemen do in the violent lurches — till 10 p.m. when I turned in to my bed on deck. I rolled myself up in my fur cloak and rug and slept splendidly, the wind roaring around. Eliza also stayed on deck all night. I have been courier, interpreter and general manager of the party for the first time in my life and I enjoy doing it immensely. We chartered a big omnibus with three horses to take ourselves and luggage — we juniors sitting on the top and enjoying the very pretty drive from Dinard to Dinan — 14 miles or more. It is a picturesque, quaint old town most thoroughly French."

This seems to have been an amusing change from travelling with Dearman and his courier, for during these few days she wrote two more enthusiastic letters to her family in Leeds, before leaving Clara with Miss Brown.

"There is a very large colony of English residents here [in Dinan] and a very good situation some miles inland. The town is very ancient and excessively picturesque with old houses, gabled and projecting over the narrow old streets till they all but meet. The town is on a sort of ridge with steep slopes, at one side a precipice of 200 ft. down to the river and a glorious view from the terrace at the top, but glorious is hardly the word — lovely is better. The country is richly wooded, the soil dry and the air bracing. The pretty walks must be endless. Miss Brown's house is large and very convenient for a school. . . . This hotel (de la Poste) has a stable-yard entrance and outside staircase, but very nice rooms. There are no bells whatever. When we want anything we have to go out on the balcony and scream down into the yard for Marie or Rosalie. These old waitresses are very kind and motherly, aged about 70, and wearing curious Breton caps with a broad white band under the chin and round over the ears, suggestive of bad toothache."

The third letter, written on Sept. 21, is from Mont S. Michel, and begins

Dearest people.
    I cannot resist the temptation of writing to you from here, it is such a wonderful fascinating place. I am writing on a narrow window ledge (no table in the room) in the open window looking out over the sea with the moon's silvery track just before me and the high tide splashing below.

Oct 15.   Sykes and son settling down and say they will make the Mill pay or soon let us know that they cannot.

Oct 19.   We hear that Maude White had been rather inclining towards the Church of Rome when she came to us for the Gloucester Festival and heard Beethoven's Mass in D. During the Benedictus she saw her way clear, and was received into the Church of Rome the following week. The truth of the Real Presence came to her.

Oct 26.   Gloucester Diocesan Conference. A very large gathering. We were long engaged in agreeing upon the rules, and the first paper, on lay help, by Wemyss Colchester did not come forward till the afternoon. About 200 were all asked to lunch at the palace.

Oct 27.   Very interesting debate on middle class education ending in election of strong committee to promote it. Papers by Canon Beadon and Gambier Parry on Cathedrals were severe in the extreme on the system, but lenient to the present possessors of canonries. Committee appointed to consider the subject.

Nov. 5.   We took Edward and Maida Mirrielees to Fairford (by train to Cirencester) to see the famous windows whose quaintness and character are unmistakable.

Nov 7.   Annie Lawrence whom we obtained as under-nurse with such an extraordinary high character from Helen Sinclair is found to have imported lice and be suffering from mild itch. Whether she has infected the children Mr Graves cannot decide.

Dec 5.   Returned home [after a week in London going to theatres most nights] and found Percy and Violet quite well, Dyer still sore, Jack looking thin and delicate and much eczema and Linda's vaccination better. Mr Graves again wishes to part with Annie, a gross unclean woman but so pleasant and well-spoken. We have had the carpets taken up in day and night nurseries, to be cleaned.

1881

Jan 2.   Sunday. 40 communicants. The wine running short Mr Emeris replenished without consecration. [Dearman had remonstrated with the rector on this subject but evidently to no avail.]

Jan 8.   We came down to Leeds this afternoon and found both Father and Mother looking very much better than was the case in October especially Mother who looks most fresh and beautiful. Father's voice is also stronger.

Jan 9.   Interview with Campbell. . . . Things look gloomy, the Mill still offering nothing which is causing a run. Expenses very heavy. Campbell sleeps badly and feels worn out . . . Warburg writes hopefully from Paris. Oswald goes to London with new winter patterns. Interview with Sykes & Son. They seem hopeful but must have six more looms.

Jan 28.   Met Edward Armitage and young Freeman[53] [in London] and discussed the proposition of the Chancellor's Visitors that James William [Brook] should have a carriage and pair, be taken away from Ticehurst, and set up an establishment in London, thinking that the change and diversion might prove a sensible benefit. This recommendation appeared to all of us most reckless and unsuitable. Edward and I each sent in an affidavit conveying our objections. The Judges almost immediately said they thought the Visitors had been misled. They granted £250 for the purchase of carriage and horses and extra £500 for expenses; but insisted on his remaining at Dr Newington's. Edward and I subsequently purchased a landau, blue with white markings, light weight, in Baker street, built by Lambert, for £110 with every fitting quite new and very good looking.
This evening I went to see Corsican Brothers with Irving and Ellen Terry.

Feb 6.   George Eshelby [Bowden] tells me that Mrs Travel's girl has been confined in her cottage of a stillborn child and that Williams has confessed that he is the father. Mrs Travel came with same story. I blame her very much after the experience she had with her other girl that she permitted her daughter to come home from service without sending Williams away. The cottage is too small. Williams says it was no seeking of his. She laid on the top of him when he happened to drop asleep over his book. Even young Morris [footman] was found in equivocal positions with her. It appears to Williams she has tried to entrap him.

Feb 22.   Dined at Prinknash to meet Sir Michael Hicks-Beach who did not turn up owing to some mistake . . . Mr Hoare unable to get his Hansom up the hill, had his horse taken out and rode up.

---

[53] Family solicitor in Huddersfield.

I wrote a long and friendly letter to Oswald urging him to relinquish London and devote himself entirely to the home trade in Leeds.

Feb 23.   Afternoon charity concert for Elmore church, then went by train to Stroud to attend dinner of Conservative Benefit Club held for presentation to J.E. Dorington by Sir M. Hick-Beach. At night we accompanied Dorington to Lypiatt Park with Granville Baker and his wife.

Feb 24.   Superb weather, country covered with snow. Large dinner party. Afterwards we told ghost stories.

Mar 3.   Inspected houses in London. Preferred 20 Prince's Gardens. Mr Hanbury asked 500 guineas after Easter. We made a bid of 400 guineas which was accepted from 25 April–1 August (14 weeks). It is a beautiful house furnished with great taste three years ago.

During March at Bowden Emily did a lot with Clara; they rode together, paid calls and studied Latin. Emily also enjoyed taking the boys, Jack and Percy, for walks. Mrs Marshall,[54] the authoress of children's books stayed. And as usual there was plenty of coming and going to Clarefield, Eliza's house in Cheltenham. Sometimes Clara would drive Emily and the boys up to the Royal William and Painswick Beacon. On one occasion they saw the people who had just put out a fire in Dearman's woods at Cranham, and a day later Emily says she was tricycling very fast on the terrace when it went over and she fell smash on to her forehead, and got a black eye. Dearman does not mention the accident. It was March 30th, and he was buying horses at a sale, but they did not pass the vet.

April 1.   There was 12 degeees of frost in the kitchen garden last night. We have had three weeks or a month of perfectly brilliant weather with cold E and NE winds and frosts more or less severe. The fields which were green a month ago are now greyer than they were at Christmas after the snow. We have never had such a prolonged winter since we came here. The laurestinus are dead, the deodaras mostly brown and probably killed. Conservatory superb.

On April 3, Clara's 19th birthday, there was evidently a census taken. The 20 people at Bowden Hall were listed as follows:—

---

[54] Emma Marshall. *Heather and Harebells*, 1880; *Hurly-Burly: Little Queenie*, etc.

Name	Age	Place of Birth	Position (servants)
John Dearman Birchall	52	Leeds	
Emily Birchall	28	Leeds	
Clara S. Birchall	19	Harrogate	
John Dearman Birchall	5	Upton St. Leonards	
Arthur Percival D. Birchall	4	Upton St. Leonards	
Violet Emily D. Birchall	2	Upton St. Leonards	
Constance Lindaraja D. Birchall	1	Gibraltar	

[Emily's family were staying and so got included.]

John Jowitt	69	Kendal	
Deborah Jowitt	67	Kendal	
Florence Jowitt	26	Leeds	
Sarah Ross	69	Leeds	Mrs Jowitt's maid
Ellen Smith	38	Coaley	Housekeeper Cook
Rachel Ryrie	23	Halkirk, Caithness	Lady's maid
Laura Dyer	35	London	Head Nurse
Eleanor Martin	52	Penalt, Monmouth	Housemaid
Eliza White	25	Tetbury	Laundry Maid
Annie Louisa Smith	23	Uley	Under Housemaid
Annie Haslum	19	Winchcombe	Under Nurse
Sarah Medcroft	21	Gloucestershire	Kitchen maid
Evan Morris	25	Swindon	Footman

April 17. Easter Day. Father and Mother joined us after Morning Prayer for the Sacrament. There were 50 communicants. Mr Emeris replenished the bread once and the wine twice without reconsecrating.

April 19. Read the Merchant of Venice at Dr Ancrum's. Emily — Portia. I — Bassano.

April 26. Our exodus to London. I came up by 11.18 train. Servants followed at 12. Emily, Clara, nurses and children with Tothill at 2.30. Owing to misunderstanding there was some difficulty getting the door opened at 20 Prince's Gardens. All very comfortable but entertaining rooms are larger than we need and more sitting rooms than are necessary.
    Dined with Drummonds, [who lived at 48 Prince's Gardens].

April 27. Archer [groom] and the horses and two carriages came today. Emily went to Mrs Hughes and ordered Court dresses. Engaged Albert Dewdney, 21 as footman.

April 29. Met Charles Sykes. He is 27 of good address and very gentlemanly appearance. He has been 2 years with Mycroft in U.S.A. and 2½ with J. Hirst & Co. He was pleased with my partners and thought Warburg knew what he was about. Quite confident he can do well for us. The trade is much more open than it was of old. Competition has compelled everybody to look about. His best customer is Holland. He thinks he might have to live in town. Oswald could never do the business coming up for 3 or 4 days at a time. I wrote to Campbell speaking favourably of my interview, and offering to agree to what my partners might decide.

May 5. Emily presented Clara at a Drawing Room. [Dearman went with them.]

May 17. Went to At Home at Mr Sinclair's. Met Mr & Mrs Hasell and Miss Janet Sinclair and hosts of people of whom we know nothing. [Thus began the Sinclair connection.]

May 20. Went to stay at Enderby [the Drummonds].
Garden Party on the Saturday. Two bands and plenty of lawn tennis, and 5 splendid fire balloons. Emily came out in her terracotta aesthetic dress and Clara in her summer costume. No one looked half as nice.

Sunday. We went to church morning and evening, dining at 8.25 p.m. It proved a very long day, no one doing any reading. In afternoon we walked round the woods in which Cecil has made some pretty walks with lovely views. Cecil has been very pleasant and genial, Amy rather cold blankety.

May 27. Drawing lesson from Mr Watson, perspective mostly but to-day he brought a cast of an ornament for me to do in chalk with view to improving myself in light and shade. Emily has lessons in Spanish. In afternoon I went to Ealing to see a procession of tricyclist clubs, Gloucester and many London ones. We saw examples of the Special Salvo, Otto, Cheylesmore, Meteor, Humber, Devon, Tom Tit and Omnicycle.

June 1. Emily had her first At Home, 4–7. Great success. 80 people came. Afterwards we went to the (aesthetic) Opera Patience; the love-sick maidens most charming, jokes amusing, airs lively. The children have measles.

June 13. I went to Bowden. The house had not even got one coat of paint all over it. Best bedroom begun papering. Ordered stables to be colour-washed. Called on dear old Mr Jones. He said, "I shall be under the sod before you come down again. I am very happy." I tried to encourage him thinking the pain he complained of in his chest was partly indigestion. Mrs Jones told me he was sinking; but I could scarcely credit it. I only stayed 10 minutes as he soon fatigued. The next day Mr Jones died aged 84. It will be a great loss. His end was peaceful without pain. He dozed away and the time when his spirit fled was not marked or even noticed by those who had the privilege of being present. May we be sustained by as robust a faith when our end comes.

Emily: aesthetic photograph by Bassano

June 24.   We attended meeting of Society for protection of Ancient Buildings. American minister in chair; William Morris, George Howard, Lord Houghton and others made most effective speeches.

June 25.   Pagets' afternoon party; extremely slow. Went on to Alexanders' Garden party, wet afternoon and so all in the house. Very amusing. Emily talked to Whistler. The Misses Hunt in costume memorable. Our ladies looked a little too much dressed to compare with the old doxies present.

June 30.   The Ellicotts' [Bishop of Gloucester] evening At Home. I took Clara. Emily and Maida called for us after attending the Meiningen play, Julius Caesar at Drury Lane.

June 1.   Dined with the Ellicotts.

July 2.   John Sinclair [who afterwards married Clara] came to luncheon and we drove him down to see Ham House, beyond Richmond, [his kinsman] Lord Dysart's antique residence. We saw two old fossils called Tollemache, two Misses Hussey and a host of other dry as dust old creatures, fit inhabitants of such an unchanged medieval abode.

On July 3, Emily wrote to her mother.

I fear I have not written a proper letter to you since Monday but you will forgive me when you hear a few of the things I have done. We much enjoyed having Maida but the time seemed to pass very quickly. The extra Richter concert on Monday was splendid, Beethoven's Missa Solemnis; solo inferior to Gloucester but orchestra and chorus glorious. I espied Robin Benson in the gallery and next him a very aesthetic looking lady, consummately pretty and utterly Burne-Jonesy in whom I recognized Margaret. I spoke to her on coming out and she knew me and was languidly pleasant. Her dress was a blue sort of sacque like Edward B's Japanese dressing gown and her whole appearance was "intense" to a degree. Her husband is quite a usual looking man. On Tuesday Maida and I went to M.me Modjeska's benefit at the Princess Theatre and it was most interesting, and Sarah Bernhardt acted. In the evening we went to the Horticultural Fete, splendid flower show, taking the boys and Sophie and then called on May Benson. Margaret Drummond was there in a more aesthetic robe than ever. Sophie was horrified but Maida and I thought it rather pretty and suited to her style. She was very friendly and is staying there. Thursday Maida and I did lots of shopping and we walked about 6 miles, and in the evening went to see Julius Caesar in German, and at 11.50 we joined Dearman and Clara at Mrs Ellicott's At Home. I talked to the poet Lewis Morris. Friday I had a long sitting with Cotman, and Maida left. We dined with the Ellicotts, a particularly delightful party of 20. Mrs Ellicott is the best hostess I ever saw. Sir Fred. Pollock[55] took me in and we got on tremendously well, perfect floods of talk. On my other side was a very nice German Baron de Stein. Dearman took in Lord & Lady O'Neil's daughter and Clara was taken in by a distinguished Yankee General, aide de camp in the war to General Grant and wounded, and had dear old Sir Montague Smith on her other side. Besides the O'Neils there were also Lord & Lady Bandon and Mr Justice Keating. Mrs Ellicott then had yet another Reception afterwards.

Yesterday John Sinclair guided us to Ham House and introduced us to his relatives who live there, a deeply interesting historic house built by James I, exquisitely furnished and decorated at that period and full of old pictures, china, and curiosities of all kinds and of historic association. We were shown all over it by Mrs Algernon Tollemache. The masters of the house seem to be Lord Dysart's great uncles. Mr Frederick Tollemache was most gracious to us and much interested in all Dearman told him about the china. We saw tribes of other people, Sinclairs and Tollemaches, it was quite confusing.

We suddenly decided to let Dyer have a holiday, so she went yesterday and is to stay till Tuesday night, Ryrie taking charge in her absence which she does most efficiently and amicably. It was Jack who suggested Dyer going. He came to me and said very seriously that he was sure Nana wanted a rest. "I have noticed her have a tired look", and he was most willing to undertake to "see to Percy" if I could arrange to spare Nana.

I have now to write Spanish letters for my master as well as all the exercises.

It is very hot here in London. Ever your loving Em.

July 6.   Took the boys to see Mrs. Jarley's waxworks.

July 14.   I spent the day at Bowden. All looks lovely and alterations and painting are arriving at completion.

Rendcomb sold to Mr Taylor, a cotton spinner for £160,000 a great reduction from what they asked. Sir Francis Goldsmith paid £170,000 for it and built a house and stables which cost over £100,000 pulling down the old house so long the home of the Guises. Dined with Eliza, returning to Princes Gardens by the night train and leaving my traps I went into the City and inspected Billingsgate, Smithfield, and Covent Garden markets. There was such an immense quantity of food, for instance of salmon there were 400 boxes from all parts mostly containing 20 fish generally in ice. There was no way whereby I could distinguish where the meat came from in Smithfield. American, Continental and English all seemed mixed together in hopeless confusion. Very hot weather, 97° in the shade. Went to afternoon party at Mrs Morse's, 96 Cheyne Walk, Whistler's old house and met Mrs Millais.[56] Afterwards watched polo at Hurlingham.

---

[55] Sir F. Pollock. (1815–88). Queen's remembrancer and author.
[56] Effie, formerly wife of John Ruskin.

July 20.   Emily's large 'At Home'. Over 100 came including Oscar Wilde. Most successful. Dinner at the Alexanders; Mr Palgrave[57] [Editor of 'The Golden Treasury'] took Emily in.

The next day Emily wrote a letter to her mother:—

We were very busy preparing; the flowers took me the whole mortal morning till 1.40, then arranging the room, and superintending the florists doing up the plants in the conservatory etc. — Then dressing — and seeing that the table was all right. We had a great spread of fruit, about 20 dishes of strawberries, peaches, greengages, raspberries, gooseberries, nectarines, currants etc. I find Clara is devoted to white currants. I thought only town missionaries were. We had of course cakes and tea and coffee and ices and claret and champagne cup etc.

I wore my new white dress embroidered by myself and very nicely made up. It looks very nice and I wore a pretty aesthetic pink sash. Punctually at 4 Sophie arrived, but it was hard not to have any of my own sisters. Then came Mr Morton the accompanyist and then the Sinclair family. The Bishop of Gloucester came which was kind of him as he does not like parties. People dribbled in and then came a rush and the drawing room was very full for a time. Oscar Wilde was the great lion; when he was announced a sort of silence fell upon the room and everyone gazed at his striking figure. The way Oscar Wilde came was that Malcolm Lawson called on me on Tuesday and asked me to give him a card for Oscar as the latter wanted to come, whereat I felt much flattered. Dearman thought him very pleasant, much more sensible than he expected. Frank Benson (Romeo) was charming. Clara took an immense fancy to him. All the people were very cheerful and there was quite a babel of talk between the music. We had not too much time to dress to go out to dinner. Mr Palgrave and I got on like a house on fire.

The three elder children came in a little yesterday, and the boys handed out the tea. Violet evoked much admiration and went and sat on strangers' knees and talked to them.

July 30.   We all returned home from London, though Emily did not arrive till 2.15 a.m. the next day.

July 31.   All to church; the place looks fresh, green and lovely.

Aug 6.   I spent my 53rd birthday on the tricycle. First went to Eliza's, 1 hour 8 mins. Lunched there, then on to Gloucester at 3.30 arriving at Club at 5.5 p.m. After drinking some tea I came home — say about 23 miles.

---

[57] Francis Turner Palgrave (1824–97), poet and critic.

Aug. 10.   Village Flower Show at Bowden. A glorious breezy and even sunny day though the glass was falling and it looked like rain. Well attended we brought heaps of people through the house, and 50 had tea in the hall.

Aug. 12.   Garden party here; but from early morn to late at night there was not five minutes' cessation in the downpour. No-one came but a few Emerises and a party from Prinknash just to condole with Emily.

Aug. 14.   Tothill complains that for years he has never had a comfortable dinner — no time is allowed. Lunch often keeps him till 2.0 or ½ 2. There is no punctuality.
The boys are always rushing about, no-one having control. The place is getting harder every year — no consideration for him whatever — it is Tothill here, Tothill there. He can never get to his plate without being rung for, and it is much worse, and especially about meals when I am away. The footmen complain they can often scarcely swallow their food before the carriage is wanted, and then they are kept out past their tea time. Tothill cannot consent to spend another winter here. He feels that being a good worker and willing he is put upon and not treated with consideration.

May 16.   Emily returned from Leeds where she went three days ago to see Helen Heaton [Linda's godmother] who is to marry Fred Newall to-morrow. Train very late. She came up from Gloucester in a cab which had a smash against a tram, so she had to change.

Aug. 27.   Charming garden party at Mr James's of Edgeworth. Mrs J. inherited quarter of a million. They are increasing and improving the house.

Sept. 3.   Staying at Oxton. Went on excursion to Castle Howard, Mr George Howard giving us a grand luncheon. Emily sat next him and found him charming. We enjoyed the pictures.

Sept 10.   Staying at Whiteholm [with Mary Birchall his sister-in-law]. This afternoon we drove over the hills some 9 miles to call at Browseholme. The view from Barnard Pastures I should say is unequalled in Yorkshire for mountainous sublimity. The Master of Harriers and otter hounds, Edward Parker, is the very Tony Lumpkin[58] of real life. He has lately married a simple young lady but he appeared too abashed in our presence to have anything to say.
A party of gentlemen returned from otter hunting and with a large drag of hounds with 3 horses looked very picturesque in front of the old mansion. The house looks lonely and ghostlike filled with old armour and china and pictures and tapestry mostly in a bad condition. The young lady seems to be engaged in disinterring curiosities every day. The china closet with open-worked door is nailed up, the china covered with the dust of ages. The carved oak rooms are really beautiful.

[58] *She stoops to conquer.*

Sept 12. We left Whiteholm Mary taking us to Stonyhurst. She had an introduction to the Jesuit College. We lunched there. The building is progressing apace. We saw Mary Queen of Scots' Missal in the Library. Clara went back with her aunt to Whiteholm and we returned to Leeds, and Bowden next day.

On September 19 they went on a driving tour with dog cart, cobs and groom (Winslade) to Evesham, Warwick, Leamington, Kenilworth and Coventry.

They returned by Chipping Campden, Broadway and Winchcombe and called at Sudeley Castle.

Sept 21. At Coventry I called and inspected the factories where the Cheylesmore, Salvo and Premier tricycles are made, and ordered a Premier of Hillman & Co.

Sept 25. Emily says: Harvest Festival, most hearty service and good singing anthem and lovely decorations. Weather brilliant. Both boys to church in morning.

Sept 26th. Jack's 6th birthday and Violet's 3rd kept also. Five Ackers children and two nurses came to spend day which was very fine and all very good.

Sept 27. Jack and I blackberried at Brockworth, and were caught in heavy showers.

On September 28 Dearman & Emily were off again, this time to Bournemouth, Isle of Wight, and the New Forest.

Oct 1. Lunched at Lyndhurst and examined the beautiful church with interest. There are two large windows by Morris, Marshall of an early period, and a large fresco in which Gambier Parry's method has been adopted. The style is far from severe and presents too great a contrast to the medievalism of Burne-Jones's window above.

Oct 2. Attended church (very high fine ceremonial) at St Clement's, Boscombe, saw the tomb of Mrs Tinling. The rectory is also built by Sedding, architect. The nunnery near is by Norman Shaw.

Oct 5. John Sinclair and Janet [his sister] came to stay until the 8th. They walked up Nut Hill with Emily.

Oct 7. The two Sinclairs and Clara had long ride. Maida, Clara, John and Emily played lawn tennis in the afternoon.

It was during this visit that John Sinclair opened a new Visitors Book at
Bowden with the following verse.

An Alphabet addressed to the family of Birchall of Bowden Hall with divers
allusions to the visit of certain guests in October, 1881.

A   announced the surnames of Ackers and Ancrum.
        At Upton I hope you'll contrive to anchor 'em

B   brings us to Birchall and Bowden and Brown
        And the beautiful beech trees we saw on the down.

With C   comes Miss Clara; but I really don't dare her
        Perfections to sing, lest I fail, so I'll spare her,
        and praise Charlie the cob with his tail cut in bob
        And the Cotswolds and china that tempts one to rob.

D   dwells on the Duties that brought us to town
        And the dear single dahlias, and good Lady Downe.[59]

With E   Mr Emeris enters my song
        An excellent man; let us hope he'll live long.

F   is full of the fun, with each morning begun
        And the fossil we found on our Saturday's run.

G   still gladdens your guests with the garden and grove
        And the grand-viewed gazebo, a place which we love.

H   harps on our hosts, the histories of ghosts
        And Heaton, whose hall's one of Gloucestershire's boasts
        And Hotspur the hound, full of frolic and bound,
        Our sticks as we hid them, he cleverly found.

With I   inspiration has vanished I think.
        For ideas will not flow and I'm wasting my ink.

But J   joins a jumble of subjects, alack!
        For I cannot enlarge on John, Janet and Jack.

K   keeps us in mind of the welcome so kind
        Which we failed not to find, more — as since I'm opined
        Like kinsmen than guests who have left home behind.

But L   will not doubt the secret let out
        That Leeds was the magic that brought this about.

L   will tell too the fame of that curious name
        Which belongs to the sweetest and last of your kinder
        Suggestive of sneezing, beginning with Linda.

M   mentions Miss Mirrielees, the brightest and best of those
        Ladies from Moscow who everywhere daily please.
        Now at Bowden alone as N needs not narrate
        The most priceless Nankin reigns from cellar to garret

O   opens my room, into which we may poke
        And gaze on the treasures of a fine old black oak.

P   pens about Percy, and Prinknash near which we went

---

[59] Viscountess Downe after her husband's death in 1832 lived at Bowden Hall with Mr & Mrs
Charles Brooke Hunt till her death in 1867. She built the Upton St. Leonards schools, architect
Henry Woodyer.

The charming piano and Pear's advertisement.
Q   is such a queer letter, I'm sure you will spare me
It lands me in such a tremendous quandary.
R   raves of Miss Rice,[60] the sister so nice
Who we hear is not seen on her old fortalice.
S   speaks of your school under excellent rule
I'm sure that it isn't a place for a fool.
T   takes us again to brave General Thackwell[61]
Miss Maida's tomatoes which some folks don't smack well.
U   is Upton, I wish an Imperial ukase
Would command one to live in so charming a place.
V   ventures on Violet, sweet little maid;
When older she'll break many hearts I'm afraid.
brings the charade Words, and brightly tinted wood
Now W   The wood we loved to ride in, though the weather was not good.
While X   will kindly make excuse for rhyme and rhythm untrue
And Y   shall tell of Yorkshire, land that brought us first to you
And Z is most unwelcome, for it bids me say Adieu!
John S. Sinclair

The reference to the gazebo is probably the "observatory" on Nut Hill behind Bowden where years later my parents Linda and Cecil got engaged; and the ghost stories were special favourites of Dearman and fashionable in those days. The first people to sign the Visitors Book after this were Sanford and Edith Scobell the grandparents of Barbara Cartland, on November 17, after a dinner party.

Oct 10.   In London. Called on Fred. Harris. Miss Harris got scarlet fever from Norman Shaw's aesthetic drains, which are not a success.

Interviewed Fred Warburg who complained about Oswald. He said Oswald was weak, never likely to manage a business and his principal virtue was his relationship to me, disappointed with him in Paris, always poor, borrowed £5 and did not pay back when he ought to have done but long after. I think more than ever that Warburg has stuck to Oswald for his name. He thinks Campbell good, but old fashioned. If Campbell has become behind the age, and Oswald has not the stuff in him to manage a business what do I propose to do? If after 12 months with the assistance of Ellis we don't succeed I shall look further.

Oct 17.   In Leeds. Had a long talk with Campbell and Oswald. Warburg has been brought to apologize to Campbell and is showing a better spirit. Campbell and Oswald to devote more time to pushing the foreign trade.

[60] The Misses Rice were daughters of a former Dean of Gloucester and sisters of Lord Dynevor. They lived at Matson House.
[61] A friend and neighbour of Eliza Birchall in Cheltenham.

Oct 24.   Talked for hours and hours with Campbell, Oswald and Warburg. We turned the business round in every fashion. We seem after much storm to have some distant prospect of a calm.

Oct 27.   Emily and I went with Florence to Newcastle and spent night at Ferndene with the Newalls. Helen very cordial. Handsome house with beautiful drawings, Turners, Barretts, Hunt, and some oil paintings by Leighton, Watts, etc. Nice china. Lovely hot houses and flowers. The country is cut up with railways and disfigured with smoke. We saw his immense telescope; the sun was clear for a short time. I noticed 3 spots. The Leatharts and Sowerbys dined.

Oct 28.   Went to see Mr Leathart's pictures. Rossetti, Burne Jones, Maddox Brown, Holman Hunt are well represented. In afternoon to see Sowerby's glass works which are marvellous. Goods seem inexplicably cheap. Saw an order for 18 thousand dozen tumblers. A penny a piece seems an average price for good quality. Saw some fancy work like Venetian. Mr. Sowerby is the illustrator of 'After Tea' and other popular books.

Nov 5.   It appears that during our absence though I had left instruction with Archer to drive Dyer and the children each day, he refused on Saturday last saying it was aganst the rules. He would not let horse or carriage leave the stables. Archer thought Dyer very exigent and contradictory in her instructions. He spent most of his time in his garden. I gave Archer a severe jobation; but I don't consider Dyer came well out of it — she likes dawdling about shopping too much.

Nov 12.   Dined Prices, Tibberton. Canon Case looks a very inferior man to what he did when living in Gloucester. His dress secular but marked with a redundancy of ornament, numerous rings, etc. He talked of Paris and London theatres like a rather blasé man of the world.

Nov 14.   I had 5½ hours at the Asylum visiting with Ancrum and Granville Baker. The earth closets have been denounced by the Commissioners, also the want of supervision over the epileptics. We ordered some old drains to be taken up, in fact the last of the old system. We have 46 male and 56 female epileptics.

Nov 17.   Gave dinner party. Gambier Parrys though Parry himself was unable to come owing to being thrown out of his dogcart and run over, Granville and Barwick Bakers, the Scobells of Redmarley who stayed the night. Mrs Scobell said to her maid "I suppose they have a man cook here", which compliment was repeated to Mrs Smith to whom it gave great joy.

Nov 29.   Went to the Bazleys at Hatherop for three nights with Emily and Clara. Other guests included the Talbot-Ponsonbys; he was brought up at

Down Ampney, an estate of 2,000 acres now on the market, — Barkleys — he has been years in Turkey and tells wonderful tales — and the Percys. Mr Percy is a Cumberland young man, very pleasant but rather too dependent on copious libations of Bazley's beautiful beer.

Nov 30. Gentlemen shooting. We had a pleasant time at the covert. I stayed until lunch time but did not shoot my foot being too fatigued. In the afternoon Miss Bazley drove us to Kempsford to see the St. Johns. The Rectory is being restored by Waller with considerable skill at cost of Queen Anne's Bounty. Clara broke a tricycle.

Dec 1. We went round the farm. Bazley has two in hand in addition to Home Farm. In 3 or 4 years he calculates he has lost about £4,000 in farming.

Dec 2. Left Hatherop. Dined at Highnam, Gambier Parry on crutches.

Dec 13. Dined with the de Ferrières in Cheltenham, a pleasant evening. Adjourned to Eliza's where we partially changed our clothes and proceeded up to town by night train reaching Paddington at 3.50 a.m. We had first rate accommodation at Grand Hotel at the most moderate charge till Dec 17. Mild weather.

1882

On January 3 1882 the Birchalls gave a ball for 229 people at Bowden. A ballroom 50 feet long was temporarily erected by Benjamin Edgington for the sum of £62.3.0. Dearman wrote:

Edgington's room looked most fairylike and by allowing a free circulation through the drawing room and out by the deliciously well-lighted conservatory prevented any undue crushing or inconvenience.

The other accounts were

Champagne 4 doz. at 60/-	£12. 0.0
Claret	1.11.3
Sherry	2.18.4
Fruit	5. 0.0
Fortt's bill	34.16.9
Lamps and candles	5. 0.0
Extra waiters	3.16.0
Tips	1. 0.0
Supper for men at Houghton's King's Head	8.15.0
Woodwards Band of 6	7.15.0
Great Western Railway carriage	25.15.0
Haulage	2. 0.0
	£172.10.4

The Ball so long anticipated with eager hopes by all the lady-kind and with some nervous trepidation by myself has passed off with the greatest éclat. The chorus of praise and admiration was too universal to leave room for doubt. God Save the Queen at 4 a.m.

Next day was the County Ball and the day following the Guise's. After that Dearman attended a Temperance Mission. The press reported that a county magistrate Mr Dearman Birchall was so pleased with the meeting that he had given two guineas towards the expenses, and a chimney sweep gave a sovereign.

Jan 14. I empowered Mr Knowles to offer £20,500 for Upleadon Court estate, 504 acres. I stipulated I would not complete the purchase until Michaelmas next.

Jan 19. Fancy Dress Ball to open the entertaining room at Barnwood. I was dressed as Mahomet Bel Hadgi, the father and Emily as the mother of Lindaraja. We were not recognized at first. After an hour Emily dropped the Moorish sheets and came out a full-bloomed Harmony in Yellow Liberty Silk with scores of sunflowers. Emily's waist on rising in a morning is 25 inches. When in corset, 22½ inches.

Jan 29. Leeds. Dined at Edward's and met Fowler of Durham who was very agreeable and recommended our going to see Bodley's church built for Meynell Ingrams at Hoare Cross; windows fine by Burlison and Grylls — one of the most beautiful churches in England.

Warburg left for France and Italy. Campbell and Oswald seem getting on in a most friendly way and both look in better spirits, though there is much to depress in the failures at the Mill — the looms mostly running on double worsteds in which they succeed.

March 2. Wrote to George Wyndham Gray accepting his offer to take the management of Upleadon Court Farm and the Home Farm at Bowden on salary of £200 per annum and the keep of one cow and two horses.

March 3. Mr Gray came over at dinner time to go round the markets to-morrow. He has been 19 years farming and was formerly a sailor. He was most successful at Agricultural College and is now invited to examine the students. He says they have lost money at Cirencester since Constable left.

March 4. Mr Price[62] invited me to bring Gray to inspect his covered yards. A complete investigation of results had convinced him that they had proved more efficacious than he had even anticipated. The cost with corrugated iron and glass was 10/- per square yard. Each animal must be calculated to take 12 yards = £6.

March 7. Mr Gray bought a lot of stock at sale at Southam.

March 9. Came to Enderby for the baptism of the son and heir of the Drummonds to whom Clara was godmother. Cecil gave a famous entertainment to the school with hundreds of presents for all the children, and tea for tenants and other farmers in the Hall — Mr Edwards preached a good sermon on the text "Take this child away and nurse him for me and I will give thee thy wages".

March 17. Walked over the Upleadon Court farm. The steam engine was at work on the land. It was a superb day.

April 1. Emily and I lunched with the Percivals at Meredith and Mr. P. drove us over to Upleadon which was Emily's first visit. We did very little walking but she was very much pleased with what she saw. The lilies and wildflowers generally very pretty, trees bursting into leaf and all so spring-like and bright. The anemones in the gardens especially beautiful and gorgeous in colour. House in course of restoration and also cart-shed blown down in the October storm.

---

[62] W.P. Price of Tibberton Court.

April 3.   Took my Premier tricycle to the Cross in Gloucester in 30 minutes — return took 36 minutes.

April 7.   Good Friday. Church in morning. Afternoon I and Theodore Crewdson (and his son Jack) rode to Upleadon and walked over the farm.

April 8.   Emily very busy doing decorations in church, two crosses, pulpit wreath, little pillars, etc. Theodore Howard arrived. Emily's parents and Susie already here so it is a family party for Easter. Jack in bed with injured leg.

April 12.   Jack's leg has been in a "splint" by directions of Mr. Bower whom we called in after the death of Mr. Graves. It looks better than it has done from the beginning.
   We attended meeting of the Gloucester Archaeological Society at Prinknash and heard Mr. Bazeley's paper.[63]

May 4.   Rode over to Upleadon in afternoon. Gray seemed getting on well; barley and oats coming up, planting cabbages. Joined my family in lodgings at Tenby.

May 7.   We are perfectly charmed with the large old parish church, its services and clergyman Mr Huntingdon, who is almost inspired it seemed to us. In the morning he preached on the text "In my Father's house are many mansions"; in the evening, "This is life eternal to know the only true God and Jesus Christ whom thou has sent". He spoke of Darwin one of the greatest thinkers who had in his last utterances confessed his true faith. His eloquence amazed and delighted us.

May 16.   I rode over to Upleadon. Audited Gray's accounts and agreed for him to erect dairy and poultry house, he to raise me a few pheasants, and to invite his brother-in-law to have a little fishing at Upleadon.

May 20.   We have taken rooms for a month at Brown's Hotel. Went to Mrs Warde's At Home. Emily had a long talk with Prof. Huxley. The two Miss Stopford Brookes were in Patience dresses. Some wondered why they did not carry sponges with them as they were only dressed in nightgowns.

May 27.   Lunched on board the *Dunedin*, a sailing vessel which has just come from New Zealand in 90 to 100 days with 500 carcases of sheep, a few dozen oxen, hares and turkeys. They were all frozen as hard as iron and the lower compartments were maintained 20° of frost all through the voyage

---

[63] Rev. William Bazeley, rector of Matson, read a paper on the "History of the Manor and Mansion" of Prinknash.

even on the equator. There was also good fresh butter. The mutton tasted very well but the cooking on board was not calculated to give it a very attractive appearance.[64]

Some gentlemen from the colonies said they only wanted a regular and assured market to send very large quantities. 100 sheep were sent to Smithfield and sold wholesale at 6d per lb. The New Zealanders told me that the agricultural tools including reapers and binders so universal out there all come from the United States, but threshing machines were mostly of English building.

May 28.   Whitsun Day. Again we attended St. Alban's and heard a beautiful and impressive sermon full of fire from Stanton. "If we then being evil know how to give good gifts to our children, how much more shall your Heavenly Father give the Holy Ghost to them that ask him."

May 29.   Attended the Wagner festival.

June 1.   I received a very manly and satisfactory letter from Oswald urging continuance of the Mill. He says, "you may say that it is easy for me having nothing to lose to lay down theories and try experiments with (your) money, but you will give me credit for sincerity at all events. . . ."

June 3.   Miss Kingdom's Concert. Amy Wakefield sang some German songs by Schumann. A very small house, so the drumming on the piano for the Misses Kingdom's duets was almost overpowering.

Horse Show. Saw a very smart roan mare. She did not take a prize in the harness class; but I asked her price as she was a good match for our roan. He would not take less than £100. Mr Gray writes that the young horse he had from Bowden fell down dead in a ditch on his return from ploughing.

Typical day for Emily. *June 19.* Spanish lesson. Florence came. We drove in Victoria paying calls. Robin Benson, Mr Cross, Lady Pease and John Sinclair called on us. Maida came to tea. Dearman, Clara and I to Lady Ellenborough's Ball.

June 24.   Emily went to Leeds till July 15. Clara and I home.

June 27.   Quarter Sessions. I drove Jumbo and the Roan. They were very fresh. On arrival at home I took up Dyer and Jack and Percy to call at Prinknash. Having been previously driven into Gloucester I thought we were secure of their good conduct. They were gay and when Archer got down to put on the slipper, Jumbo who was on the near side began rearing, plunging and kicking. Archer got hold of his head. I hitched the reins up and slipped down to get Dyer and the children off thinking he would kick the

---

[64] This was the first experiment of sending frozen lamb from New Zealand.

trap to pieces. Before I could effect my object they plunged forward throwing Archer down and darting away towards Cheltenham. The slipper must have kept in down the hill, but they galloped all the way to Cheltenham without coming into collision with anything. Archer and I followed running with the horrible consciousness that they were in danger of death and mutilation. We got a trap at the Cross Hands and followed at a better pace. All the village was out at Shurdington looking aghast. We soon met two traps that told us the trap had been stopped on the Cheltenham side of the railway bridge. We found our darlings uninjured. Dyer had stuck to the trap heroically; nothing could be nobler.

Clara had been much alarmed for a travelling musician had come to tell of the accident bringing a broken trace and Jack's hat to verify the story. Tothill set off in the basket trap and met Archer driving back.

The mercy of God has preserved these dear children from a frightful death and us from unutterable woe.

The Dean of Gloucester wrote:–

The Deanery, Gloucester 4 July 1882.

My dear Mr Birchall
    In the midst of bodily suffering I cannot but rejoice in signal mercies bestowed upon others. I rejoice with you in the marvellous preservation of your children. You must receive them as given back to you from heaven. Believe that their lives are not twice given to you in vain. Assure Mrs Birchall that I am happy in your happiness. Most truly yours. H. Law.

June 30.   I made a first and final offer for Whitley Court of £10,000, with no valuation for timber or anything else.

    Mr Gray spent the morning here. He is about to obtain a summons against a boy for fishing in the Leadon without leave and setting him in defiance.

July 2.   I asked Mr Emeris to return thanks in church for our children's delivery.

July 9.   We have storm and unusually heavy rain every day last week. Six extra men for haymaking have never been able to touch it. This week they have been making believe to work in chopping up firewood and mowing down thistles. We have about 50 ewes over here from Upleadon with a view to get our lawn small enough to mow with lawn machine.

    Keen has gone on a tour of garden inspection. He is to see George Simpson's, Wray Park, Cubitt's Dorking, William Fowler and Gurney Barclay's at Walthamstow, Lord Salisbury's at Hatfield and the Baroness Rothschild at Gunnersbury besides the Botanical Show at Regents Park and some nursery gardens.

July 14. I went to Reading Royal Agricultural Show and purchased two pedigree Jersey heifers from W.A. Peel of Rickmansworth, Dream and Doterel.

July 17. Very large and important meeting at Asylum . . . we suspended Hawkins and Hopkins who are unfavourably connected with recent death of Partridge on whom Coroner's inquest brought in verdict of wilful murder against some person or persons unknown.

The Commissioners urge us having more male attendants and giving them shorter hours and fitting up places for rest and recreation. They praised the cleanliness of the wards but pitched into the bread and complained of some bad smells in earth closets and sewer gas from W.C.

July 19. Emily's 30th birthday. Dined with the Ancrums, very lively, dancing, etc.

July 24. Committee at Asylum. Dr. Toller has sent in his resignation. Dr Bowes aged 42, recommended by Wemyss Colchester and who has lost his money by purchasing a bogus practice in London, was appointed as the new head.

Aug 9. Flower Show at Bowden. We had the tent on the lawn and a very large attendance, no end of merry children, fire balloons, two bands, and the bedding was immensely admired. Sports were kept up till 9.30. Miss Maria Rice stayed and dined with us.

Aug 12. Drove to see Eliza's new house. Helped her choosing wall-papers. It is called Lanesfield, in Lansdown Road.

Aug 15. Stayed at Hatherop. Mr Bazley seems more retiring and less inclined to visit or go about than ever and says he never travels because it disarranges his digestion. He is sadly troubled about the farms in hand, and is attempting to let them by auction, at 12/- or 14/- an acre.

Aug 16. It turned out Bazley had no real bidding though the room was full of tenant farmers. Various reasons have been assigned. Some don't like farms to be let by auction. All admit he makes a good landlord and why he is really left in the lurch one does not see.

Aug 17. I told Clara all about John Sinclair. [On June 14 Dearman had made the following entry in his diary without any other explanation. "Met John Sinclair at the Oxford and Cambridge Club at 10.30 a.m. He was very frank and pleasant; had gathered from my letters I was rather more determined to admit no intercourse than I intended; said if there was an absolute obstacle he would prefer to be warned."] I told Clara first because she was forming uncharitable views of Mrs Sinclair's and Janet's conduct from not rightly apprehending the position of affairs, secondly because there being no chance of his turning up at present Eliza thinks it unfair she should be exposed to the chance of other love affairs without knowing of John Sinclair.

Aug 20.   Mr Stow of Cheltenham took the service owing to Mr Emeris's illness. He is on the lookout for a country living to purchase. He talks of ritualism being nearly played out now that all the churches have surpliced choirs, good music and cheerful abbreviated services.

Aug 22.   The Bensons of Canada [he was Emily's uncle] came to us. George their son is at Uppingham and the girl to remain at school at Finchley.

Aug 23.   Mr Benson, George and I spent most of the day with Ackers, inspecting his herd; the former was immensely pleased and said he had not enjoyed anything so much for years. Mr Benson says that opinion in Canada is now rather going in favour of Herefords and polled Angus cattle. What is wanted is the best grazers to cross ordinary Montana or Texan cattle in the ranches in North West turning bulls out, a race is expected to rise having great merits. Ackers says he can have no idea how his cattle will sell; one bull Lord Prinknash III he said might sell for £25 or £1,500. He will not today take a thousand guineas a piece for two Maids of Gloucester II & III.

Aug 24.   Mr Benson and I went to Upleadon. He was wonderfully pleased with the farm and said he thought it would be worth the money I paid for it in Canada, that is in the eastern states.
I agreed to go shares with him in a Ranch investment he is proposing with a number of others in the Bow River, North Western Canada. The freehold is 5,000 acres but there is 80,000 acres of grazing and when Government require this they allot more further west and grant double for the freehold land. Risk at £200 a share, afterwards might risk to extent of £2,000. He has his eye on a capital judge of cattle and honest man he is going to send out to manage it.

Aug 29.   Garden party at the Scobells, Down House, Redmarley. We had a very pleasant drive, but it is 28 miles there and back.

Aug 30.   Garden party at Barnwood House. The place looked lovely. Emily and I tricycled thither.

Sept 6.   The weather has been changeable, but all else *couleur de rose*.

Sept 9.   I took a days tricycling. Started from Bowden at 8.30 a.m. Standish Rectory 9.45 (7½ miles), Berkeley Road Station 11.27, Pier View Hotel 12.20, Sharpness Point 3 o'clock, Berkeley Road Station 3.50, arrived Gloucester Club at 6 having done 40 miles, home 44 miles.
Cowley Manor with all the timber and furniture has been sold by

Richardson Gardner to Mr Baring Bingham for £76,000 about 1,800 acres. Gardner gave the same price when he bought it from Mr. Hutchinson, but he paid in addition a valuation for the timber amounting to £4,000 and say furniture another £4,000 so that the total loss amounts to about £8,000.

Sept 12.   Emily goes to lunch at Eliza's to meet John Sinclair. Clara is staying there.

Sept 25.   House Committee at Asylum. After it I tricycled over to Tibberton with Granville Baker, and meeting Gray there. Mr. Price showed us his covered yards and shorthorns. If his beasts sell at 6/- a piece more they will pay interest on his expenditure in covering them over. At the Asylum we agreed to erect two Thompson's Smokeless ovens, heated with Dowson's water gas.

Sept 26.   I drove Mary [Birchall] to see the new Asylum at Barnwood House, Brockworth church and House; at the latter they have found the arms of Katherine of Aragon.

Jack's seventh birthday. The Fowlers called from Miserden. He is very depressed at prospects for agricultural land. Lord Bathurst has laid out £9,000 more than he has received on his estate the last 5 years. Fowler expects a lower price for wheat than he has ever obtained. He looks for great revolution from discoveries of silver; the Rocky Mountains are made of it.

Oct 1.   Took the pledge of total abstinence from intoxicating liquors as a beverage.

Oct 9.   Emily and Maida tricycled to Gloucester in spite of "Mop Fair".

Oct 14.   Went to stay with the Lewis Starkeys at Norwood Hall, Southwell. The porter at Leeds station sent my portmanteau to Gloucester, labelling it on seeing me without listening to my remark that I was going to Nottingham. Met Emily and Clara at Nottingham without my luggage. It never turned up in spite of telegraphing all over the country. Fred Starkey and his wife formerly Snow, daughter of the Vicar of Bibury here, and Jack Starkey, eldest son, fitted me out with clothes. Second son just returning from the war, with 4th Dragoon Guards to which regiment he volunteered for service in India. Weather most cold, damp and unpleasant. The country and house are not particularly interesting.

Oct 15.   To Southwell Minster which is being restored and they are trying to raise money to pay for a Bishop. Distinguished stone carving.

Oct 17.   Stopped at Newark and saw wonderful new Queen Anne coffee tavern, which is being erected by Lady Ossington with the architects Ernest

George and Peto. Most beautiful, in the style of Norman Shaw. There is accommodation for 100 horses which crowd in on market days. The billiard room and skittle alley are very good. Contract for erection was £15,000.

Oct 28.   I exchanged Jumbo for roan cob, own brother to our roan mare, giving Mr. Harvey a cheque for £15. The roan being very raw and shying violently when I was riding it with Emily and afterwards kicking in the dogcart with Archer, I sent him to Bowles the breaker to be fairly tried for saddle, and single and double harness.

Oct 31.   The glass having risen I took my tricycle by train to Monmouth and then ran over to Chepstow, 16 miles, roads heavy at first became almost impassable as the rain commenced. I stopped at Tintern for an hour refreshing myself inadequately and on arrival at Chepstow was wet and fagged. I trained to Gloucester, dined at the Bell Hotel, and attended Freeman's interesting lecture on the Cathedral.

Nov 2.   Dined at the Palace, all parsons, a sort of duty dinner.

Nov 7.   I could not leave Leeds. Had painful interview with English and Fearnside. Their salaries had been so much increased during more prosperous times that the business could not now afford them. The former I reduced from £2.18.6 a week to £2.8.6 the latter from £300 to £250. I continuing my donation of £20. These old and valued servants were painfully affected and I was compelled to assure them of Warburg's noncomplicity in my action for they attributed all the evil to him. Spent evening at Elmhurst; Benson now advises paying Warburg out, as he sees he does not care to work the business unless he sees a new firm at the end of it.
    On the same day Emily at Bowden wrote to her parents. "We are getting on very well in Dyer's absence. Violet takes sole charge of Lindaraja from 9–11 a.m. They are alone in the Hall or Morning Room and Violet is most old fashioned and dependable. She always takes Lindaraja up and down stairs, washes her hands, brushes her hair, etc. and amuses her by the hour together, generally without toys or anything. Jack is also most kind to Lindaraja and she quite clings to him. She calls herself "Little Gibraltar", or "Jacko's baby Gib". She talks quite as plainly as Violet and much more distinctly than Percival."

Nov 19.   A letter from Warburg agreeing to retire from the firm on receipt of the balance last stock-taking less subsequent drawings. An intimate friend of Campbell's has recommended a Mr Shaw, a first-rate energetic man in the foreign trade.

Nov 21.   This day we signed deed of dissolution of partnership so far as Warburg is concerned. It is a great relief in many ways; but it will be rather an anxious time until we make fresh arrangements.

Dec 1.   Emily and Clara went to the Chapter House to hear Gambier Parry's lecture on the artistic side of the cathedral which was most brilliant.

Dec 2.   Interviewed various applicants for the job we have to offer in Leeds. Mr Nathan managing partner with Reichenheim spoke warmly regarding Emil Kafka, nay enthusiastically. He said he was the best man who went out of Bradford. He would do business if it could be done; but he would need reining in to some extent. Other enquiries were equally favourable as to his energy, business capacity and industry.

Dec 8.   Another interview with Kafka in which we were fully confirmed in the good impression he formerly made; but we were staggered to find that he insisted upon having £1,000 per annum and a fine of £500 supposing we did not go on with him, and the same to be paid by him if he inclined to go.

Dec 9.   Emil Kafka has accepted our offer of £900 per annum or three years but the agreement to be terminated on either side with three months notice at the end of first or the end of second year, £500 being paid by either side wishing to conclude the agreement; this dates from Jan 1st 1883, but he will probably really commence a fortnight sooner. I returned to Gloucester.

Dec 22.   Kafka has had a depressing visit to London. He was not met by buyers with the cordiality which he expected as representing J.D. Birchall & Co. They seemed mostly to indicate they could not do with us. They say he came home flat and *disillusionné*. We settled for Oswald to go to the States for about three weeks. He knows all the ins and outs of the business and will see how the land lies with regard to appointing an agent, or otherwise.

Meanwhile Emily is busy. On December 18 she reports a Shakespeare reading at Bowden *Much Ado About Nothing.* "Most pleasant and successful; 22 people. And a long call from Mrs Ellicott." On the 19th she had a quiet evening reading Gibbon, after calling on the new bailiff's wife. On the 20th Temperance meeting; Dearman read speech. On Christmas Day everyone went to church. Christmas tree in the afternoon and grand display of cards. Muggy warm weather. On 27th Emily and Eliza went to a concert at Painswick and had to walk all the way up Upton Hill because the horses jibbed. On the last day of the year they all went to church and the Dead March was played for the old clerk Freeman who was buried the Friday before.

1883

In January Dearman took Emily and Clara to London for a short visit. They much admired the Rossettis at Burlington House, which "have amazed everybody and taken the town by storm".

The Children were all ill with temperatures and Jack had earache, which prevented them going on to Leeds, as they usually did at this time of year.

Feb 13. Spent the day at Upleadon. The day was fine throughout for a wonder. The country is soaking. The Oxford Down ewes are beginning to drop their lambs. Gray has made as good a lying-in hospital as possible, covering the ground in a yard with brushwood and with straw and litter for warmth. One ewe had three lambs today — one is dead, in fact she disowned the third altogether.

Feb 14. Opening of Assizes. Neither I nor any of the Visitors at the Asylum were on the Grand Jury and the coroner told me he had not called us because Hawkins the attendant was one of the prisoners. He is charged with the manslaughter of old Partridge at the Asylum. Before this occurred he was thought to be a humane man and I fancy there is no direct evidence to incriminate him but that of a lunatic who says he saw Hawkins knock Partridge down and stamp upon him.

Heavy thunderstorm following almost incessant falls of rain. The Severn valley is all under water, the Maisemore road only passable with boats and this is the fourth or fifth time this winter. No settled fine weather since early autumn last year.

Feb 15. I returned from the Assizes rather late, say 6.30, and found Emily in an easy chair in the bedroom, very faint, saying she was very ill, continual hemorrhage. Clara and the boys were in the morning room and would have fetched Dyer in a moment had she known Emily was ill; but the latter never called but merely reclined with the window open and quite dark.

I got Dyer and we put Emily to bed, but she fainted first. We sent down and most fortunately secured both Mr Bower and Mrs Addis. She was made comfortable. The pain went on and at 11.30 a little girl still born arrived. Emily had only taken chloroform for about ¾ of an hour.

Hawkins was discharged. There was no evidence to sustain the prosecution without the lunatic and he was evidently unreliable.

Feb 16. Sam Bowly[65] gave an address at the Coffee Room (Temperance meeting) and was a great success. I took the chair. Mr Bowly is 81 years of age and has been a total abstainer for 47 years and his wife 46 years.

---

[65] Born in Cirencester, he worked as a youth for his father at Arlington Mill, Bibury, and later became a well-known Temperance Reformer.

Jack

Percy

Violet

Violet and Lindaraja

Feb 18.   Emily much better in all respects today. Mr Bower did not come. Mr & Mrs Ackers called to enquire.

Feb 27.   Clara and I had tea at Lanesfield in honour of Eliza's 64th birthday.

March 1.   Bower says that Jack slightly, Percy and Baby badly, and Clara, are all suffering from Scabies acarus — it is most grievous and we are perplexed what to do. Bower is convinced Clara has caught it in one of the cottages and brought it back to the children. She is wonderfully strong, a marked contrast to the younger children who have none of them quite recovered from the feverish attacks from which they have suffered severely. Jack is a boy who naturally requires more nourishment and his nerves calmed. His body is weedy, not nearly so healthy in flesh as Percy.

March 27.   I rode over to Upleadon. We have now 320 lambs. There are only 18 ewes left to lamb — several dead ewes and lambs from the beginning — but the frosty weather of the last month has agreed well with them. They are getting barley excellently sown today. The land works so well after frost. Fields that were intended for wheat in the autumn when the bad weather started are now going into barley and oats.

April 3.   Clara's 21st birthday. Owing to continuance of malaise of one sort and another we have postponed the celebration of it until our return home.

April 6.   Emily and I with the 4 children and nurses came to Harehills.

April 7.   I went over to Oxton by tricycle, going past Scarcroft I called at Hill House, and had pleasant interviews with Sam Clement and his mother who looks little older than when I left 14 years ago. The peach trees I planted in the beds of the orchard house have turned out a most splendid success. One of them ripened 600 peaches last year and Clement had thinned out 1,200 from the same prolific tree.

Eliza and Clara are staying at Oxton. The last frosts have been very severe and have killed down many of the young laurels that had grown from the roots of the thousands slain in the frosts of '80, '81 and '82.

April 9.   I tricycled home from Oxton, say a good 15 miles to Wellington Street by the York road in 2¾ hours. After dinner party at Harehills, we tried thought reading but absolutely without success.

April 18.   Had long conversation with Kafka who is full of spirits, very brisk and bent on making a success of his department. He had great difficulties to contend with; but thinks he will do an increasing trade in Italy, France and Germany. I urged him most strongly to work with as little expenditure as possible, and to constrain his inordinate friends in their demand for patterns.

April 19.   Emily and I took the 5 children to Ilkley to Mrs Hainsworth's lodgings where they will remain for the next nine weeks with Eliza while we are abroad. They all look vastly better than when we left home. The lodgings are most comfortable and the prospect of their enjoying themselves seems assured. We agreed with Miss Milton who keeps a boys' school to take our boys for 2 to 2½ hours every day. When her boys return it will be more lively and they are to be drilled on a Saturday.

On April 20th Dearman and Emily left Leeds for London and next day they crossed to Calais and then proceeded to Antwerp. Thus they began their visit to Russia for which Emily is reputed to have learnt Russian during the previous three weeks with her usual flair for languages. Her children were under the impression she knew seven languages which must have been French, Spanish, Italian, German, maybe Latin or Greek, Russian and obviously English. The object of the visit to Russia at this time was to stay with Emily's friend Maida, whose family were stationed there, for the coronation of the Czar. They did not arrive in Moscow till May 24th travelling leisurely through Holland and Denmark, and taking Clara and Emily's niece Dora Howard with them as far as Germany.

Emily wrote to her parents from

S.S. Orion. Lubeck to Copenhagen. May 16th, 1883.

Dearest People.
    It is so amusing and unexpected to be thus en route between the above two places that I must write to you from our present very agreeable quarters. In Hamburg we paid a call on the Hirsts. Mr Thomas Hirst the father of Julius lives at Uhlenhorst, a pretty suburb. He is nicer and more presentable than William and Joe of that ilk, rather a pleasant old gentleman. I was specially requested to sit on the sofa, and solemnly conducted to it, you know it is the place of honour in all German rooms. We were a large party including Willie Hirst a shy bearded man of 6ft 4½in, and our four not small selves. Yesterday Clara went for a long day's excursion with this Hirst lot and a tribe of German cousins of theirs. She seems to have enjoyed it very much. Meantime Dearman devoted himself to business, going the round of the old merchants and people he had known 30 years ago, interviewing his agent and generally enjoying himself prodigiously. Dora and I walked all about Hamburg, through the lovely woods in the environs, the Botanical Gardens, etc. We met Dearman at a most delicious chocolate shop for lunch. He took us to see the Exchange. We went up into the Gallery and saw the enormous crowd below, 4 or 5000 men moving about and looking just like a great hive of bees, while the murmur of their voices ascended to us in a sort of steady even mass of sound. One realized what "the roar of many voices" means, no words, no articulated sounds, but a roar like a railway train or a tremendous storm of wind.

Then we went to see the new church built by Sir Gilbert Scott and opened about 20 years ago. It is most beautiful. These Lutheran churches are as different as possible from the Dutch ones, much more like ritualistic or even Roman Catholic churches. It has been terrifically hot all day, we have been nearly boiled, and the change to the delicious air on board this nice steamer is most refreshing. Goodnight.

Thus far I wrote on deck yesterday evening till my paper was nearly blown away. It was such a nice steamer with a charming Swedish captain. The cabins were most comfortable, the food excellent, and everything delightful. We all enjoyed the voyage, even Clara. It was very smooth, an exquisite moonlight night and lovely summer lightning. Clara is becoming quite sensible about the sea. It was a 16 hour voyage. We got into Copenhagen soon after 7 a.m. and I write from the Hotel d'Angleterre, Kjöbuharn, where we have lovely rooms, and feel it great fun to be here.

Your loving Em.

May 21st. Kiel

Dearest People.

Just arrived from a night at sea. We left Copenhagen at 7.20, train to Korsaer, then to Kiel on a very large steamer. We go back to Hamburg by train. I have such an awful lot to say I shall have to simply not say it. Thorwaldsen must have changed the face of Copenhagen. One sees statues and friezes by him at every turn. One evening we went to the Tivoli gardens and finally got so lively that I had at last my heart's desire and went on a Merry-go-round, and such a gorgeous one too, a set of life-size boats, which went up and down exactly like a very rough sea. It was a stupendous lark, Dora and I got in, and then the dignified Mr Birchall jumped in too and we went whirling around swinging up and down in the most ludicrous way, all shrieking with laughter and enjoying it hugely. Clara, meantime, looking on from a distance in dignified isolation, till she had to look away as it made her feel giddy to see us.

Dearman and I called on the English Ambassador (Hussey Vivian). He was most polite though we had no introduction whatever. He made out a passport and gave us a card and a private letter to the Russian legation, and sent a footman to show us the way. There we were received by the Minister and Secretary, a Prince Bariatoff, a very handsome and agreeable young man, and were shown into a room with splendid Persian carpets. They offered Dearman a cigarette and we all sat down and began talking in a most sociable way in French. Prince Bariatoff *"visait"* our passport then and there himself. Now goodbye. Do comment nicely on our movements. Ever your loving Em.

On May 24 Emily wrote to her parents from Moscow.

Dearest People.

Here we are after a most comfortable and not at all tiring journey from
Sunday evening till Thursday morning, 4 whole days and nights without
undressing, and we both feel as fresh as larks. I sent you postcards from
Warsaw and Smolensk. I have not very much to narrate as our journey was
calm and uneventful. We had a fearfully busy time in Hamburg arriving
there between 9 and 10 and having to leave by 4 train. We had to see the
Hirsts, arrange our packing, send some things home by Clara, get Sunday
things mended, and Dearman had to buy a hat and I a dress, bonnet and
gloves etc. I got a blue silk brocade dress for small mornings or quiet
evening and it was altered to fit me in those few hours.

At 3.30 we parted from the girls who we hope have by this time reached
England with the Hirsts. It has been very nice having Dora. I like her
extremely. She has been a most pleasant lively addition to our party. She is
so merry and amusing and sees the ludicrous so quickly that we have been
far livelier with her than we would have been without her, and she is nice and
strong and does not get tired quickly. She was much more ready to practise
talking foreign languages than Clara who was unaccountably "took shy" in
this respect, I can't think why.

Well we travelled peacefully to Berlin and there took tickets and registered
our luggage right through to Moscow, and went for a walk *unter den
Linden*. On our return we found the station in a tremendous bustle and
excitement, no end of gorgeous officers about, all the sleeping carriages to
Warsaw engaged beforehand for the two princes and their numerous suites.
They were the Prince of Bavaria and Prince Albrecht of Prussia, representing
the Emperor. We felt them a great bore that night as they absorbed the
attention of the officials, so that we could hardly get places at all. In the end
I got a beautiful ladies' carriage entirely to myself and had a capital night,
but Dearman was less fortunate, though he did pretty well in the end. But
we are more than ever confirmed in the opinion that German officials are the
rudest, most over-bearing beings on the face of the earth. The Russians are
extremely nice and polite and as soon as we left Germany behind we met
with every civility and courtesy. At the frontier there was a grand reception
of the Princes, the station gay with flags, crowds of people looking on
behind barriers, no end of magnificent officers and bands playing the German
national anthem. We had a couple of hours in Warsaw but a good part of the
time was occupied in driving from one station to the other over awful
pavements. It is a melancholy looking place with dirty wretched people
especially the Jews with their long curly beards, long ragged coats down to
the ground and a sort of wolfish expression on their dirty savage faces.
Poland is a miserable looking country, great tracts of marsh and swamp with
scattered villages of wretched huts looking like shabby cattle sheds or pigsty
erections. One does not wonder at insurrections in a country so visibly

oppressed and miserable though I suppose now they have no spirit left even to rebel.

Russia proper looked better, great forests of larch and fir and some birch woods, the ground less marshy and some cultivation. Smolensk is really a very fine looking place with many domed churches and charming looking country houses dotted about the undulating hills around, while the Dnieper winds prettily along. It was interesting to cross the Beresina and pass the battlefield of Borodino and to see the hundreds and hundreds of miles of dreary pathless wastes over which the poor French army had to drag themselves in mid-winter.

We had a very pleasant young man in our carriage, French but living in Russia. We never changed carriages between Warsaw and Moscow so it was most comfortable, plenty of space to move about, and sofas for the nights on which we slept our 3rd and 4th nights splendidly. We got excellent coffee and lovely bread everywhere, and there was plenty of meat of all kinds; but we only took a little meat once a day whereas the people in the next compartment plied their knives and forks at every buffet, besides bringing in provisions and feasting in their carriage.

We reached Moscow at 8 a.m. today and found a magnificent reception awaiting the Princes, in which we took our share, as far as walking on a carpet between lines of soldiers and being stared at by crowds behind barriers — goes. One of the Imperial Princes was there and about 50 other officers in every variety of dazzling uniform. The Mirrieleeses did not come to meet us having thought we could not possibly be here till to-morrow; but we got on all right as I remembered the address and made the coachman understand it. We took two little droschkys, ourselves in one and our luggage in the other, tiny little things, and we drove in bright sunshine and through streets gay with flags, to this house where we had a warm welcome from Maida and Archy. It is a large house and very pretty. Ever your loving Em.

Moscow. May 25.

Dearest People.

I shall not send this to-day but I think whilst Maida is writing I will begin a letter. It is perfectly impossible to give you any idea of the wonders of Moscow. I never realized it even from Maida's excellent descriptions so how can I hope to give you the faintest impression of it? It is a place that must be seen to be realized. We are both of us astonished and delighted and feel that the half had not been told us. We walk about the city staring and gaping, we keep stopping in the street to gaze and Maida has infinite difficulty in getting us home in time for meals. The place is curiously fascinating, it is so entirely different from all other cities, so unique. We are seeing it under very favourable circumstances, the streets alive with soldiers and all the houses gay with flags and other decorations while at every turn we meet carriages with royal flunkeys in cocked hats and scarlet flowing robes down to the ground. These are in attendance on the innumerable Imperial guests. It is the liveliest place we have ever seen rather like Naples in this respect, crowds of people, droschkys darting about and troikas dashing along — the 3 horses harnessed very loose and wide apart and the coachmen shouting wildly as they gallop along. The private coachmen are all either enormously fat or else stuffed out with pillows to make them look so. Tartars and orientals abound in the streets. The Russian common people all dress in very bright colours, a scarlet shirt being universal among working men and the house dvorinks (hewers of wood and drawers of water) have the scarlet shirt and a long black velvet waistcoat over. These bright colours give a very gay appearance to the streets. Moscow is, as Dearman says, a curious mixture of gorgeous splendour and semi-barbarism. You see the wildest looking people about, and in many of the best streets the palaces of princes are next door to the shabbiest of little hovels. The irregularity is picturesque, and there are trees everywhere in fresh foliage and lilacs and laburnums in flower.

As for the Kremlin it is more beautiful and wonderful than I ever imagined and immensely bigger as indeed is everything in Moscow; the scale is perfectly enormous. The Kremlin covers two square miles of ground. We have been to it both yesterday and today and find it quite fascinating. Photographs give no idea of its great beauty which is its variety of colour, golden and silver domes flashing in the sunlight, one church with little blue domes, the palace a light brown orange colour and green roofs, red houses, wonderful old green tiled steeples on the towers, yellowish and reddish walls, all make up a marvellously varied scene.

We went to the Kremlin yesterday past a very holy shrine (there are hosts of them, and all the Russians cross themselves as they pass) and at this particular shrine we saw every person stop and cross themselves many times, ten or twelve times or more, many prostrated themselves or went into the shrine to kiss part of the sacred image, rich and poor, and no-one too hurried to stop.

There are over 700 churches in Moscow and the number of domes is bewildering, I counted 80 this morning in sight from one spot. The great new cathedral of the Saviour is surmounted by five golden domes, the middle one of stupendous size and all covered with real gold. It is to be opened by the Emperor in a fortnight. The priests wear long cloaks down to the ground and very long hair far down over their shoulders as they may not cut it. They look unkempt and wild. We got into one of the Kremlin churches in which the early Romanoff Czars are buried. I never saw anything so gorgeous, it is all decoration and gilding, ikons in gold frames, shields of burnished brass all polished up in honour of the Emperor.

Ever your loving Em.

Moscow. Sunday May 27.

Dearest People.

I sent off my last yesterday morning but there were several details I forgot to mention e.g. at the Restaurant at which we dined on Friday all the waiters were clad in spotless white from head to foot with sashes of coloured ribbon and at the same gorgeous establishment there are 65 cooks.

The fire extinguishing system of Moscow is very complete. In every quarter of the city there is a fire-tower with a high platform and is patrolled by two firemen night and day, and as soon as they see a blaze anywhere they give a signal and the fire engines at once hasten to that particular place. The circumference of Moscow is 36 miles.

Yesterday morning we came in for a pretty sight close by here the proclamation by a herald of the Coronation ceremonies. There was a band, a Squadron of the Chevaliers Gardes (the crack regiment, all over 6 ft. in height and wearing cuirasses and helmets of burnished brass), ushers and flunkeys in gold lace and cocked hats, and then the herald, a small Russian nobleman robed in a long white flowing cloak and with immense plumes of ostrich feathers, with which the horses' heads also were adorned. The proclamation was saluted with a roar of Hourras, all the crowd raising their caps and shouting.

In the afternoon we went to one or two churches to hear the singing which is wonderfully true, though they have no instruments. We heard the nuns sing at a convent and remarked how pleasant they looked. We heard afterwards that a mine was lately discovered, starting from this very convent and that immediately on its discovery the abbess committed suicide.

Dearman went yesterday with Archie to call on the English ambassador in the hope of getting some tickets to see the Coronation procession today but all in vain. They were told that even the 1st Secretary did not expect to get one himself, and that efforts had been made without success to get one for the Consul at St. Petersburg. We thought however we would make our way to the Kremlin and see what things looked like and managed to get in by one gate inside the Kremlin enclosure which was packed by an enormous mass of people. We got some places to stand on, a sort of high form, so that we were above the people and could look over the sea of heads, straight across to the reserved seats which faced us, and on which the occupants had to take their places before 8 a.m. and between us and them was the raised way by which the Emperor was to pass, after his coronation, back into the Palace.

Suddenly at 12.20 the big guns boomed forth, to announce that the Czar Alexander III was crowned, at the same moment a universal shout of Hourra, every hat went off and many of the people sobbed with joy while the guns went on firing (101 times) and the Kremlin bells clanging loudly overhead. At 12.40 the procession moved out from the church. We saw a line of grand officials all on foot, between the guards and then deafening roars of Hourra rent the air, as the great Boldachino appeared and the Emperor and Empress walking beneath it, their crowns on their heads. The Boldachino was of gold with plumes of black, yellow and white (the Russian colours). I never saw anything like the enthusiasm of the people. It is a relief to everyone the Coronation is safely over, the nihilists appear to have remained quiet; but now they wait to see what he is going to do about a Constitution.

We had a tremendous struggle to get out of the Kremlin enclosure afterwards, such a squeeze in passing through the gate. Maida was carried right off her feet but Dearman had her by one arm and a kind dvorink by the other. I was with Mr. Cazalet and got on very well. I enjoy being in a great crowd. When we got clear we left the energetic Dearman to hang about on the look out for whatever pageant might come his way and Mr. C., Maida and I went to the English church, and then to lunch with the Bernards. Mr Bernard is charming, very nice looking indeed, I have taken a great fancy to him. His sister is rather dim. A gigantic Mr Raikes was there, a cleric, the only other person besides ourselves so to speak who has come out from England on purpose without being either a diplomat or a correspondent. I walked home with Willie Cazalet; it was fully four miles, while Maida went with Mr Bernard to call on some people.

Mr Trotter came to dinner and then we all went to see the illuminations; but Archie soon came back because he has a headache and we had enough gentlemen without him. Mr Trotter took me; we kept together mostly but were constantly getting separated. The illuminations were most splendid especially the lovely electric light decoration of the Kremlin, and that stood the weather better than the candles for it was not a good night, raining off and on most of the time. We did not come in till 1 a.m. Ever your Em.

May 30th. On train Moscow to Troitsa.

Dearest Florence.

I will begin a note to you as I never find a moment of time to write in the house. I am sitting next Mr Trotter, Miss Bernard beyond him; opposite us are Maida and Mr Bernard (reading Contemporary Review together), Mr Raikes reading the Times, and Dearman reading Murray. I have been talking to Mr Trotter for an hour and a half and now think it only fair to let Miss Bernard have a little of his society. He is extremely nice. We had a most delightful day at the datcha. We went in a large carriage with three horses (a troika) and enjoyed the pretty drive to the full, Maida, Willie Cazalet, Mr Maude and I. The datcha is like a Swiss chalet, small but very charming and perched in a lovely situation on the crest of the Sparrow Hills with a really glorious view of Moscow and the neighbouring churches and monasteries, and lovely birch woods stretching for miles, so truly rural though only about 4 miles from the great city. We were a lively party 4 ladies and 10 gentlemen. Maida says that is a larger proportion of the fair sex than usual here. Some of them played lawn tennis and we sat about and strolled in the woods and gathered flowers, and generally enjoyed the lovely day and pretty place. We had a very nice dinner and then watched the illuminated

city from the hills, a most fairy-like sight and started to drive home about
10. We found the streets a scene of absolute splendour, words fail to give
any description. We drove for 2 hours between lines of illuminations of
endless variety and could do nothing but gaze and ejaculate "Oh! Oh! Look,
look". It was finer than the Paris fete because so much more extensive being
universal over the whole city, and also because of the wonderfully picturesque
outline of the buildings of Moscow which lend themselves so splendidly to
illumination. The Kremlin towers encircled by spirals of incandescent lights
and lighted alternately with red, green and blue flames were most exquisitely
beautiful. I suppose the Times will describe the scene. Everyone says it is the
finest illumination there has ever been. We have seen it all three nights now
with never weary enjoyment.

Train back to Moscow. I continue after our Troitsa visit. The Troitsa
Monastery is indeed a wonderful place, and the country around very well
wooded with some lovely lakes and all looking fresh and green. We saw the
Treasury with its enormous wealth of jewels, huge vestments covered with
embroidery of real pearls, diamonds by the thousand and emeralds by the
hundredweight. I never saw such a sight. We also saw about 1000 pilgrims
being fed; and saw catacombs where till quite lately extra holy monks have
lived all their lives in darkness and deadly damp. It has been a glorious day,
rather warm I should say. This is a stupid letter. Much love, Yours Em.

Moscow. June 1st.

Dearest People
We have had I think 14 letters. They have been accumulating owing to the
office being closed for the holiday. We had a most amusing epistle from
Clara, two capital letters from Dyer and one from Tothill, but no newspapers have come as they are all being read through by the censor. A long
paragraph in last week's Punch was blackened out and quite illegible, the
one under the picture called "The new craze". It seems like a dream that we
have been in Moscow, for this delightful pleasure is already a thing of the
past, and I am continuing this letter in the train to St. Petersburg. The
Mirrieleeses have been most tremendously kind to us and have entertained
us regally. Archie has been most hospitable, but very seedy part of the time.
Our Spectator has come but with a whole article cut out — the one on the
Coronation.

I wrote a very stupid letter about Troitsa though we had a most interesting
day there. The most curious sight was to see the pilgrims feed. Hosts of
them come every day, many having travelled from the furthest confines of
Russia, such strange looking figures: and all who come are fed by the
monks, with soup in great wooden bowls, half a dozen pilgrims to each
bowl.

On Thursday Maida and I visited the dwelling of the first Romanoff Czar
in 1620, with furniture and treasures that had belonged to him. This home of

their ancestors had this week been visited by all the Imperial family and so we saw more than Maida had ever done before. We met Dearman in the afternoon and went for a charming drive in their own droschky, and D. in a Lichatsch which means a droschky at a higher price than the ordinary ones with a fine horse and looking just like a private one. Dearman and I did some shopping. We were seen off at the station by Maida, and Messrs. Trotter and Cazalet. Mr T. got us a charming sleeping carriage to ourselves. These trains are most luxurious, like hotels upon wheels. The railway is guarded by soldiers all the way from Moscow to St. Petersburg. We pass soldiers every few yards.

Yours Em.

St. Petersburg. June 4th.

Dearest People

After the inexhaustible and ever varied delights of Moscow I privately find St. Petersburg rather tame, though I have not dared to hint at such a thing to Dearman. He thought it would be nice. There is of-course a great deal that is well worth seeing, and the Hermitage alone is worth coming from England for; but a city that dates entirely from the last century cannot possibly be as interesting as one of the remote antiquity of Moscow to say nothing of the semi-barbaric and oriental character of the old capital. St. Petersburg is very handsome, very well built, very spacious: the distances are enormous. The air is so clear, and so perfectly free from smoke that a church dome looks quite near and you find it takes half an hour to walk to it. The palaces and public buildings are on a huge scale and the river is very beautiful indeed; but except for the Russian names one would hardly know one was not in Paris, Berlin or Vienna. It is wonderfully light in the evenings. Last night I read in the window at 11.15 by day light and just now I am writing at a table quite away from the window and it is 10.30 p.m.

We walked about 8 miles in the streets yesterday and visited St. Isaac's church with splendid pillars of malachite and lapis lazuli. There are never any seats in the churches. We noticed that at the Coronation the select 500 who were squeezed into the church had to stand from 7.45 till 1 p.m. We get on very well as to languages for everybody in this hotel seem to be German and in the shops French or German is always spoken, very unlike Moscow. It is extremely hot. I am longing for cotton dresses. We passed the scene of the later Emperor's assassination this afternoon. A little shrine is built on the spot and no carriage is allowed to go along the street now. We spent 2½ hours in the Hermitage and are enchanted. There are 2000 pictures, all good.

It is out of season and all the grand people are in Moscow. Unluckily too all Maida's friends are away. It was delightful having such an able cicerone as Maida to guide us about. Her house was extremely pretty, much larger than I expected and with just the slight mixture of foreign piquancy with its English comfort.

10.50 still writing by daylight.

Your loving Em.

St. Petersburg. June 6th.

Dearest People
   We received no Leeds Mercurys at Moscow though one was sent every day; but here we got three yesterday including one of June 1st with a most outspoken article about Russia and the need of reforms, and actually this seems to have escaped the Argus eyes of the Censors altogether.
   I don't think I have mentioned the superstitious regard for pigeons enter-tained by all Russians. They believe they are sacred ever since the Holy Ghost appeared like a dove, and so no Russian will kill one and they fly about in millions all over Moscow and St. Petersburg and are perfectly tame.
   These little droschkys are capital things for getting about and they go like the wind and are wonderfully cheap if you bargain. We tell them where we want to go in an interrogative voice. They reply "40 Kopeks", we say "No, 20". They reply "35". We walk away calling as we go "30". Then they call entreatingly "Pajalst" which means "please" and indicates concession to the 30, and we get in. We can go quite a long way for sixpence, so it is not an expensive luxury. The last two days have been tremendously interesting. St. Petersburg seemed flat on Sunday but it is lively on week days, and as to the Hermitage it is one of the finest picture galleries in Europe, though English art is almost unrepresented. We engaged a guide and asked him if we would get into the Winter Palace. He said certainly not, no one had been allowed in since the death of the Empress. However when he came yesterday morning he said he thought there was a chance if we applied ourselves to the Commandant. So we went straight to this dignitary and I made my request in my most elegant and insinuating French. The Commandant listened politely and then an order was given us to pass anywhere in the Winter Palace. We spent over 2 hours in it. It is all guarded, soldiers everywhere and special attendants for every suite of rooms and all these locked up and un-locked for us. It is lavishly gorgeous. The Duchess of Edinburgh's rooms are extremely charming and in beautiful taste. Poor thing! Clarence House must have been a sad coming down to her after this. We saw the scene of the explosion under the dining room, and the rooms of the late Empress, and of poor Nicholas, just as they were when he died there, a tiny narrow camp bedstead, his military cloak flung over it, his coat, boots etc. close by, all in a simple plain room looking more like a valet's than an Emperor's. It is curious how both he and Alexander II lived in absolute simplicity in the plainest rooms in their luxurious palace. In the private cabinet of the late Emperor there was a frame containing vignettes of all his grandchildren, with an inscription presented to him in 1881, very shortly before his death. Then we saw his bed, just a plain narrow camp bedstead like that of Nicholas. It was most impressive and sad.
   Ever your Em.

Central Hotel, Friedrich Strasse, Berlin.

June 10th

Dearest Florence

I do so wish you were here, you would so love this hotel. It is almost worth the journey to Berlin to sit in this luxurious reading room the finest I have ever seen. It is more than twice the size of the one at the Grand Hotel in London and is exquisitely decorated, lined with scagliola marble and furnished in the most enchanting way with sofas and divans, and easy chairs, and rocking chairs, and full length lounges of the most tremendously comfortable character. I feel inclined to try every chair in the room in succession, but when I get into the first I find it so delicious that I am too comfortable to move.

These luxurious chairs are all covered with plush of the loveliest aesthetic colours, and some of them with fine Indian stuffs let in, the colouring is all soft and harmonious just the opposite of what you would expect from Germans. The hotel, quite new, is lighted with electric light and is first class throughout, endless restaurants, ladies' salon, winter garden and superb concert grand piano. I wish you were here to play it.

Yes our babes are still at Ilkley and are enjoying it so prodigiously that they keep begging to be allowed to stay a "long time longer", according to Dyer. The boys thoroughly enjoy school and the drill sergeant, and the moors are an endless delight. Jack is revelling in the wild flowers, and they all go to church, even Lindaraja.

We shall have a very short time in London and Dearman says we must get home now. Dearman thinks no place has altered and improved so amazingly within his remembrance as Berlin. The buildings are magnificent and the large shady trees in streets and squares prevent it looking new and bare. We had a capital sight of the German Emperor whom, in spite of my French proclivities I do acknowledge to be a very magnificent looking old man, broad chested, upright as a dart, with firm step and fine soldierly bearing despite his 86 years. Dearman felt rewarded. He came to Berlin on purpose to see the Emperor, I believe!

Ever your Em.

Dearman's diary explains some of the references in Emily's letters. The datcha in Emily's letter of May 30th is spelt Datchka by Dearman and is Archie Mirrielees's "little country place which he shares with Mr Trotter so that the latter was joint host with Maida" on the occasion of their visit. The party included the Rev. M. Bernard who soon afterwards married Maida Mirrielees. Dearman wrote — The party mostly played Lawn Tennis. I went up the village and there saw a very interesting funeral of a poor woman. The coffin was open. The lid was carried on a man's head. The service was most solemnly chanted. The spectators joining the relatives kissed the hand and face of the corpse with fearful lamentations, and the lid was then nailed down and the procession formed to the grave.

Emily with Violet and Lindaraja in Russian national costume

Dearman also recorded the Mirrielees household in Moscow: Anton Yegorovitch (butler) and his wife Maria and daughter Josephine; Feodr, coachman, and occasionally his brother; Victoria, cook and her lame boy; Anton's father-in-law and his child's nurse; Victoria's husband who waits in white gloves when there are visitors.

Anton, he says, called him Ivan Samuelovitch, and Emily Emilia Ivanovna.

The success of the illuminations are explained. In spite of the wet and muddy streets the illuminations were at once universal and indescribably pretty with festoons of incandescent light enclosed in various coloured globes of ribbed glass, and when mingled with the fresh foliage of the trees quite enchanting; millions of electric, wax, oil and gas illuminations.

June 16.   I went down to Bowden by the early newspaper train this morning and found all looking most beautiful, the foliage at its best. We have not been home since April 6th and all seems to have gone on well. Returned to London for another ten days.

June 23.   We found Carter's Hotel in Albemarle Street decidedly inferior to Brown's but with very high charges £47 or £48 in 10 days. I made a complaint but with the effect of grieving Mr & Mrs Carter who were most kind and attentive and not in any way reducing the bill.

July in Gloucestershire and the Garden Party season had come round again, and Maida Mirrielees now engaged to Mr. Bernard was staying.

July 24.   Excursion to Berkeley Agricultural Show by rail. Mr Beale Browne with us and very comic. The ground was soft and muddy and the sky threatening but it did not rain much.

July 25.   Emily and I to Gloucester and back on tricycles. Clara Armitage left. She is not yet 20 years old, and reminds me of Clara's mother — her bright complexion and open face please all who have made her acquaintance.

July 27.   Splendid day. To Thornbury Castle with the Archaeologists. We went by rail to Charfield and drove thence. Country lovely. Mr. Stafford and Lady Rachel Howard invited us to tea.

July 28.   Superb day for our Garden Party which went off brilliantly. 200 people here, Probyns, Gambier Parrys, De Ferrieres, Guises, Bells, Gibbonses, etc. Violet and Lindaraja in Russian costumes made sensation. It was the finest day since we returned home. Dawes Band played.

August 4.   We had the Upton Feast before us on the Bench. A man called Page was fined 10/- and expenses 27/6 for being drunk and assaulting the police whom he struck and kicked; Middlecote 5/- for being drunk. The evidence showed a disorderly and disreputable gathering.

August 5.   Last week 13 gallons of milk came in per day. Mrs Warner made 20 lbs of butter in the week; we sold 8 lbs and used about 12. She says that 30 quarts of milk per day are ample for all our requirements — it is getting wasted for want of vessels. Mr Gray proposes that Mrs Keylove shall make the excess milk into butter and sell it.

August 7.   I took the train to Stow-on-the-Wold passing the pretty village of Bourton-on-the-Water. Lunched there and saw the church with its fine picture by Gasper de Crayer. Leaving at 1.30 on my tricycle I came home without a break except for a glass of cold water at Seven Springs. I passed Naunton Eyford where I saw Sir Thomas Bazley's place now let to a Mr. Cheetham, then near but not in sight of Guiting Grange John Waddingham's, Cold Comfort, Andoversford, Seven Wells and home; 28 miles from Stow to Bowden. The brake worked so badly I had to walk down hill as well as up. I did not arrive till 7 p.m.

August 9.   Excellent Village Flower Show of fruit and flowers but the afternoon was stormy and the garden muddy and soaked. We had 68, all our neighbours, to tea in the hall.

Aug 11.   Emily and I went to Whiteholme [Mary Birchall's] picking up Florence in Leeds on the way, for the grouse shooting.

August 13.   We joined the Townhead party on the moors, Edward Birchall, Charles Armitage etc. It was very warm and fatiguing. I never saw half as many birds before. We shot 49½ brace.

August 14.   Very stormy indeed. We went up again and tried driving. We shot 43½ brace.

August 16.   Athletic Sports at Gloucester. Superb day, very hot. Took Jack and Percy. My prizes produced no competition. Some change must be made in the arrangements or I ought not to offer it again. Robbins who is President of the Club made a very poor show; in fact he was in thick clothes and had not trained and he weighs 18½ stone.

New ladies' maid, Elizabeth Rea, came. Agnes Rudd, half sister of Eliza's cook has secured £50 a year for 3 years at a school in Edinburgh. Emily went to London to interview cooks, laundry maids and under housemaids.

August 23.   I tricycled over to Peers Court, Stinchcomb and lunched with the Brooke-Hunts, 16½ miles; then on to Hempstead, to a garden party and home by Gloucester, 36 miles in all. I rode Clara's tricycle and sustained a flying fall in going down a sudden pitch. I was not hurt and enjoyed my day immensely.

August 27.   County Asylum at 11 a.m. Very large meeting. Afterwards I went to Upleadon on tricycle to see the reaper and binder at work. They are cutting a big field of fine barley.

August 29.   Emily and I went to spend a day or two with the Bazleys at Hatherop Castle. Emily went by train and I tricycled, 25½ miles.

August 30.   The party attended a Bazaar at Northleach, Gardner [Bazley] and I attempted to follow on tricycles but his machine lost both its india rubber tyres and was otherwise incapacitated. The rain also commenced to fall so we came back after riding a matter of 4 miles. Sir Michael and Lady Lucy Hicks-Beach dined; Emily says she had very pleasant talk with him.

August 31.   We netted the river for Jack Pike with great and unexpected success; took a vast lot, also a number of very large trout which having cannibal propensities are said to be quite as destructive to young trout. I tricycled home, in midst of rain and filthy roads.

September 3.   Our large party assembled for the [Three Choirs] Festival, Lord and Lady Ellenborough, Janet and John Sinclair, Colonel and Mrs Lemprière, Fred and Mrs Starkey, David and Dora Howard, Canon Venables and Captain Kelso, R.N. The Dean puts his dining room at our disposal for the Festival days and the quiet luncheon party seemed more attractive to our guests than the more bustling parties assembled elsewhere. The children have gone for the week to Buckholt.

September 4.   All 15 of us went to the Elijah, and most of us went to the Concert, Hubert Parry's Ode, very fine. The Deanery dining room is a great success. We took some to the Palace. Lady Sudeley asked us to a garden party at Toddington.

September 5.   New piece, Mary Magdalene by Stainer; Cathedral poorly filled. After lunch Beethoven's Mass in C. — most beautiful. In the evening the novelty Senacherib; after which we had Mendelssohn's Hymn of Praise. Our party were most enthusiastic.

September 6.   Gounod's Redemption completely filled the Cathedral — the words are if possible more solemn than the Messiah. It went very well and was most favourably received.

The greatest hospitality is being exercised in the matter of luncheons and teas. To-day the High Sheriff Mr. Knowles [Andrew Knowles of Newent] gave a gorgeous spread in the Shire Hall. Some of us looked in, but did not remain as it was so crowded. The Palace has lunch laid out to the full extent of the Abbot's Hall every day, and the Canons Harvey and Evans and the Curtis-Haywards all vie with each other in their kind invitations.

September 7.   The Messiah scarcely so well attended as the Redemption.

September 8.   Our guests departed, warm in their thanks. John Sinclair told me that he thought he was not appreciated and would not press his claims further, in fact to do so would savour of persecution. I have not observed him paying any attention to any lady here (least of all Clara) and his nervous fidgetty manner is not very attractive in conversation.

As far as can be ascertained there will be a deficiency to be made up by the Festival stewards of about £515, rather less than last year, and it will be spread over a larger number. The charity will not suffer, but the individual stewards.

Lines written in the rhythm of Longfellow's *Hiawatha* (very easy to parody) by Emily's sister Anna Dora Howard referring to the Three Choirs Festival of Sept 1883, just one year before Emily's death.

> Shall I tell you how we gathered, gathered in goodly number,
> In the hospitable mansion, in the fair and stately mansion
> Of our brother Dearman Birchall, for the Gloucester Festival?
> Thirteen visitors we mustered, on the third day of September
> First there came Lord Ellenborough, with my lady and her sapphires.
> Never railed a fiercer Tory on the sins of Mr Gladstone
> Than his Lordship, four times meddled, ever in his grey alpaca,
> Ever talking politics.
>
> Next arrived the handsome General, General Lempriere of Gibraltar
> Everybody thought him charming, and his wife is quite perfection
> In her manners' easy grace.
> Then there came the dear old Canon, Canon Venables from Lincoln
> All his life a strain of music, walking through this world of discord
> Breathing round him as from heaven, love and peace and harmony.
> All the quizzings of his lordship fell like blunted futile arrows
> From his panoply of love.
>
> Next the Starkeys, pleasant people, of a type that's not uncommon
> Honest hearty English feelings, fond of home and countryside.
> Then the Sinclairs, John and Janet, proud of Scottish ancestry,
> He a parson, too self-conscious, she a quite bewitching damsel
> Beautiful in mind and face.
> There was also Captain Kelso, gallant captain in the Navy
> He not handsome but true hearted
> Every inch a gentleman.
>
> Next I count my sister Florence, music flowing from her fingers
> Like the fair St. Cecily.
> Last of all your humble servants, of whom nothing need be said.
> But to tell you of the forethought, taste and tact of our dear hostess
> Passes far my humble powers, only can I say most truly

Never have I seen her equal, at the head of such a household.
Carriages were always ready, carriage closed and carriage open
Suiting all our tastes, to take us twice a day to the Cathedral.

There our souls were ever feasted, with the strains of heavenly music
And when rather tired and hungry, straightway had our fairy hostess
Spread for us a cozy luncheon, in the Deanery dining room.
Or near midnight when returning famished from the Festival,
In the frescoed hall of Bowden, gladdening all our eyes and spirits
Sat our fairy making coffee, so we held a deep carousel.

Oh the pleasant lazy hours, when we wandered in the garden
In the golden afternoon, and the four dear little children
Jack and Percy, Violet and the blackeyed Lindaraja
From their cottage on the hilltop, came to see the company.
Saturday came all too quickly, dreamlike was the bright week over
But the ever sweet remembrance of that visit will not fade.

September 13. I went to Upleadon on the tricycle and walked the farm
while Mr Knowles shot with Gray but all the birds were in the corn, and we
saw no hares.

September 14. I sent 14 of our people to Chepstow and Tintern. The
weather was splendid and I think the party which included all the gardeners
and a number from the house, Tothill being conductor, enjoyed themselves
exceedingly.
    On this same day Emily wrote to her father.

Bowden Hall, Gloucester. Sept 14. 1883

Dearest Padre
    A Thousand good wishes for you on your birthday to-morrow [he would
have been 72] and may you spend a very happy day though shorn of all your
daughters. But she, fairer than all her daughters, is with you, and I know
you enjoy your *tête à tête* life now and then like this, and the faithful Benson
and Carrie are at hand to congratulate you and wish you well.
    I send you by this post a bill-case as Florence said yours was getting
shabby and so I have had this made for you but it looks to me rather large. I
told them it was to go in the breast pocket. If it is too big, tell me and I will
get them to make a smaller one. Please accept it with my dearest love.
    What delicious weather we are having now. I hope you are having daily
drives and making the most of it. We went on Wednesday to an afternoon
concert at Brockworth. The music was very fair though local talent fell
rather flat just after the Festival; but oh! the stuffiness of the room, a tiny
school room not so big as the library at Harehills, packed tight with people
like herrings in a barrel, no window that would open and the sun pouring in
on an extra hot September afternoon. All the rank and fashion of the neigh-

Bowden Hall

Mr Keen and all the gardeners

bourhood seemed to be there, carriages and pairs and flunkeys. We had gone in the "clothes basket" with no servant, Clara driving.

Yesterday we went to a Flower Show at Matson House combined with a bazaar, a concert and a great tea. We all had tea in a tent. I had to pour out and had Mrs Barwick Baker next me on one side and Jack and Percy on the other, but most of the party were farmers and cottagers. We sat down 240 at once and a good many stragglers came afterwards, amongst others a tall policeman. I poured out his tea and Jack waited on him, and was highly amused at the proceedings. We walked home, the boys laden with my bazaar purchases, 6 parcels.

To-day we have sent off a party of 14 (6 gardeners, 7 from the house and Archer) for a day's treat as they have worked so hard lately. They are gone to Tintern and Chepstow. I am so glad it is such a glorious day for them.

Now with very dearest love from us all.

Believe me ever your loving Em.

September 15.   Emily and I tricycled over to Upleadon and met Clara and the boys when we lunched on sandwiches in the wood and walked over the fields picking blackberries. The weather was superb. Emily did not appear at all fatigued and went to dress as soon as she returned as we were dining with the Percivals for the first time in their new house.

On Sept. 22 Emily wrote to her mother.

Dearest Madre

Very many thanks for your most kind letter, but I do wish it had said "Yes" instead of "No" to our earnest entreaty (to visit us).

You will be sorry to hear that poor old Percy broke his arm this morning. He was running on the servants' form in the hall just before prayers and somehow fell with his arm doubled under him. Dearman at once saw that it was broken and put him on the sofa and contrived a temporary splint with newspapers and of-course we sent off at once for Mr Bower. Percy was very brave and never cried at all but groaned a little. He was rather faint once or twice with the pain; but we kept fanning him and eau de cologning him. Mr Bower got here at 11 o'clock and found the break just above the elbow. The arm looks black and a good deal swelled. He could not set it, as it required a proper rectangular splint made to measure but he did it up in the propr position with cotton wool and bandages. Percy was most plucky all the time Mr B. was examining him, feeling and moving and bending the arm, though it must have been very painful. Mr B. said he never saw a child bear it so well. Then he got him to bed and cut his clothes off, and Mr B. is coming again with the proper splint this afternoon, rather awkward as we are having a tennis party, but it cannot be helped. It is lucky that Mr B. was at home as he is going away next week for his first holiday in nearly 4 years. It is well it is the left arm, and it is much better than a leg.

I don't think I told you that on Wednesday morning we at last accomplished seeing the celebrated Severn Bore. We drove over, Clara, boys and I in the Clothes Basket, and Dearman went on his tricycle. We went to a place near Elmore where there is a fine bend in the river. We got there at 9.30, found lots of people who had been already waiting half an hour. It did not come till 10 but it was well worth waiting for, the great mass of water rushing up with a head breaking in high clouds of foam against the banks and then when it had passed, the river not only 10 ft. higher but running rapidly the wrong way. It had a most curious effect.

On Wednesday evening we had a most amusing party at the Ancrums, such a cosmopolitan party I will ennumerate them as they sat at dinner. 1) Mrs Ancrum, lived in Chile. 2) Rev. G. Swinney missionary in Zululand. 3) E.B. Glamour of Russia not yet faded. 4) Mr Upperton fresh from Italy. 5) Mrs Ackers, been at Brussels Deaf Congress lately. 6) A Portuguese Mr Fernandez, very handome and as black as a nigger. 7) Clara (hopelessly British). 8) Mr. Mutchhutchee, A Parsee. 9) Mrs Percival, lived in India. 10) Dr Ancrum, 20 years in Chile. 11) Mrs Swinney lived nearly all her life in S. Africa, a sister of Bishop MacKenzie. 12) Dearman. 13) Miss Mutchhutchee, a Parsee. 14) Wayland Ancrum. 15) Mrs Upperton. 16) Mr Percival, 23 years in India. The Parsees were quite charming. He in a sort of fez, she in a very becoming matinée dress, a long flowing pale blue robe embroidered in gold, a lovely girdle and gold head dress, half turban, half cap and is very pretty and nice. They talk English beautifully. They are Persians but live in Bombay and knew the Percivals there as did also Mr Fernandez. The next day we entertained them all back to tea here. Mr Upperton is very fond of china and was enchanted with ours. He spent 1½ hours looking at it.

Ever your loving Em.

Sept. 24th Bowden Hall.

My dearest Madre

I can give a very good report of the invalid. He was much pleased by your kind messages. He is exceedingly gratified by enquiries and expressions of sympathy and he keeps remarking "I expect all Gloucester knows about me" which seems to afford him infinite consolation. He is going on very nicely. Mr Bower came to set his arm on Saturday afternoon just in the middle of our tennis party. Dearman and I went up with him and Tothill was also present to hold the arm. At Dearman's request Mr Bower gave Percy a little chloroform so that he escaped the pain. Mr B. set the arm beautifully with a rectangular splint made on purpose, bandages and plaster. I fancy it only aches a little now and he has slept pretty well both nights. He is a very calm and placid little invalid and never seems to want to do anything or be amused and he does not care as much for being read to as Jack does; but he seems quite happy being still.

Every your loving Em.

Sept. 27th. Bowden Hall

Kindest of Parents

I am so much obliged to you both for all your kindness to the boys. Madre's never failing thought of Jack and most generous and kind present to him and Padre's delightful letter to Percy which has given the little prisoner immense pleasure. He says "it was kind of Grandpapa; he is a very kind gentleman." He is always saying "Moth, when are my grandparents coming again? It seems such ages since they came here."

Jack's birthday was a very bright and happy day. A stormy morning gave place to a most brilliant afternoon and we were glad we had sent for the Haywards. We had of-course both to fetch them and send them back — the nine miles of a very hilly road. Mrs H. [Carrie Somerset that was] and her three little girls. They arrived about 12 before I had half written my letter. Then they had to be shown all over the house dwelling at least 15 minutes in every single room and Carrie going into long reminiscenses of her youthful associations with each room.

Punctually at 3 came the little Hyetts, very nice little girls and Jack was in his element marshalling his fair young friends and leading them in procession all about the place. He had 8 girls in tow. The children had a grand tea in the Dining Room with gorgeous birthday cake and a dish of lovely honey presented by Tothill. All our children were adorned with wreaths and bouquets. Just as they were sitting down came Selwyn Bazeley on his 3rd birthday (and there are two younger) and chaperoned by his tall and solemn father and the Hon able. Maria Rice, and a nurse. He was shy at first but soon grew quite lively. Then we had to pack all the Haywards off again for their drive home to Winstone in the dogcart.

Ever yr. loving Em.

Sept 25.   Tothill tells me he has had legacies left him which will keep him comfortably for life. He does not wish to leave me under six months or so but wishes to buy some little place where they can settle. His fortune is far more than he ever anticipated.

Dr. and Mrs Needham brought about 20 patients from Barnwood, ladies and gentlemen, for afternoon tea. They were most appreciative and seemed to enjoy themselves.

We dined at Eliza's and there met Mr Campbell who came back with us at night.

Sept 28.   Mr Campbell returned back home. I did not get much out of him. He looks very well and says he is a stone heavier than during the Warburg period. He wishes the business to go on but would feel great diffidence in being left my only partner if Oswald went out; but he had no suggestions how we could surmount the difficulty of Oswald's impecuniosity. He likes Oswald and is full of praise for his present attitude in all respects.

Sept 30.   Harvest Festival decorations exquisite (mostly done by Emily). Collection: £29.0.0.

Oct 1st.   Gray says he has still 18 acres of wheat and 30 acres of oats out. The delay is caused by the dreadful weather and because the reaper did not work properly at first but made the sheaves much too large.

Oct 4.   Visited the Infirmary and saw the father and mother and 6 children who have all been laid down with typhoid fever from drinking water of a contaminated well in India House Lane.

Oct 28.   London. We drank tea with Fred Mirrielees to see Maida who leaves for Vienna to be married to-morrow.

Nov 10.   Gray has purchased an estate near Castle Carey and thinks I should let Upleadon from next Michaelmas. He thinks he can go on managing till then.

Nov 13.   We went to Cheltenham to attend the Fancy Fair and Bazaar. It was a great success and very pretty sight. Carrie Hayward was helping at the Duchess of Beaufort's stall. In the evening we went to the Theatre to see Frank Benson[66] in Romeo & Juliet; but the house was nearly empty and miserably cold. The Fair was partly the cause of the thin attendance. We slept at Lanesfield.

Nov 14.   Emily, Eliza and I went to Thirlestaine House to see Mr Fenwick's pictures especially Catlin's North American sketches. Fenwick married the daughter of Sir Thomas Phillipps of Broadway. They were very kind and showed us round. Frank Benson came home with us, so we dined at 4 and he left at 5.30. He was most charming and very amusing.

Nov 17.   Dined at Lanesfield and then to Theatre to see Frank's Shylock, really magnificent.

Nov 24.   Fined Thomas Bridgeman, and Henry Perry, 10/- each and 20/- costs or 14 days, for trespassing in Pope's Wood in pursuit of game.
   Letter from Mary (his sister-in-law, his brother Sam's widow) saying she is expecting Sir Spencer Wells to operate next week; is prepared but feels it an anxious time. Her nurse has been a treasure to her; all are so kind, the Queen herself could not have been better waited upon.

Nov 26.   I came down to Leeds after taking a meal with Eliza at Lanesfield.

---

[66] Frank Benson was a cousin of Emily's. He had his own Shakespeare Company.

Nov 28. I left Leeds by 3 train, and took a carriage from Clitheroe arriving at Whiteholme at 7 p.m. I sat half an hour with Mary who seemed much interested in everything. She is thin but looks nicely in the face. She is much affected by the warm sympathy her illness has called out. There is a united prayer meeting of the church and dissenters in the village (Slaidburn) this evening to pray for her recovery. The operation is to be at 12 to-morrow and after lunch Sir Spencer Wells wants to get off to London by the 2 o'clock train. His fees are for first visit 150 guineas, 2nd visit 250 guineas, surgeon with him £50 and if Sir S.W. remains after an operation he charges 5 guineas an hour or 100 for 24 hours.

Nov 29. Mary had a good night and felt refreshed. Sir Spencer Wells and Mr Keith came at 11.45. She had some new kind of anaesthetic. Mr Wilkinson (a relation of Mary's) and I sat in suspense for more than an hour, then he came down saying it was not the success he had anticipated. Only the fluid portion of the tumour could be removed, the solid portion was so inseparably connected with the bladder and intestines that complete removal was impossible, and if attempted must have been fatal. He had operated on seven cases since he was here a month ago — they were all doing well — this is much the most serious case.

Mr Keith who stayed on told me that Mary walked into the operating room without assistance. She took bicarbonate of methylin without repugnance and never felt anything.

Nov 30. This morning Mary sent for me and said "I thank God for all his mercies. Sir Spencer told me I should soon be well and I believe it." She also said "I thank you, dear Dearman for all your kindness." I said I was going to Leeds, but would come back to her, as the doctors insisted on her being quiet now. I left at 2, and went to Leeds where I dined with Edward and spent an hour at Harehills.

Dec 1st. I went to Bradford about Bank business. On my return about 12 I received a telegram from nurse "Return at once!" I went back and so learnt that Mary died at 9 o'clock this morning. She began to be worse last evening and was more or less sick all night. At 8 Mr Wilkinson went in and was so shocked by her appearance he burst out crying. She said "None of that; I am going home", and afterwards, "A plain funeral, William". Mr Keith says hers was the worst case he ever saw. It seems a tragedy.

Dec 4. We followed Mary to the grave, a solemn walking procession, the coffin on village hearse drawn by one of her own horses driven by William Wilkinson. No strangers but all the tenants. Every blind was down in the village, the people kept inside. The church was fairly filled. Mr Jones (the vicar) read the service most impressively and did not break down till the end. The two nurses to whom William gave respectively £5 and £2 went home after the funeral. They have given the utmost satisfaction. On the plate was simply "Mary King Birchall, Died December 1st 1883". The coffin was placed in the same grave as my brother Sam. At 1.30 we had a tea lunch and in evening Mr Jones dined with Edward and myself.

Dec 5.   This morning Edward and I bid adieu to Whiteholme. It was a superb morning and all looked bright and lovely.

Dec 7.   I came home and spent a couple of hours with sister Eliza on my way.

Meanwhile Emily's diary records that on Nov 22 Dyer left and Miss Irvine came. On December 3 she heard of Mary Birchall's death and went to Cheltenham immediately to buy mourning, and again the next day to have her dress fitted, and for Clara to stay 2 nights with Eliza. Both Clara and Eliza had been very fond of Mary.

On December 19 she bought 102 Christmas cards and 11 presents in 1½ hours in 5 shops in Cheltenham. Christmas Day was misty and muggy. Dearman read "A Christmas Carol". A turkey and goose were sent to Harehills, to the partners Campbell and Oswald, and to sister Sophie Atkinson at Beckenham. 14 male employees at Bowden also received presents of food; but Tothill reported dissatisfaction amongst the women in the house as to the supply of meat which he said had been gradually diminishing. He admitted there were plenty of pies, puddings and vegetables; but said Mrs Moore was very close and allowed them very short he thought, and there should be more liberality.

Feb 22.   I spent the day at Upleadon, very fine and bright. The soil has been so soaked all this year that so far they have not got their spring corn in but they are hoping to get on the land in a few days. We have now about 200 lambs for 110 ewes. They seem doing very well. Gray says he is in no hurry to leave me.

Feb 25.   Dined at Hardwicke. Mr Baker very much better. Willie and Mrs Hicks Beach there. It was pleasant to see Mr Baker at the end of his table again. He is 75 years old and suffers from a frightful cough but which, he says, does not hurt him much. They have had no company for 18 months. Mrs Baker looks much aged.

Feb 26.   Clara sang at a Temperance Meeting at the Coffee Room. The Keens, especially Willie, and some other of our outdoor men performed.
   Benson Jowitt agreed to be my executor along with Theodore Crewdson and Edward Birchall, and he did not object to Emily if she wished it. He advised me to express my wishes that none of my sons should go into the Army.[67] [All Dearman's sons went into the Army and two were killed.]

Feb 28.   Rather solemn discussion at Meeting at the Infirmary of the catastrophe which has occurred in the death of Annie Frost through an overdose of chloral hydrate prescribed by Dr Ancrum as Syrup but which Wayland put down omitting the word syrup. The dispenser should have called attention to the dose which was ten times as strong as was intended. We passed a resolution calling the doctor's attention to the bye-law which states that prescriptions must be initialled by the physician ordering them. Dr Ancrum said that none who were mixed up in the case would ever forget the warning it conveyed.

Emily was still concerned about Percy's (broken) arm. In her diary there are frequent references to her taking Percy to see Mr Bower, and Lindaraja hurt a finger and had to have a nail taken off. She and Dearman stayed at the Grand Hotel in London. At the Lyceum "Mary Anderson was lovely as Galatea." She and her sister Susie called at the Mansion House, where they were kindly received. Back at Bowden she went to the Cathedral Society's meeting in the Chapter House. "Mr Gambier Parry read a charming paper on glass." Organ recital afterwards. Jack was now included on their rides. In London again; "to Ruskin's lecture on "The storm cloud of the 19th Century, at the London Institute — huge crowd." Then they went to stay with her parents in Leeds where there were 25 in the house besides the servants, but "no dancing because of the Assizes." However the Harris cousins at Oxton gave a ball, attended by the cavalry officers from regiments quartered at York and Leeds, and the next

---

[67] A last Quaker echo?

day they took a party of 14 to Lady Hawke's Dance though "the frost was very severe and so many open windows made the house almost unbearable to non-dancers." However Emily says she danced "a good deal, and Dearman did any amount."

On March 3rd they heard Arthur Severn lecture at the London Institute and Ruskin afterwards for ¼ of an hour. The next day Dearman and Emily left for Paris accompanied by Eliza, Edward and Clara, and were met by Anna Harris, who had crossed the day before.

Paris March 5. 1884

Darling Percy

We all wish you very many happy returns of your birthday. [He was 7 on March 7.] We hope it will be fine enough for you to enjoy going to Upleadon. It is very fine here today and we have been walking about the streets all day. We send you four pretty cards, one for each, you can choose which you like best as it is your birthday. We left some presents for you with Miss Irvine, a puzzle of the map of the world which Jack can help you put up, a knife, a book and a game of Happy Families. Your loving Mother.

They then travelled by train to Rome via Pisa, where they saw the Leaning Tower by moonlight. "Rome never looked more superb", and there they remained till March 17th, when Dearman and Emily left for Naples. Dearman went up Vesuvius and found it much more angry than in 1873, while Emily spent 4 hours in the museum. They also saw Casamiciola on Ischia where the earthquake on 28 July 1883 had killed so many people. "No-one is attempting to reconstruct a single house or even remove the rubbish". Back in Rome on the 22nd they bought embroideries and costumes for the children.

Violet and Linda were painted in the Russian and Roman costumes, which have survived nearly 100 years.

Dearman also "bought of Cantagalli a few nice things from the grand exhibition at Turin"; but he does not say what they were. Perugia, Florence, Bolognia, Ravenna, Venice, Milan and Lucerne followed; and home on April 8.

Lucerne April 4, 1884

My darling Percy

We got here this afternoon and were delighted to get Miss Irvine's letter giving such an interesting account of you all. We were extremely sorry to hear of the sad accident which has caused the death of Miss Rice. I hope you did not forget Sissy's [Clara's] birthday yesterday. We drank her health in soda water and lemons. Champagne was out of the question as she is such a staunch blue-ribbonite. We are so pleased to hear you enjoy your gardening so much and you may tell Keen that flowers are so cheap here we could buy six to nine lovely hyacinth blooms for one penny. Mama always goes about with an immense bouquet of them until we see people in the railway carriages bobbing their heads and feeling faint from the strong scent of her lovely jonquils and hyacinths. You would not believe me if I told you the wonders of the St. Gothard railroad. One tunnel was 9¾ miles, say as far as the other side of Cheltenham from Bowden, and going up the mountain we could sometimes see a train above our heads and one down in the distance a thousand feet below. It is so beautiful and sunny here and the lake is blue and bright. Give the enclosed note to Tothill immediately — very important. Dear love to you all and very kind regards to Miss Irvine from us all. I am your affectionate Father.

On April 12, Emily was busy decorating the church and wrote the daffodils were lovely, and Jack had his first tricycle ride, 4 miles.

Easter Day. They all went to church including Lindaraja (aged 4).

Mrs Marshall was staying and she and Emily went to a Bazaar on April 16 at St. Mary de Crypt Schools where Emily talked to Lord Fitzhardinge, and the same day she and Dearman went to the Stantons' dance.

April 18. Yesterday I threatened Trew that unless he could make my W.C.s work right, I should get someone from London to do so and bring an action in the County Court against his company for the expense.

On April 24 Emily went to stay at the Queen's Hotel Eastbourne with her parents, and Dearman went to Leeds.

April 26. Leeds. Interviewed Mr Stockart, a Saxon born in St. Petersburg where his father went as Professor at the University, a very nice quiet earnest face, he offers his services to us as sub-manager under his son-in-law Mr. Kafka. Kafka is about to go to America and says he must be back the first week in July in order to go to Italy. I strongly urged a reduction in the agents where Kafka visits.

April 27. Called on the aunts at Chapel Town [these were Emily's aunts, the sisters of John Jowitt, Elizabeth and Esther Maria. Another sister Mary Ann Jowitt had married Edward Whitwell.] The aunts were in, and had their nephew Robert Whitwell and his bride née Brown staying with them. [They had been married on April 17th. She was the daughter of Colin Brown of Hillhead House, Glasgow, and their daughter Crommelin afterwards married the 12th Duke of Bedford, when he was Marquis of Tavistock.]

April 30. Left Leeds at 11.45 p.m. last night and arrived home at 5 a.m. I took a long walk round by Barnwood and all round my hill; though the trees are coming out, the grass is scarcely moving at all. It does not look half so well as the park at Harehills. Some of the bottom fields look dreadfully bad from rushes, even where I have drained, and this seems to arise from the long succession of cold dull sunless seasons.

May 10th.   I went to London to see a few houses we thought of taking for 5 weeks from 6th June. I saw Hamilton Cuffe [afterwards 5th Earl of Desart] at 2 Rutland Gardens. He asks 20 guineas a week; no stable but his agent says you could get one for 2 guineas a week. I inspected 76 Ennismore Gardens and 9 Rutland Gate; but these houses are in poor condition.

May 28.   Sent Archer to London to see about stables. Miss Irvine [who had succeeded Dyer, the nanny] gave notice. Reasons: overwork, too much responsibility, too little salary; food served to children and herself shameful; Mrs Birchall never comes up and sees that things are nice. Violet, a delicate child, has to eat hashed veal and burnt pudding. It ends in her taking not half enough. She never was worse done for in the way of food. I told her she had been very captious and was acting most unkindly, and would regret leaving. She heard we had paid that miserable cook £50, and she who had the responsible charge of our children in which she had done her duty to the utmost of her ability, got only £30 and was grossly underpaid.

Emily fell on getting out of the new Stanhope. She caught her dress on the step and hurt her knee. Her parents came to stay.

June 6.   We have taken 2 Rutland Gardens from today. Sent Tothill to take the inventory.

June 7th.   All left by 9.15 a.m. train. When we got there Mrs Scutts [the cook] fell down the area and broke a rib.

June 8th.   Cecil Drummond called and Lord Ellenborough. Clara accompanied me to Moody and Sankey's in the evening. It was an interesting service. There were many soldiers looking most devout.

There then followed, anyway for Emily, a perfect whirl of engagements, dress-makers, dinner parties, calls, dances, concerts, in spite of the fact that Mrs Scutts was removed to hospital and Miss Irvine left like a raving maniac. However, good news for the children, on July 10th Mrs Hawkins came.

Emily was forced to send Dearman the following note.

Darling D.
    Miss Irvine is in a perfect fury and refuses to go! Will trumpet abroad our conduct throughout Gloucestershire, refuses the testimonial, and I am afraid she will meet Miss Chapman (a temporary appointment before Mrs Hawkins arrived) who is due about 4 or soon after and will poison her mind. Do settle her off and send her away. She is like a raving maniac.

On July 12 they were all, except Dearman, back at home. "Bowden looking very pretty but dull after London", wrote Emily. Dearman had enjoyed the medieval market, a charity they took part in, and had been exclusively in charge of selling "Mr Holland's charming Rhenish Pottery". He disposed of it "remarkably well", selling to friends, the largest piece to Lord Ducie and others to Cecil Drummond, Capt. Kelso, Lady Sudeley and Lady Adeliza Manners. Dearman also had opportunities for making business contacts, and discussing and rearranging stocks and shares. And he had the pleasure of taking Clara to a ball at the Mansion House, and introducing her to some "officers fresh from Egypt, who danced beautifully". Lord Ellenborough's ball was "very beautiful; his flowers and ferns were exquisite". Every Sunday they sampled at least two different churches. The Hon. Hamilton Cuffe was paid a total bill of £89.7.0. Dearman then went to Leeds.

July 12.　　Leeds. Kafka looks very well and entertains a most exalted opinion of the advantages of the American trade. He had a fine passage, but was disappointed with the towns in the Eastern States except Washington. Spent the afternoon at Harehills. Mother looks at her best, Florence fairly well and Father much more himself though the cultivation of his beard gives him an altered appearance.

July 16.　　I went to Crewe en route for the Royal Show at Shrewsbury and got a bed made up in the reading room of the hotel.

July 17.　　Bought a St. Bernard "Leicester Lion" from Mr Potter of the Black Horse Hotel, Leicester. He obtained 2nd prize among the St. Bernard puppies at the Crystal Palace. He was born August 5th, 1883, and is registered in the Kennel Club Stud book.
　　The Royal Show was very good. The Herefords are a very good class and seem to be more in fashion than any other breed. The Americans buy them more freely. Four classes of Jerseys are all decorated with either prizes or commended, not one was unmentioned. Ackers took prizes on Shorthorns, the two first for bulls and their offspring.

July 19.　　Moody, interviewed by the correspondent of the Pall Mall on his departure for America, spoke very flatteringly of England. Its rich men were acclimatized to wealth, and there was more done for every class in London than in any city in the world. There is more sanctified wealth. England has improved in temperance, in charity and in sympathy. The Church of England has awakened. He has had an average daily congregation of 9000, 7 days a week ever since he came.

Emily wrote in her diary on July 19. My birthday [she was 32]. Children all gave me lovely flowers.

July 22.　　I tricycled to Upleadon and rode over the farm on Mr Gray's mare. 140 tons of hay are well won and stacked. They start cutting the wheat this day, the crops promising 40 bushels to the acre.

July 23.　　I called at Prinknash, which consists of between 4 and 500 acres. If

Ackers cannot sell as a whole when he tries in October, he will sell the house and surrounding 200 or 250 acres. He has bought the Huntley estate which has better shooting, and is easier to get about, and has a commodious house, and no separation from his friends. Ackers has seen Miss Irvine and heard her tale.

The last entry in Emily's diary was on July 27, a Sunday. We all went to church. I read the Giant Killer to Jack.

Dearman's diary for August 9th.

Emily was very uncomfortable to-day. At 9 p.m. we sent for Mr Bower and Mrs Addis. They thought it was a false alarm and Bower went back in his hansom at 1.30 a.m. We had to send again, and he did not arrive until 3.15 a.m. At 4.45 a.m. on Sunday August 10th a little boy was born. My third son 7 lbs. Emily very nicely.

August 16.   Emily suffers great discomfort from veins in her leg. Bower calls it a threatening of phlebitis. He orders constant linseed poultices and occasional fomentations.

August 19.   Emily had a very disturbed night with constant pain in her leg all the way from foot to thigh.

Aug 23.   Emily has had a much better day. Florence came to stay.

Aug 26.   Emily improving. Violet has mumps.

Aug 30.   Emily very nicely. Daily gains ground. Florence and I dined at the Ancrums, a very musical party which we enjoyed.

Aug 31.   Emily's pain almost entirely gone. The swollen leg a little better. Good spirits. We read all the evening.

Sept. 2.   Clara and Florence drove over to see Eliza, returning to luncheon. Jack and I tricycled to Gloucester leaving Emily bright and cheerful, though her night had been rather wakeful without pain or feverishness. The groom galloped down to us to say Emily was taken very ill. I sent Dr Washbourne and Jack up, and went with Bower. We arrived at about 12.45, all to no avail. My darling had been taken from us about 11.40 without a parting word. She said "I feel faint" and shortly expired. The passage of a clot of blood from the improving vein in the leg to the heart absolutely stopped its action. No doctor in the world could have afforded the smallest relief. It was the will of God and we must bow to his decree. In his inscrutable wisdom he has taken a beloved wife and mother of five little ones who need her care. May he grant us grace to bear this crushing blow with fortitude. Poor Florence went to Leeds with Rea [Emily's maid] after the event as I feared the effect of the announcement on her beloved parents.

Bower was pleased to learn that I was perfectly satisfied with all that had been done. He said this deplorably sad event could neither have been foreseen or provided against by any doctor in the world and added, "It is sad for me I have lost not only a good patient but the best friend I had in Gloucestershire. I never saw a lady with such a well-balanced mind." Bower's certificate of death is Embolism of the pulmonary artery. Emily had cross-examined him on this danger; but he said if you get into a train you have a danger of death but the risk is so small you do not take it into account.

On the same day September 2, Florence, on her way home, wrote to Maida Mirrielees (now Mrs Bernard) in Moscow.

Dearest Maida

I wrote to you last on Wednesday. Emily went on as well as possible, the bad pain all left, and she slept better; she has been wonderfully lively and always so cheerful and patient. Clara often said "Mama's room is the brightest place in the house." She was as well and bright as usual this morning. I read all the letters to her and then went off to Cheltenham for a drive with Clara, returning to lunch and Dearman went to Gloucester. What was our surprise to meet Dr Ancrum near Bowden. He stopped us and looked fearfully sad. He said Mrs Birchall had been taken very ill. We instantly saw she must be dead. It seems that at 11.30 when Mrs Addis was dressing her (she was entirely in bed but moved from one side to the other for the day and night) she was faint. They tried in vain to restore her. She was unconscious in a minute and never came round at all. Poor Dearman was in before us. He seemed dreadfully crushed, but he was crying, naturally, and thinking of the parents and everyone.

I know what a dreadful blow this will be to you, dearest Maid. I am so glad you have your husband to comfort you in it. Of-course I cannot realize it the least yet. We arrived back at Bowden at 1.30 and tried to eat a little lunch, later, but we could not. The children, none of them realize it at all not even Jack. I am so thankful they have this sweet nice Mrs Hawkins with them, and Jack is going to school at Canon Girdlestone's at Sunningdale this month. Miss Birchall will come to Dearman and Clara this evening.

Emily looks so beautiful, with her fine features all white, and a most peaceful expression. I want to tell you how very nice Emily has been, far nicer than before. That little scene about your letter was the only break of any kind to our perfect harmony and happiness. I do so wonder what she is doing now. I think she will be with Lily. Perhaps Lily's work will be to fit her entirely for the life and work in heaven, "and her soul at home with God", keeps running through my head over and over again. She has been so wonderfully patient and so much more affectionate to us all than is her wont. I have never heard a single expression of discontent or impatience all the time I have been there, and she has been so unselfish, insisting I should go drives, etc even if it left her alone. I think she has been much more peaceful too.

It seems as if Clara had been kept free from her lovers, etc. to take care of Dearman and the children and house, poor girl, what a responsibility it is to her. It is awfully sad for poor Dearman to be left a widower a second time. Tothill has been so nice doing everything, and so intensely kind. He saw me off and said how much he felt for Mr & Mrs Jowitt, so nicely. I am now on my way home with Rea as Dearman would not let me come alone. We shall reach Leeds at 11 p.m. and so shall stay the night at the hotel and I shall go to Harehills as soon as parents have finished breakfast to-morrow. Susie left them yesterday and Benson and Carrie are away so they are absolutely alone. I have asked Dora to come to us. She came after Lily's death. I am thankful to have had this sweet visit to Emily. I felt at first awfully grieved I had left her this morning; but I think it is all for the best as she was not conscious at all after the faintness came on. What a wonderfully easy thing death seems, and how close it seems to bring the Unseen World to us.

Ever dearest Maid. Your loving Florence Jowitt.
To Mrs Bernard
c/o Messrs. Muir & Mirrielees
  Moscow.

The next day Dearman wrote to Maida. "You will know my bitter grief; my right hand cut off without a moment's warning."

On September 6 Dearman describes the funeral in his Diary.

At 11 a.m. the said procession started. The coffin covered both top and sides with exquisite flowers. Ten of our men with George Barnes and Mills were bearers, six at a time. I walked first with Clara. Benson and Jack followed, next then Eliza and Edward. All the village seemed out and I trust they will feel the solemnity of this most awful occasion showing as it does that no position is exempt from the saddest trials and in God's providence rich and poor are all alike.

Emily seems to have inspired everyone we were intimate with, with a sense of her gifts, her power, her goodness, her beauty, I may well estimate my loss by the testimony of my friends plus all I know of her loving devotion to myself.

Sept 7.   The little boy born on 10th August was to-day christened by Mr Emeris in the name of Edward Vivian Dearman. Theodore and David Howard, Eliza and Clara all stood sponsors.

Mrs Hawkins and Percy both very bad with the mumps. Benson was a great comfort to us. Mr Emeris preached two most feeling sermons. He seemed much moved.

Florence wrote again to Maida on September 5 from Harehills.

My dearest Maida
  We all feel so much for you, Dearest Maid, so far away where none of us

can speak to you and answer all the questions you would like to ask. We have been all most wonderfully helped and supported. I stayed at the Queens Hotel on Tuesday night. I lay awake most of the night but was not at all miserable. The Almighty and all-embracing power of God's love seemed to take all unhappiness from the deep sorrow we all so keenly felt. It is such a mercy Emily is safe with her Eternal Father, and we can so confidently trust her to his care. I am afraid poor Dearman is very miserable, his pessimistic views of life make sorrow very hard to him. He seems as if he could not "let love clasp grief" which is the secret of joy in sorrow.

I came up here after breakfast on Wednesday. Parents looked amazed to see me and did not guess the cause of my coming till I began to tell them how very ill Emily had been on Tuesday. Father is most sweet and calm and resigned, but his feelings are quite blunted with age. Mother has a more acute and sensitive sense of loss and grief than any of the others of us. Her first thought was longing she could have died for her. She feels so intensely for Dearman and the children; but I am most thankful to say she most fully realizes that God has called Emily away in love, and she is able to leave Emily in God's Fatherly love and care with perfect trust. Dear Benson came at once to us on Wednesday. His firm faith in God's love and wisdom has been a great comfort and strength. How pleased Emily would have been to see how strong his love to her came out. He went off to Bowden today to comfort Dearman. Clara's character is coming out beautifully. She has so much sense and presence of mind.

I am so anxious dearest Maida that our friendship should not drop at all now we have not Emily as our common link. I hope you will continue to write to me once a fortnight, as you did to Emily. I shall now need your friendship much more than ever.

Your most loving Florence Jowitt.

Emily's eldest sister Susie wrote to Dearman:–

So it has been to me to-day in thinking of my precious tender Mother missing the greeting on her birthday of her dear loving, warm-hearted, admiring Emily. Never was anyone so loyal to her own family as our dear one, and though she had been so admired and was so popular, she was never one bit blasée. Her love and pleasure in simple things was as keen as ever. A thought that flashed into my mind this morning and gave me much comfort was this: the tender mercy of our Father in Heaven shown in the way he took our darling without giving her the pain of saying goodbye to all her dear ones which in her deeply loving though reserved nature would have been very hard, consciously leaving a world which surely looked unusually bright and full of promise and interest and pleasure to her who had a strong love of life. So He took her straight to Himself where the knowledge of His love would burst upon her before she ever knew she had left the earthly for the heavenly.

My poor Dora [her daughter] is so sorrowful. She loved her darling beautiful aunt with such an intense love, far beyond anyone else except just this household. It is her first deep heart grief.

Ellen Heaton, a friend of Ruskin and Rossetti, wrote:—

My last view of dear Emily was the day she went with me to see Christina Rossetti. We had a pleasant talk with Christina who I saw was much impressed by Emily and she said to me afterwards that it was a pleasure to sit and look at my friend, she was so beautiful and charming in appearance. Dear Emily how many thought so, and to those who knew what was within the outward loveliness how much there was to love.

Mrs Hayward (Carrie Somerset) wrote from Winstone to Florence Jowitt:—

You don't know, no one does, all her goodness and warm hearted love to me. So many of my songs, so many of my books came from her, have her name or initials on them. She would send my children pretty presents at Christmas, and often besides. I find it so hard to realize I cannot see her again or hear her voice, I keep remembering her in a thousand little ways and speeches not to be put down. I loved her dearly. On Saturday we drove down in very pouring rain to see the last sad service and I could hardly command myself at all. It was all as bright as the lovely flowers and music could make it; but the rain poured steadily all the time and perhaps it was best so, more in unison. What Mr Birchall will do I cannot tell. She made the best sunshine of his daily life.

This Bishop of Gloucester wrote to Dearman:–

I do indeed mourn that on this earth I shall no more have the happiness of conversing with that bright, cultivated and gentle spirit, your dear wife. It was always a pleasure to talk with her, so intellectual, so kindly, so right-minded: and it is a real grief to feel now that the eye is not permitted to see her again. Yet my dear friend doubt not that you who were so closely bound to her, are bound to her in spirit closer than ever. Our dear God and Father never permits the holy family tie to be severed. The eye may see not; but the blessed bond remains. Deep indeed is the consolation in that article of our creed, "I believe in the communion of saints". May God in his great mercy, for Christ's sake, support you. We shall daily remember you in our prayers. God bless and comfort your dear children.

Emily's sister Dora Howard wrote:—

I do so want you not to give way to a sort of dreary flat discouragement when the routine of ordinary life must be taken up again, feeling as if none of us would care to come and see you now the bright and beautiful one is not there (oh how she did shine as a hostess), for we cling to you all the more, you are such a dear brother, and your tender, ever devoted care of her will live in all our hearts. You made her so happy, and this will be a happy thought to you now.

Finally Dearman wrote to Maida on December 12th.

My dear Maida

I cannot tell you how truly grateful I feel to sister Florence Jowitt for occasionally allowing me to see your letters giving as they do such a vivid picture of your daily life and discoursing of persons in your entourage so familiar to me from that bright and eventful visit to Moscow last year. I am so thankful we took that journey, it gave her such delight and had been the strongest wish of her later life. She was always thinking of you and I don't think either her marriage or yours seemed to place the smallest obstacle to your long continued intercourse. I am sending you back some "Retrospects" written entirely without my cognizance, and never seen by me until Susie found them in her drawer. They are to me touching beyond description. I never knew that she could write so openly of her feelings, even to you, and I thank God that she was able to speak so lovingly of me. I feared my want of intellectual capacity and reading would have disappointed her; but these posthumous papers show her devotion, and her happiness in the sphere in which she was placed.

During the happy years of our married life I was never parted from her for more than a few days and she never wrote to me more than a superficial note so that I have no letters. I wonder if I should be asking too great a favour if I asked if I could see any letter she wrote of a recent date?

We have had a very sad time during the last fortnight. Susie has been with us. She is a most wonderful person. She took to evangelizing everyone in the house. Her energy and business talents were most conspicuous. Had it not been for her assistance I should have been like my poor father who never could open his wife's drawers though he outlived her 14 years. There are some little things laid aside as remembrances for you; but we think we had better keep them till you are in England when we hope you and your husband will come and see us. Of-course it will indeed be different; but having a husband will take off the effect somewhat, and my darling Clara will do her utmost for your comfort as she studies incessantly and with great success to do for me.

We are going to have Jack back next week. He loves his school and we have a capital account of him from Dr Girdlestone. We are all going to my cousins Anna and Sophia Harris at Oxton for Christmas. I could not bear a Christmas spent here, for we have always had a family party, and if not very jolly it has been a season of most solid happiness.

Accept my love.   Yours most sincerely J. Dearman Birchall.

1885

Dearman was unwell with gout during the early months of the year. Vivian was sent to Eliza's to be looked after for a year. On February 13 Dearman had gout so badly when he was staying in Herefordshire that Tothill was sent for to take him home. "I had to get down stairs on all fours (my knees) and felt very faint and ill. At Leominster I was carried across the station in a chair." He was thankful to get home and to bed.

Feb 22.   Jack says there are only 16 boys out of 40 attending their lessons, the remainder are confined upstairs with measles.

Feb 24.   I visited the prison. Major Knox kindly had all the prisoners down stairs in the airing courts to save me the fatigue of visiting the cells and going upstairs.

I wrote to Dr Girdlestone condoling on the subject of measles and called his attention to Jack's spelling and the futility of teaching Latin until he could spell English fairly well. Linda is gone for a week to her Auntie's [Eliza.]

Feb 27.   Dr Girdlestone writes Jack is getting on exceedingly well and is having the almost exclusive attention of one master in consequence of the illness of the rest of the class.

March 15.   In the evening Clara and I went to the Cathedral to commemorative service for poor General Gordon. We had seats kept for us by the Tinlings, and were well placed before the nave pulpit. The Cathedral was densely crowded; hundreds outside because they could not find standing room within. Handel's Dead March from the Oratorio of Saul.

March 16.   Small committee at Barnwood, Sumner, Colchester-Wemyss, Graham-Clarke and myself. Saw Lady Durham. She looks brighter and very pretty. Needham thinks it quite possible she will recover, and thinks it would have been absurd for her marriage to have been annulled.

March 20.   Keen was at Highnam today. They are giving up a gardener, a footman and two stoves or peach houses. Gambier Parry has lost money in Wagon Works and in Crawshays Iron Works and seems despondent.

The children and Mrs Hawkins went over to Upleadon to gather lent lilies which are now in full bloom.

April 1st.   Had lunch with Jack at Reading and sent him home for the Easter holidays. Spent a few hours with Charles Brooke-Hunt at Slough. The old gentleman was especially lively and cheerful; most interesting reminiscences of Battle of Trafalgar and Nelson's death.[68] He well remembers his grandmother who was born in the reign of George I.

April 9. Great excitement that the Russians have attacked the Afghans and defeated them — a rapid retreat and 500 left dead in the field.

April 23. Eliza and I took Percy to Miss Saunderson's school in Cheltenham. He bore up well but is an affectionate little fellow and feels leaving his little sisters and us.

June 29. Fishmonger had caught a sturgeon this morning at Awre, 9 ft. long, weight 260 lbs. It was still breathing when I saw it.

July 1st. Very hot fine weather; getting on well with the hay, an immense crop of strawberries and roses which I am sorry we are about to leave. [He and Clara went to London next day for their "season".]

August 24. Garden Party at the Doringtons at Lypiatt Park. We took the Greens and enjoyed a very pleasant expedition. It took us nearly two hours with barouche going by Stroud — a mistake — returning Miserden way; it was a most superb day and the company numbered over 200, all the best people in the county, and the Greens were much struck with the beauty of the place and agreeable party and the picturesque country.

August 25. Garden Party at Hardwicke 3.30 — 7. A smaller party than yesterday. Mr Baker was walking about and seemed very cheerful. The garden looked in nice order; but the grass plot much cracked from the unusual drought which has prevailed for at least a couple of months.

August 26. We took the Greens to see Prinknash which looked most charming this sunny day. Ackers tells me he wants £45,000 for the house and 427 acres including timber valued at £10,000.

Dr & Mrs Ancrum [whom Emily used to call the Ancra] with two appendages, an Emeris, Dr & Mrs Needham [from Barnwood] and Mr Gray [the manager at Upleadon] dined with us. All went very well; but I felt Emily's absence was most affecting [she who once said after a party, "All the gentlemen smoked so I was in heaven"].
It is the first time we have had anything like a dinner party though small.

---

[68] Tennyson on the reported insufficiency of the fleet.
"You — you — if you have failed to understand
The Fleet of England is her all in all
On you will come the curse of all the land
If that old England fall
Which Nelson left so grand."

August 27.   Adeliza Davis came over from Well Close to see me and showed me a letter her mother had received from Mr Davis [her father] saying he was going to cast in his lot with Clara Downham [daughter of a local pub-keeper] and would she sue for a divorce. In the afternoon I called and saw Downham and pointed out what an awful responsibility he would incur if he allowed his daughter to go off. I tried to frighten him, and Adeliza was to see her father.

Aug. 28.   Adeliza writes she has managed an interview between her father and mother and matters had assumed a more favourable appearance. She thanked me very warmly for my interview with Downham which she says has produced an excellent effect.

Sept. 16.   Tricycled to Upleadon. The Grays commence their departure on Saturday. The place looks very nice. I then went on to Huntley to call on the Ackers. The house struck me as looking very dull and uninteresting. [This was by S.S. Teulon, and would probably not compare very favourably with Prinknash.] Ackers says how bad everything is. He cannot get an offer for Prinknash and has to keep it up, and cannot sell the Prinknash herd of shorthorns. He has now the three houses and is going to give up butler and footman and keep waiting maids. I had been 32½ miles.

Sept 18.   School Treat. 184 children. We gave 20 girls cloth for dresses and 20 boys suits. These children were chosen for the number of their attendances. It was a splendid day and all enjoyed themselves.

Sept 22.   Sale of Mr. Hobbs's stock at Park Farm; very bad prices realized. Things are now probably lower than for 20 years. The season has been good and stock is plentiful, importations continuing the prices continually fell. The horses brought exceptionally bad figures. I bought a colt for £13.15.0 Mr Davis purchased sheep and horses. He looked very wild. I believe Mr Hobbs would have remained at Park Farm if Mr Davis had given him a sensible reduction from his rent of £500 p.a.

Dearman wrote to his sister-in-law Florence Jowitt on mourning paper with a black edge ¼" thick.

Bowden Hall   Sept 24. 1885
Gloucester

My dearest Florence
    It seems some time since I have sent you a line and I am sure it is not from lack of interest in your proceedings but rather from preoccupation that has hindered my writing. I trust all is going well and that our beloved mother is the better for her change. How I wish I could peep in at Westleigh and enjoy a sight of your beloved circle sitting round a fire I guess and nice and cosy

and someone reading aloud. Susie darting at intervals when a thought of some absent sufferer crosses her mind or some note forgotten. I hope Father's voice is stronger with the change of air.

All our party got off to Scarborough yesterday morning. They seemed in very good spirits. The whooping was not entirely gone but I expect the change will soon cure them. I think Jack has had it the worst. He looks very white but won't allow there is anything the matter with him. Eliza insisted on the necessity of Mrs Hawkins and the two nurses going, so with Rea [the lady's maid] and Brown the footman the party is very large.

Tothill has again postponed his departure *sine die*. He has kept us in order lately and been very cross and he is fully alive to the difficulty we have in replacing him and well aware how I detest changes.

We have had a visit from St. John Ackers and our present Conservative M.P. Reginald Yorke who is about to contest this division and never was I so surprised as at the meeting we had in our schoolroom. It was crammed and we were greeted with plaudits rivalling the most excited Yorkshire welcome. I have heard that the Liberal meeting in the same place 2 months ago (with Dr. Ancrum in the chair and Sir William Guise[69] as speaker) introducing their candidate young Samuelson was only attended by 8 residents and 8 visitors. I never anticipated such a result and cannot account for it. We did a bit of canvassing next day and we three with Jack went round amongst the women at home. They nearly all told us that their husbands had bad legs. Can the Upton air cause this complaint to be so well nigh universal amongst the old men? The young ones have nearly all run away. If Upton was the arbiter a radical like Samuelson could stand no chance.

This day my Upleadon farming experiences have terminated for the present. I have been all day at the sale. When I got there I did not at first go to the ring or recognize anyone. I wandered about and could scarcely realize that I was the owner of the crowds of beasts and sheep and implements and wagons that covered the field. I felt like a wandering spirit returned to earth after death and taking unknown cognizances of what my successors were doing with my effects. No one seemed to take much notice of me and I listened to heaps of comments made by people who little guessed that I was the unfortunate owner of the property they were buying at such inadequate prices. They were indeed desparately low; it is quite ruinous. Farmhorses, great big animals went for £17 to £30. Cattle dreadfully low, and sheep at a bad price; but the latter did the best, the flock has been so deservedly admired. What intensified the depression was the want of support from my new tenant who could not sell his stock in Devon so has hired a train to bring his family and all his flocks and herds, a complete exodus. My carts, wagons, and ladders were nearly given away.

---

[69] Sir William Vernon Guise, 4th Baronet of Elmore where he lived all his life, 1816–1887. First President of the Bristol and Gloucestershire Archaeological Society, 1876.

I have been at Barnwood this week. *Entre nous* we have another well known Yorkshire man, Johnston Scott of Woodhall, Wetherby, brother of Lord Abergavenny's wife. Lord A. used to be Lord Nevill when he lived near Scarcroft and he was my proposer at the Junior Carlton, of which he has always been president. I am dreadfully sorry to hear that his eldest son, and of course nephew of our patient, is also out of his mind. Is it not sad to have such a skeleton in the closet.

After leaving Upleadon yesterday on my tricycle I visited the Bakers at Hasfield Court and found the young lady Mrs Bourne Baker in process of being painted by no less an artist than Alma Tadema. She has only been married a short time, and has a handsome face, and the pair remind me of Jack Sprat and his wife. Baker is a little spare creature. He is not a dwarf, but next to it. She is tall and stout and twitched like a wasp. I saw her playing tennis vigorously one day and looked on with wonder and amazement not unmixed with apprehension as to the effect of such violent exercise on so artificial a figure. I had done my 30 miles by dinner and today I have again done 25 and spent the day in the open air at the sale; very cold it was I assure you standing there.

I parted with Mr Gray with the utmost regret; but he is coming to me twice a year just to look over the farms and take rents and for this I am going to pay him £20 p.a.

I go down to Scarborough at 8.50 p.m. on Monday. Clara is to leave me on Wednesday, and Eliza Eveleigh comes to take her place. Sister Eliza is much better since her return from Switzerland. Accept my dearest love, Yours affectionately J.D. Birchall.
Our address at Scarborough is 63 Esplanade.

Sept 27.   I called on Mrs Davis. She has Adeliza with her. She has had an interview with the Commissioners in Lunacy; but afterwards her brother and Mr Davis's brother objected to such proceedings. Davis has had a prize fight in Gloucester fields. He knocked a Mr Hopton down who won't summons him. One day Davis dined with the wood dealers in Chalford, returning he had his trap upset and was found insensible on the ground. His watch was stolen but afterwards recovered. Davis is about to remove his furniture from Well Close to Park Farm and employ Downham to manage the Farm for him. He tells Mrs Davis he is looking for her death with joyful anticipation. Mrs Davis thinks the Downhams have a conspiracy to get all his means from him. He has cut down the elms at Well Close.

Sept 29.   Arrived at Scarborough and found all the children with renewed whooping cough owing to the cold winds.

Oct 8.   Clara has had a letter from Adeliza Davis describing her visit to the Percivals and from there making a raid on Well Close with two furniture vans and effecting an entrance by a window in the dead of night and clearing off with their belongings at 4 a.m.

Dec 4.   R. Tothill left after 12 years faithful service. It is 13 since he first came to me but he spent one year away after being with me three, and then returned. I gave him a silver tea service and Clara a kettle to match. (He has bought a house at King's Stanley, having had a legacy.) Robert Kew, aged 33, came. He is to remain a month and then bring his wife and children.

Dec 22.   Mrs Barnard[70] and Anna (Harris) leave us. There was a fancy dress ball (yesterday) at Barnwood and Clara went in Roman costume and Anna richly gowned in beautiful brocade with splendid jewels and hair finely elevated and artistically arranged by Mrs Barnard. Mrs Barnard has worked extremely hard, scarcely giving herself time for meals during the day light in order to finish the portraits. She has completed darling Emily's, Violet and Linda (in Russian and Roman dress) and a smaller one of Vivian which Clara has had done to give to Eliza at Christmas. Anna and Sophia have generously presented us with Violet and Linda's pretty portraits. The two ladies have been capital company and most kind and bright.

[70] Emily Barnard, portrait painter.

1886

In January Dearman and Clara went to Paris, and in February to London where Clara stayed with the Drummonds. On Feb. 14 they went to church together at St. Peter's Eaton Square where the Bishop of Truro preached "attacking the sins of the higher classes and showing how disaffected the masses were getting, and how full were the publications read by them of denunciations of the luxury, idleness, avarice, and immorality of the upper ten."

On February 15 he was back to attend the monthly, quarterly and annual meeting at Barnwood Asylum. "I took the chair on pressure. Granville Baker, Col. Wemyss, Broome Witts, Sir Thomas Crawley-Boevey etc. were present."

A few days afterwards he attended a meeting at the Infirmary and afterwards visited all the wards. "There are now no fever cases in hospital." Another day Sir William Guise was very lively at the court where we had no business. He told me all about the last days journey to Bombay and back of Willie Price. Mr Price met him at Marseilles, and brought him home where he died. "Curtis-Hayward has sold all his wheat this day at 3/10d a bushell. He has held it some time and sees no chance of going better. Everything is very low. . . Excessively cold. We have had a very prolonged winter."

Dr Girdlestone reported well of Jack. "He is doing very well. . . he does a fair latin exercise, and is getting on with Greek grammar. He has got to the top of his class and is showing great improvement. Average marks in class 168, Jack's 208."

Mrs Curtis-Hayward had a concert at Quedgeley. "Hilda Parry sang. We saw the dairy: he is milking 36 cows." Another day he and Clara rode to the Grays at Parklands. "The cinerarias are certainly very effective, all massed together — they are from Veitch's seed. In other things they cannot compare with us."

March 2.   Davis, the cowman, caught and killed a fine badger. It was sleeping in a corner under the manger at the stalls. He was feeding the cows and first stuck his foot into its rump, and beat it on the head. They are getting rare. I do not remember one being caught here before though we have often found their holes in the wood. They are not in the least destructive of anything one wishes to preserve. We had it stuffed at a cost of 20/- and put into what the taxidermist called a menacing attitude.

March 7.   The cold weather continues very severe, the pond frozen but won't bear as the nature of the ice is very rotten from snow. The wind continues in the east. It freezes every night and there is little or no thaw during the day. We have had to buy hay. The fields are much browner than any time previously this winter.

April 2.   I ran up to town by early train and saw the Millais exhibition at the Grosvenor; Holman Hunt and Mrs Allingham at the Fine Art Society, the former most striking including The Light of the World and the Scapegoat. Arthur Tooth has Millais' lovely Bubbles.[71]

April 4.   Inspected draft deed of partnership between John Kelly and Edward Birchall,[72] terminable on either side at 6 months notice. Capital £100. Kelly's office to be kept up in London and Leeds. Of existing contracts each is to get 90% on their own for share of profit; but all future contracts to be divided 60% Kelly and 40% Birchall. Works Kelly has in hand now are:– Church of Holy Rosary Sheepscar, All Hallows Leeds, Our Lady of Grace Chiswick, Emmanuel Leeds, St. Agnes Burmantofts, Our Lady of Lourdes Acton, Holy Cross Fulham.

April 6.   Dined with the Magistrates. Sat between Admiral Christian and Granville Baker. Afterwards I went down to Leeds by the 8.56 Scotch Express and slept at Queens Hotel. The train which had 8 first class compartments was almost empty with only 3 first class passengers.

April 21.   My Monasterboyce cross[73] carved by Farmer and Brindley under Aldam Heaton's direction of Parian marble now completed. The inscription — In loving memory of Emily Dearman Birchall. Born 19 July 1852, Departed this life 2nd Sept. 1884. (Cost £171.10.0).

The 5th May was the Golden Wedding Day of John and Deborah Jowitt. Dearman did not attend because he had gout, nor did the other widowed son-in-law Theodore Crewdson. However "the parents were bright and well and happy, and all passed most successfully". Later in the month Clara, Mrs Hawkins and the children were sent to Tenby for a holiday.

June 5.   I went to Cheltenham and lunched with Eliza and then we went to see the sports at Miss Sanderson's. Percy was down to run in two races and also one in sacks. He did not run in one because he had failed in some trial the night before and in the sack race he was far behind. He was in capital

[71] Sir John Everett Millais, 1829–96. After 1870 devoted some of his painting to portraits of pretty children under fancy titles.

[72] Works completed by Edward Birchall F.R.I.B.A. [Dearman's brother] before 1886.
Tylney Hall, Winchfield for Charles E. Harris; Residence at Harrogate for T. Hattersley; House at Ilkley for H. Richardson; House at Scarborough for J.P. Webb; House at Durker Roods, Meltham, for Capt. Armitage; Schools at Leicester, Otley, Tadcaster, Selby and Leeds; Churches at Enderby near Leicester, Sawley, Wath near Ripon, Tadcaster, Bardsey and Meltham; All Hallows, Emmanuel, and Beeston at Leeds. Convalescent Home at Meltham. Police Courts at Kirby Lonsdale. Town Halls at Birkenhead, Chorley and Pontefract.
    [Edward separated from Kelly in Sept. 1893 the year their R.C. church in Soho Square was opened.] 'Possessed of ample means, he did not push his practise, but carried on in a somewhat leisurely manner,' wrote W.H. Thorp who worked in his office.

[73] This survives in Upton St. Leonards churchyard.

spirits and looked very bright and jolly. He was very much taken up with the relations of a boy friend of his called Campbell, the Lucys of Charlecote Park, Hampton Lucy.

Cheltenham looked most delightful, quite at its best with the great variety of flowering trees and shrubs all in full bloom, and the foliage in its spring freshness.

June 12.   Went to the prison to remand a young woman who is to be brought up for murdering her child. It was found in one of the empty cottages at Coney Hill. Capt. de Winton and I also inspected the gallows erected for the execution of Hewit for the murder of his mistress in Gloucester.

Dearman then took Clara to London again for a short season where they saw many of the same people they saw at home like the Ellicotts and Ellenboroughs; but there were concerts, entertainments and parties and on Sundays they were able to sample a variety of preachers, and could hear for example a very interesting sermon on the text "Are not two sparrows sold for a farthing".

He does not often refer to the younger children; but on September 1st Clara took the 2 boys and 2 girls with Mrs Hawkins to spend the day at Huntley (with the Ackers family). Clara did not understand Edith's conversation (Edith Ackers was a deaf mute.) A few days before there were athletic sports in Gloucester. Mrs Hawkins took the two little girls, the boys went with him on their tricycles. The sports were dull. Most of their friends had deserted to attend a Conservative fête at Sir John Dorington's at Lypiatt.

Sept. 17.   I tricycled to Dursley with the intention of going to lunch with the Powers who have taken The Ridge [from the Bengoughs] for three months. I had a headache and was rather seedy and it was extremely hot, so I lunched at the Bell, and then returned home by the beautiful ride over Uley Bury and past Woodchester Park, down to Stroud and through Stonehouse and so home. To Dursley 18 miles; home by Uley 20 miles = 38 miles. The matter of the unch was put right on the 28th when he and Clara lunched at The Ridge. "It is a great rambling place, very high, and must be very isolated and almost in the clouds in winter."

On the 21st Mr Coleman, the head gardener at Eastnor Castle had gone to Bowden by appointment professionally to advise about peach growing. He admired the bedding out and said it was the best arranged, with the most pleasing colours and altogether the most successful he had seen that year. However, he said the Japanese maples had not the least chance in the miserable soil they were in. He was to write a report. On October 2 Dearman sent Mrs Morris at Manor Farm £5.5.0 as honorarium for the week Mrs Hawkins was there with the children. Mrs Morris was "extremely obliged" for the present which she considered handsome, and they may go there again at any time. The same day Percy came back from school for the day and the little Percivals joined them and they kept Violet's birthday (her 8th). Dearman notes that Dr

Marindin of Eton is Mrs Percival's first cousin, so he may have started thinking about his sons' further education. (The Percivals were near neighbours at Kimsbury.) Later the whole family went to Scarborough, and on November 7 the children went to stay at Harehills with their grandparents.

In December they went to a dance at Hatherop Castle — Dearman writes that "Clara danced merrily". People they knew were the Crippses, Wingfields, Chester-Masters, Mr Bulley who was about to marry the eldest Miss Bazley and Canon Dutton Vicar of Bibury who brought the Maharana of Sarawak and Hilda Parry.

Dearman also attended the Installation of Dean Spence in the Cathedral, and he notes the death of Barwick Baker of Hardwicke whose life work was connected with the prevention and treatment of crime. Lord Greenock, son of Earl Cathcart, was taken as a patient at Barnwood, with acute mania. He smashed his father's windows; but Dr. Needham thought he would recover, and he did, and later left for a cruise in the Mediterranean.

1887

Feb 17.   I attended the execution of a young man Pritchard for the robbery and brutal murder of a boy Harry Allen at Stroud. Berry from Bradford was the executioner and all was silently and solemnly performed.

Feb 21.   Visited the prison and found Admiral Fenwick the government inspector there. He comes once a fortnight. He was investigating a charge of drink brought in surreptitiously for Berry the executioner. It seems that functionary demands a pint of champagne the morning of his employment.

On March 13th Dearman wrote to his sister-in-law Florence Jowitt.

Bowden Hall
Gloucester

Dearest Florence

After luncheon on the 7th I set out on a tricycling expedition and made my way over Birdlip and the Cotswolds to Cirencester. The roads were infamously bad and on the rise to Birdlip muddy as well as stony. The wind was keen and biting. I was more than three hours, and put up at the Cirencester hotel where they made me very comfortable. Travelling was not facilitated by the weight of clothes necessary in so cold a season. Before starting I had in the morning visited the prison with Russell Kerr.

The next morning I had a jolly run to Cricklade calling at the Bowlys; but I found them away in the south of Europe. There is a pretty old town cross at Cricklade and the cottages are excessively pretty all about that country with eaves windows in the roofs, wood painted green, and everywhere covered with vines and red-berried plants. There is a large bronze Russian cannon in the main street.

I saw heaps of men and ladies riding off to the meet, two of the latter looked much weather-beaten and though engaged in such youthful pursuits I judged them to have seen near 60 summers.

At Swindon I got into the train taking my machine to Reading where after a little late luncheon I went over Huntley & Palmer's biscuit factory. It is indeed a most gigantic enterprize. They take 500 sacks of flour a day turning out 100 tons of biscuits every working day. Their goods are appreciated in the interiors of both China and Africa. They use a vast quantity of coconuts, almonds, treacle, ginger, butter, eggs, lard, arrowroot, rice water, and isinglass. I saw a large parcel of macaroons and coconut cakes come out of the ovens for a special order from Windsor Castle. They have over 3000 hands and there are many very interesting mechanical dodges invented by the Palmers. The income is immense but the two young ones work incessantly instead of spending their money and living in idleness. Reading is a prosperous looking place much more so than either Gloucester or Hereford which seem in rapid decay.

Wednesday I opened some clothes fresh from home and dressed up with

Dearman on his steel horse

chimneypot hat and Sunday best and trained off to Sunningdale. I found Jack looking extremely well, most hearty. The school was in every respect of which I was competent to judge A1. The numbers are certainly lower, only 33, but they get every attention. I dined with the boys on roast beef and apple pie, all so clean and nice and fancyable. The house is most fresh and healthy, each boy with a separate cubicle. I made up my mind to send Percy there after Easter and the greatest satisfaction was apparent not only in the Girdlestone family but especially with Jack who was quite delighted.

After luncheon Theophilus Girdlestone a pale cadavorous blackeyed heavy moustached youth of interesting expression accompanied me as a sort of guide to Eton, and we were received very warmly by Mr Marindin, the master whose house Jack is down for in January 1889. It is a large new red brick house with 40 boys. He was sitting in a beautiful library full of the most interesting things. We also called on Miss Evans an old lady who has a most popular house. She told us about Herbert Gladstone who was with her. When his father spent a day there he could tell the name of every boy he had been at Eton with years before, an almost unparalleled feat of memory. We also saw Billy Busfield (the son of Anna and Sophia Harris's sister) who has only been at Eton this term but was very happy decorating his room with Bramham Moor Hunt lithographs.

I went from there to Slough in a hansom cab and dined with the Brooke-Hunts. He is 94 years of age but his mind is bright and vigorous and his memory unimpaired. I got back to Reading and started by tricycle early next morning for Henley where I sat half an hour in a boat thoroughly enjoying the placid expanse of the river and the recurrent gleams of sun and cloud. Then on to Dorchester with a beautiful church restored of late years and seven small windows by Clayton and Bell as beautiful and chaste an imitation of 13th century work as I have seen. In the little village inn there were five youngsters from college presumably field naturalising with a tutor. They had thrown aside huge packets of Oxford sandwiches and cakes and were cramming down quantities of fried ham and eggs, washed down with bumpers of hot whisky and water, and getting their flasks filled with port wine.

I dined at the Clarendon at Oxford and next morning went all over Magdalen, New and Christ Church colleges and chapels. Mr Lloyd was much astonished to see me at the last where he is organist. I then took the train to Witney, a very nice cheerful looking place as unlike Batley or Dewsbury as you can conceive, no smoke whatever and a large open green with a beautiful old church. I did see a cart or two with blankets of gaudy coloured edges or I should not have realized that this was the birthplace of that most valuable domestic commodity.

I now mounted my steel horse again and made my way under great difficulties of stones and bad execrable roads to Burford and eventually to Northleach. The roads were so infamous I could get no further that night but slept at a little country inn where they did their best to make me comfortable. Yesterday in snow, north west wind alternating with sun and cloud I reached Eliza for luncheon and ended the day by getting home at tea time having tricycled 105 miles, and seen a great deal by train and road.

Prinknash is let for two years with option to purchase to a Mr. Dyer-Edwardes who lives in London but is at present spending the winter in Algiers on account of his wife's health.

I have written a long letter and I hope you won't be bored with it. With dearest love in which Clara unites. Believe me your most affectionate brother J.D. Birchall.

In May Dearman took Clara to the Italian lakes for over a month and they fraternized with the other English visitors who included the Hicks-Beaches. This was followed by a stay in London, separated by only one day at Bowden, June 6th on which Dearman wrote:–

Found the little girls, Mrs Hawkins and Vivian all very well. The garden looks backward between cold and rabbits, the roses deplorable. The season has been miserable and they have scarcely had any fine weather during the last month. However on June 14 Clara decided to go home, the heat is so great in London she does not think she can stand the fatigue of the Queen's Jubilee in town.

On July 7th he wrote to his sister-in-law

Dearest Florence

Thanks for the sight of Maida's letter. How curious it is to see so strong minded a lady so completely changed in her tastes and interests by her husband's influence. Just contemplate her devoting a summer to the microscopic examination and dissection of the corpse of a frog. If she rises from the contemplation of vertebrate animals with a quickened sense of the goodness, far-seeing intelligence and all-prevailing oversight of our almighty Creator, well and good; but most physiologists seem much more penetrated with the idea of their own sagacity in discovering delicacies and intricacies in animal life which they attribute to blind chance or natural selection, and are as often as not mere materialists.

Yesterday we made our first call on the Dyer-Edwardes at Prinknash. Mrs Dyer-Edwardes is a very sweet looking delicate lady who has to spend her winters out of England. Algiers where they passed last winter they found a grand climate, warmer and more equable than the places on the Cornice. We are most anxious for them to stay and purchase Prinknash; but they are both High Church, and the Rector's dull empty church and Mrs Emeris's sour evangelicalism will I am afraid have some influence against the realization of our wishes.

I am writing this letter in the train on my way to town to attend the wedding of my friend, and your distant cousin, Robert Benson. He is making a great match — Miss Holford of Dorchester House, Park Lane, and of Westonbirt in Gloucestershire. Her father used to be M.P. for our division. He is a man of immense property and owns a superb gallery of pictures.

Robert Benson through American investments and the favourable result of
his great railway — the Minnesota and North Western — is now believed to
have become a very rich man. They are to be married today at St. George's
Hanover Square at 2.30 and then we go to a reception at Dorchester House.

5.40 p.m. I am sitting in Aldam Heaton's Studio where I have dropped in
to see a great altar he has designed, and he is out. We have had a most
gorgeous affair today. The church was closed against all but ticket holders
and each person — some hundreds — was presented with a white button
hole which became the passport to Dorchester House. The bridesmaids
were like Kate Greenaways with mob caps, the pages had scarlet coats in the
fashion of adult clothing 150 years ago. The bride looked rather small with
her old father, 80 years of age. Some of the ladies and little girls were as
beautifully dressed as I have ever seen but some of the Benson young men,
especially William, were very excentric-looking with olive trousers.

Robert Benson's presents were the most numerous, the donors' names
attached to each article. The collections of old silver, Queen Anne especially,
old engravings, paintings, 1st editions of costly books like Ruskin, dressing
cases — three or four with superb silver mountings, old china, watches,
clocks cameo-mounted articles from Italy, in fact such a sight I never saw or
imagined nor am I able to throw any light on the regal magnificence of the
display unless all his clients have to a varying degree profited by his unequalled
good fortune. I saw for once in my life I had come in for a real experience
like those imaginary ones concocted by Lord Beaconsfield in *Lothair* for the
admiration of a luxurious and sumptuous age.

I think this may be called a circular.

I am your most affectionate brother J. Dearman Birchall.

In September Dearman and Clara went to stay in Scotland with their cousin
George Lees and his family who had a deer forest on the Isle of Skye. The other
children were sent to Weston-super-Mare with Mrs Hawkins. Dearman, as
was his wont, only half took part in the sporting activities.

On November 7, Susie Howard wrote to Dearman giving an account of
taking her motherless nephew Dillworth Crewdson[74] to Sunningdale.

"We had a lovely clear sunny day and this helped poor Dillworth's spirits.
Theophilus Girdlestone showed us the Fives courts where Jack is quite a famous
player. Jack and Percy came in just before dinner looking so nice, Jack very tall
and much less shy and Percy most bonny — poor little Dill looked such a little
shrimp compared with them. All the boys gazed at Jack in a smiling way. We
had a very good dinner, nice clear soup and the tenderest roast beef and jam
roll. I asked Jack to be most specially kind to Dill. They walked to the station
with me and their tongues now loosed, they chatted away."

---

[74] Joseph Dillworth Crewdson of Syde Manor, Gloucestershire (1875–1947). Married Margaret
Hicks-Beach of Witcombe Park.

1888

January 15.   Waller [the architect] has gone up the Nile with his brother-in-law John Collier.[75]

We fined a man Wilks of Hucclecote 10/- and costs for tearing up the roadway after a frost with an ill-adjusted skid on a stone wagon. He was charged under an Act of County Highways bye-laws for damaging Upton Hill.

Mr Dyer-Edwardes has bought a field of Job Morris,[76] 6 acres for £1,000 to enable him to make an excellent road to Prinknash Park. The road will be a mile and quarter and have easy gradients and some lodges.

January 21.   I got C. Cloke (tenant at Upleadon) to walk over Castle Meads with me. He said it was a very useful piece.

January 25.   Lunched with Dr Warre, headmaster of Eton. Called on many house-masters and felt inclined to choose the Rev. T. Dalton.

On March 30th Florence wrote to tell him of her engagement to Arthur Baines, aged 40, who had been for some years in Australia as secretary to some institution at a salary of £300 p.a.

He is at present in no position to maintain a wife; but he has gone back for a year and will then return and endeavour to obtain a suitable job in England. They seem much in love, and Florence would rather marry to comparative poverty than a rich man for whom she might not have so warm an affection. Mother approves it and Florence says that in religion, aims in life, intellectual and artistic tastes, poetry and music, she thinks his character remarkably well suited to hers. His hard life and want of success whish is his one great drawback, has been borne in such a brave, manly and upright way that it has only ennobled and deepened his character and left not the least bitterness or hardness. Benson and Carry and Aunt Esther Maria[77] most cordially and kindly approve. He has returned to Port Darwin as neither he nor Florence are in a position to marry at present and they feel quite happy to wait until the way opens.

April 4.   We left Gloucester a party of 14 consisting of myself and Clara, Eliza and Edward and Mrs Hawkins, Jack, Percy, Violet, Linda and Vivian, Craddock [butler], Berry [footman], Rea [Clara's maid], and Elise [nursery maid.]

---

[75] The Hon. Sir John Collier, artist, who later painted Dearman's portrait.
[75] Job Morris of Manor Farm, Upton St. Leonards.
[77] John Jowitt's youngest sister. She died at Woodfield, Newton Hill, Leeds on Sept 7. 1889 aged 64. She left £40,000 to be divided between 6 Jowitt and 4 Whitwell nephews and nieces.

They travelled by train to Southampton. There were snow storms. The crossing to St. Malo was on the same boat that Clara had crossed on eight years before when Emily enjoyed it so much more than anyone else. The rolling this time was only slight, however Elise was violently ill and never held up her head during the passage. Dearman had rented a house at Dinard called La Conchée, a comfortable house over and behind a handsome grocer, and an Italian ware-house full of fresh and pretty furniture. He hired a good cook at 50 francs a month, a housemaid at 40 francs and *aide de cuisine* at 20 francs, and was well pleased with all.

The next day he and his architect brother Edward went to Dol to examine the early pointed Gothic cathedral which though built of granite has beautiful and delicate ornamentation and fairly fine old glass. Edward liked it very much. Mr. Talbot Baines (a first cousin of Florence's fiancée Arthur Baines) called and said he would introduce them to the English Club. Dearman thought he must be living at Dinard for economical reasons. Thus the holiday continued till April 27 with the grown-ups making expeditions, sometimes taking the two older boys with them.

Linda, aged 8, remembered this holiday, particularly for being the first time that the young family made a combined attempt to tease their elder half sister Clara, whom they were forced to call Sissy, but privately for some unexplained reason called the Camel-leopard. The roof of La Conchée evidently had very elaborate tiles which resembled devils and this gave the children the idea that Clara, who was very religious, must be praying to the devil every morning. The suggestion was made just plain enough to cause Clara disquiet. Clara, encouraged by her father, made great efforts to be a mother to her small brothers and sisters, but somehow the traditions of their real mother were kept burning brightly in their hearts. Poor Clara: she was at this time invited to go on a private yacht for a Mediterranean cruise with comparative strangers. Dearman writes in his dairy "Sister [Eliza] and I both thought the offer too attractive to be refused, and we therefore telegraphed our acceptance." There is no mention of consulting Clara who considered herself a bad sailor.

Linda also remembered the shame when she and Violet got locked into a lavatory and had to be rescued by the footman Berry who climbed up the drain-pipe.

On April 21 Dearman wrote that they were all photographed by Ordinaire, Dinard, who took much pains to group them artistically. It is a kind of pyramid; Dearman stands at the back with one hand on the seated Clara's shoulder. Perched on some kind of platform parallel to Clara is Vivian with long hair and apparently dressed as a girl and clutching a boat. Jack is standing on the right looking at Vivian. Violet has been made to lean her head against Clara's breast. Percy sits beneath them on the equivalent of a straw bale while Linda sits on a chair opposite in a pretty velvet dress and holding a doll.

May 24. Bowden. The Campbells left this afternoon for London; she has a cold. They have been very nice. We did not talk much business. They have engaged a Mr Nutter for 12 months at £350 p.a. I am struck with the failure

The Birchall family at Dinard

of Campbell. He has not the grasp he had and seemed to have lost his
energy. He agrees in remarks about Oswald; but does not seem to have
much fight left in him. His health has been better; but he has not energy to
do much tricycling.

June 18.   Came up to town to stay with the Dyer-Edwardeses at 5 Hyde
Park Gate. He is very fond of the house. His father for whom he has a
veneration lived here and furnished it. Sandhurst his other house is to be put
up for auction. He used to be fascinated with that but the society is now too
exclusively military.

June 19.   Dyer-Edwardes and I had an afternoon in the Italian exhibition
which we admired very much.

On Sept 29 Dearman should have received the following letter.

Highnam Court
Gloucester
28th Sept. 88 (2 a.m. 29th)

Dear Mr Birchall
    It is my painful duty to write and tell you that my dear father passed
peacefully and painlessly away at 11 p.m. to-night.
    As one of his intimate friends I feel sure you will sympathize with us in
our great sorrow.
            Yours very truly
                E. Gambier Parry
                Major.

Dearman was away staying with Anna and Sophia Harris at Oxton for one of
their huge house parties; but he returned for Thomas Gambier Parry's funeral
on Oct. 3rd at Highnam. Parry was born in 1816. His first wife and young
children died and that is why he dedicated Highnam church to the Holy
Innocents. He married his second wife Ethelinda in 1851. His sons included Sir
Hubert Parry, the composer, and Sidney Gambier Parry the architect. Thomas
Gambier Parry is best known for his decorative painting in Ely Cathedral as
well as the frescoes at Highnam and in Gloucester Cathedral.

Nov. 24.   We made representations to the Emerises regarding the effects of
the close air in Upton church and suggested that there was some opening
which permitted exhalations from the flooded vaults to ascend into the
church. Eshelby quite agrees and says that he is always much more tired on
Sunday evening than on other days. [Readers of the *"Diary of a Cotswold
Parson"* will remember than when Mrs Howell, of Prinknash, who died in
the same sad sort of circumstances as Emily Birchall but some forty years
earlier, was buried, she was interred in a vault inside Upton church.]

Waller's report on the church subsequently stressed that the unwholesome smells in the church must come from the vaults below and render the building unhealthy. He proposed to put down 6 inches of asphalt all over the floor and lay wood blocks under the seats and stone paving in the passages.

Dearman visited Harehills about this time and reported that Emily's father was now extremely confused, mentally worse than before, and her mother now looked rather sadly anxious. John Jowitt died on Dec 30th. He was 77.

1889

Jack went to Eton for the first time on January 15. Dearman took him but when they got there they discovered it was a day too soon owing to their having misread Dr Dalton's letter. Mrs Dalton, however, was very kind.

During the beginning of this year Dearman suffered very much from gout. On February 24 he went to church after 5 weeks absence. His sister Sophy visited him and he records that they had some famous laughs, and Eliza, ever sensible, gave him sound advice. She reproached him about his nervousness concerning Clara's health. She never saw a girl looking more blooming and hoped that Clara would marry in his life time. She did not like the idea of Clara becoming an old maid and exposed to the persecution of those who might be attracted by her fortune.

There was a visit from Maida who was very much struck with the beauty of the views from Bowden, and appeared to take a great interest in the children. Her husband was studying at Jena under the most distinguished German evolutionists.

They went to an amateur theatrical performance at Painswick School room in which Mr & Mrs Scobell of Redmarley and Mr & Mrs Meath Baker of Hasfield took part. *"Freezing a mother-in-law* and *Naval engagements* were performed most admirably to the profit of the Convalescent Home, enlarged lately by Mr Seddon the vicar and his rich wife."

On May 1st Dearman rented No. 59 Pont Street for 3 months and there followed such entries in the diary as, "Clara went with her uncle and aunt Drummond to a great function at Buckhurst for the coming of age of Lord Cantalupe. A special train took a party of 30 or 40 down from town", and "I took Violet and Linda to Beckenham to lunch with Sophy. Weather and country equally beautiful. William [Atkinson] photographed us twice, first with a flash light in the house and secondly on tricycles in the garden. The sun shone in our faces; it can scarcely prove a great success."

May 27.   Went down to Bowden. Meeting of County Council.
  I went with Emeris into the church. The gallery, pews and pulpit all removed. The ground was strewed with rotten wood. We found a vault in the aisle by the door of our pew. It had 18 inches of water in it, and 2 coffins, one of Mr Byles[72] of Bowden Hall who died in 1835 and the other of a baby daughter who died in 1820. There are at least three other such vaults in the church which must be filled up and proper drains made.

On June 4th Dearman had his first experience of Eton's celebrations for the birthday of George III. "There was a cricket match going on of no importance". On June 20th Florence Jowitt was married to Arthur Baines at Bickley church. Dearman was accompanied by all three daughters. "Mother looked remarkably

---

[78] James Byles bought Bowden Hall in 1817.

well in face; but was sadly burdened by the great weight of her widow's mourning."

There followed two days at the Royal Agricultural Show at Windsor Great Park, where they had the boys out from school, dinner in London with Aldam Heaton, the Conversazione at the Royal Academy. A meeting of the Iowa Land Company, seeing the Princess of Wales at a Sale of Work, the Old Boys match at Sunningdale (Jack made 29 and Percy 26), a Royal Concert for the Shah of Persia, the Lambeth Palace Garden party, the Eton and Harrow cricket match at Lords, ". . . Eton very badly beaten. We did not think Michael Baker,[79] Billy Busfield or Jack looked at all well. Eton is I fear too relaxing for them." So the season passed; but it was obviously not as entertaining as when Emily was alive, and the habit of going to church twice on Sunday continued. On July 14 they went to St. Paul's to hear the new Archdeacon of London William Sinclair (brother of Clara's admirer John). "It was moderately interesting but rather long and had the most soporific effect on some of the canons."

Instead of returning home Dearman took the young family to Cromer for a' holiday. While there he heard from Mr Emeris that he had resigned from the living of Upton St. Leonards, giving as the only reason Dearman's remarks urging shorter and brighter services, after the restoration of the building. Dearman hoped his remarks had not had undue influence. The Bishop now offered the living to Edward Scobell of St. Luke's, Gloucester, a very fortunate choice for the Birchall family as it turned out.

August 8. Flower Show at the Playnes.[80] We went by train. The Midland station at Nailsworth is only a mile from Longfords which is in a singularly pretty situation. We found a remarkable show of flowers, fruit, table decorations and industrial arts. We were glad to meet Beatrice Potter[81] [the future Mrs Sidney Webb] with whom we had a good deal of talk in old times. The great and varied knowledge she has obtained during her temporary residence with the working classes in different parts of the country has made her more conservative and less socialistic. Hyndman calls her an advertizing fraud.

August 24. In the afternoon the boys and I walked up to Prinknash to 4 o'clock Service (Sunday). The new chapel was very full.

Sept 21. Campbell writes me that Kafka has returned from Canada and was immediately served with a notice from the Divorce Court. He appeared disspirited but offered to retire from the business if we preferred it to suffering from the reflected obloquy of unsavoury proceedings in court. I wrote and suggested that Campbell should approach his father-in-law Stockhardt

[79] Granville Bakers' eldest son, later father of Olive Lloyd Baker.
[80] Mrs Arthur Playne was an elder sister of Beatrice Potter.
[81] Notable both as a social researcher and reformer, she was one of the most influential of modern Socialists, and was at the centre of British intellectual and political life for nearly 70 years.

and try to get some arrangement to obviate the necessity of going through the exposé of the court; but both Kafka and his wife desire the custody of the only child a boy.

Oswald Birchall had of late been doing very little to help the business along owing to a prolonged and possibly hyperchondriacal illness. A friend of Eliza's had called at Oswald's house at Ilkley and reported seeing two servants and a gardener at work in the garden. "She is opposed to Oswald's proceedings, and cannot bear his wife, so poor and proud."

On October 4 Campbell saw Oswald's doctor. "His progress is very slow but he thinks he is gaining ground. He hopes he may be fit for business after Christmas, or it is doubtful if he will manage it at all. He is stout, sleeps well and has a good appetite."

Later in October Dearman met Kafka in Paris, and they discussed how the business was to carry on. Kafka was most anxious to get his father-in-law Stockhardt out of it, and neither knew if Oswald would ever be any use again.

The boys came home for the Christmas holidays in December, Jack with a capital report having come 4th in trials out of 280 in Remove and thus getting into the upper school. Mrs Hawkins went for a fortnight's holiday. She had her own family of children, little older than the Birchalls. Marie the Swiss maid [probably she who gave the Birchall girls such bad French accents, although they spoke fluently,] also went home. Dearman said he felt depressed on Christmas Day which always "seems to revive painful memories".

A most beautiful sunny day ushered in the new year and decade.

January 8.   Clara and Mrs Hawkins with all the children went in to the servants' party and had a good dance.

Jan 11.   We thought the Dyer-Edwardeses had left for Nice; but he tells me today his wife and Noëlle have been very ill with influenza.

This was the epidemic of Russian influenza which now made victims of the Birchall family, first Clara, Jack and Percy. The newspapers were full of melancholy accounts of the epidemic which seemed to attack the upper classes most, and the death column in the *Times* was crowded. Then Violet got it, and Mrs Hawkins and most of the servants including the French maid Eugénie who was usually bullied by the others. Even Craddock the butler hated foreigners. The Eton holidays were prolonged for an extra week. The unfortunate Oswald had returned from his wife's home in Ireland pretty well but now succumbed to the epidemic. Finally Linda's and Vivian's temperatures rose to the same heights as the rest of the family's, or nearly, Violet's still being 105 at 9 o'clock in the morning. This turned into pneumonia.

On February 7 Dearman went to the County Ball in Cheltenham without Clara who was not considered sufficiently recovered. There were "galaxies of pretty girls and the room decorated with Cypher's superb orchids".

On Feb 17 he set off with his brother and sister and of course Clara on a prolonged tour of the Riviera. By March 5 they had arrived at Nice and drove up to Fuon Santa the Dyer-Edwardes's villa, "a tremendous pull out of the town and takes nearly an hour. Edward and I walked all the last part. It is a handsome house surrounded by orange groves and flower gardens. We were most warmly received and had a pretty lunch which included Noëlle and her governess. Dyer-Edwardes spoke of the thrifty character of the people, the entire absence of appeals for charity, the badness and inefficiency of the gardeners and occasional dishonesty in selling the plants during the summer, and assurance in the autumn that they have died of the heat. He has made a fine rockery and is improving the place. They sell flowers from his farm." The Dyer-Edwardeses took them to various "At Homes" where they met "English, French and Russians all mixed together".

On March 12 they arrived at Menton and called on the Hanburys at La Mortola, and on the Ducies. Lady Ducie looked "the picture of rude health" and gave Clara flowers. A few days later they went to La Mortola again by invitation. "We got a very bad pair of horses that nearly turned round at the Custom House and in coming away charged a large stone and tree breaking the harness which had to be repaired with rope. Mr Hanbury devoted himself to us showing his treasures for about an hour. He has a room almost devoted to portraits presented to him by Royalties and to visitors' books. The portrait of his great uncle William Allen he places next to the Queen's because when the

Duke of Kent was embarrassed with debt, Mr Allen undertook to arrange with his creditors and succeeded in enabling the Duke of Kent to abandon his intention of taking his family to Canada. Had it not been for this good man's assistance our present Queen would have been born in Canada and thus been ineligible for ascending the throne. The Queen mentioned these circumstances to Mr Hanbury and told him how much her father loved and admired Mr Allen to the end of his life.

The soil seems miserably poor but with great diligence Hanbury has acclimatized an immense number of trees and plants from hot sunny climes previously unknown in Europe. His agaves are very fine and flower in about 12 years. He just cut a bloom stalk down, 30 ft. in height weighing 460 lbs."

They travelled on to Bordigherra where they found Mr Emeris who was reading prayers in the English church. In the cemetary they discovered the grave of Henry Hilton Green the former rector of Upton St. Leonards. Dearman thought it was a curious coincidence that Emeris should have "pitched up in the very place unknowingly where his predecessor in the living deceased". The whole story is indicative of the prevalence of the winter migration to the Continent among the more fortunate inhabitants of Gloucestershire, both churchmen (for there were English churches every-where) and laymen. In the space of a few days they had met their neighbours the Dyer-Edwardeses and the Ducies and their former rector at Upton, and his family.

They got home on April 2. "Bowden looked lovely, the garden bright and the conservatory gorgeous."

April 12.   We drove up to Minchinhampton where we tried the golf with Sir Edward Stanton and Queeny, afterwards drinking tea with them at the Culver House. They are moving shortly to Ashmead near Dursley.

April 14.   County Council. Much discussion on the making of main roads.

April 16.   Florence Somervell has a little boy[82] Susie was with her. This makes Mother a great grandmother for the first time.

Poor Florence Baines has been frightfully ill and had a still-born baby. Bright's disease of the kidneys.

May 1st.   Jack went back to Eton. Much as he enjoys his work and play at school he always seems to go back with a heavy heart and looks depressed days before leaving home. Dillworth and May Crewdson have been staying and appeared to enjoy the company of their more excitable cousins Jack and Percy.

---

[82] Theodore Howard Somervell, Medical missionary, Travancore. Joined Mount Everest expeditions in 1922 and 1924.

Family group with Bruno the St. Bernard

Percy under the gunnera leaves at Bowden

May 14.   Clara was driven to her music lesson in Gloucester this afternoon by Archer with the pair of cobs, and near St. James church Victor had a little frolic, quite playfulness; but he got his near hind leg over the pole and thus frightened they bolted. Archer and Berry (footman) pulled at the reins with all their might, and after galloping a couple of hundred yards they pulled them into a wooden fence. After plunging a little they succeeded in getting the harness unfastened; the only positive damage done to the Victoria was the breaking of the splinter bar. Clara was no worse but only frightened. She went into Mr Sweetapples and was eventually driven home by Mr Sampson who has performed the same kind office in two other cases of late, for the Hyett's little girl who was thrown from her horse and has concussion of the brain, and Ethel Ancrum who broke her nose in a pony phaeton when coming down Matson Pitch.

Scobell is going to open some evening classes for men and boys, and wishes to have the Village Room once a week.

May 28.   Capital Dog Show at Gloucester. Over 100 exhibits of St. Bernards including the own brother of our Bruno.

In August there was a Royal Archaeological Congress in Gloucester. A Mr and Mrs Theodore Bent stayed at Bowden.

August 14.   I went with Bent to Charles Bathurst's Lydney Park, a lovely spot and outdoor Roman remains. We had Arthur Evans[83] and Oman[84] of Oxford. Bent was at school with William, John and Hugh Sinclair. John was rather the dunce of the family but he likes him much the best. The others are so very ambitious, always looking for titled people. He believes if the Baroness Burdett Coutts had not married, William would have taken her. He thinks William and Janet very pedantic; Hugh is very clever and likely to make a name. Bent heard of John's proposing to Clara before I went abroad and expected all would have been settled. I remarked on his nervousness and love-making by deputy.

During August Dearman had a tutor to keep the boys occupied, and in September he took them to Scotland.

Sept 20.   Jack and Percy left Oban by express for London. We were sorry to part with them. They have been exceedingly agreeable since we have been away and enjoyed the trips to Staffa, Iona and Skye which was a great experience for them and above all going on Mr Stevenson's yacht.

---

[83] Sir Arthur Evans (1851–1941). He was keeper at the Ashmolean 1884–1908.
[84] Sir Charles Oman (1860–1946). Oxford historian.

Oct 25.   Wrote to Oswald, and said I felt very deeply the wrong he had done me in keeping up house and paying servants the year he had spent away. I thought most men with a scrupulous sense of honour would consider that all that was not spent on actual necessities belonged to a fund towards making some payment in discharge of the debt he had incurred to me.

I was not inclined to relax the words of our partnership. I was keenly alive to the struggles I have had in his interest to keep him square for a number of years, home influences I feared have pulled in another direction; but he has at last arrived at a crisis so far as expenditure is concerned for he has drawn £9 more than the limit for 12 months and the exchequer will remain empty until 31st March.

Nov 15.   Attended at Court; another futile prosecution of an old woman for cruelty to a donkey.

While in Nice earlier in the year Dearman wrote the following letter to his children.

My very dear Jack & Company
The last letters received from Eton and Sunningdale were very welcome but what were you thinking of to ride upon an engine? Had that driver been seen by the superintendent of the South Western Railway or a Director he would probably have received his congé which being interpreted into the vernacular means getting the sack, so I hope none of the quintette I am addressing will try such an experiment again.

You never saw anything so confusing as the clocks here. The sun arrives here 20 minutes before it gets to Paris because we are so much to the east; but the railway insists on having the clocks kept to Paris time and the town are equally determined to have their clocks correct by solar time, so the clocks have two hands, one steel the other brass, and one is 20 minutes before the other.

There are no end of street singers. The markets are full of superb flowers and every garden is brilliant with ripe oranges and lemons. The Dyer-Edwardes have been most sociable. Noëlle and her friend divide their attention and anxieties between two life-like dollies, a monkey and a lovely little marmozet. We all send dearest love
                    Your ever affectionate Father.

Vivian, Lindaraja and Violet on ponies, Jack, Clara and Percy standing at the front door of Bowden Hall

Clara driving her Norwegian cobs with Archer in attendance

January 26.   I went to Wotton Asylum to see a man called Taylor, who was married at Upton Church on Saturday to a good-looking young woman, and at 2 o'clock in the afternoon was declared to be insane and taken off to Wotton. He is an engineer at Fielding & Platts and he met the girl at Leeds when doing some work at the Great Northern station. He corresponded, and led her to believe he had made some great discovery and would be much enriched. She believed all he said and had lived two months with him at Weston-super-Mare. The strong point was that he tried to kill his mother when she wished to prevent the marriage.

This January Percy joined Jack at Dalton's house at Eton. Dearman went to London till the middle of February. On 21 March he attended Jack's confirmation at Eton. Everyone spoke warmly of his boys and said they were doing very well and Mr Dalton said he wished he had more of them.

It was about this time that the girls at Bowden wrote letters to their brothers about the problems of keeping white mice.

"My dearest Percy
   We are going to drown your youngest mouse as she always quarrels with every mouse so has to live alone, also she kills all her children and bites our fingers when we put them near her. It would be cruel to sell her as she is quite young and will have lots more children and no doubt eat them all. We will, however, wait till Tuesday to hear if we may act like this, and hope you will say we can!
   Yesterday at dancing class Bruno came right in, was not it funny. Your very loving Violet.
   P.S. Give my love to Jack"

The census taken on April 5th reveals that Dearman was 62, living on his own means. Clara was 29, Jack 15, Percy 14, Violet 12, Linda 11, and Vivian 6. Mrs Fanny Hawkins, children's nurse, was a widow aged 41, William Craddock the butler was 36, Harry Berry, footman 21, Ellen Connor, cook 50, Eugénie Raymond, Clara's maid was 25, Head housemaid Mary Stephens, 39, and there were three other living-in maids. Harold Atkinson, a nephew aged 22, was staying.
   The next day Mrs Hawkins took the five children to stay with the Theodore Howards at Westleigh, Bickley. They returned having had a grand time, Susie was always a popular aunt, and they brought the news that their cousins Dora and Millie Howard were determined to go out as missionaries, if they could be passed by a doctor as fit for the work. They wished to go to Japan. Dearman says he is "cast down and it is a deplorable job; but the parents while regretting it can only admire their self-sacrifice."
   In June Dearman took Clara to Norway, staying at Leeds on their return. "Mrs Heaton gave me a piece of silk from Burmah. She is to have a blue

Nankin pot in exchange." During this visit Benson Jowitt told Dearman that Campbell was looking very depressed. Benson's sympathy seemed to draw Campbell out, and he told him how faithfully he had served the firm for 20 years. He found it very heartbreaking to lose all in winding up. Benson was touched with his trouble and said, "My brother-in-law is a generous man; he will never allow you to lose. You may make your mind easy. I will talk it over with him." Benson then said to Dearman, "I hope you will shield Campbell from loss and I strongly urge you to let Campbell know to relieve him from anxiety."

Dearman then copied out in his diary the letter he wrote to Benson as if to justify himself.

Dear Benson
   You are the most conspicuously honest open hearted man I know, and I love you accordingly but you allow your feelings to run away with your judgement. You have unwittingly done me much injury. I took Campbell, an accountant into a prosperous business. His share amounted to many thousands of pounds a year and was increased in every fresh partnership. From being nobody he has had a position of visible head of the business for many years. He has been party to if not chief instigator in getting rid of the only money makers I have had, Webb, Cheetham, and Warburg. When left to himself and Oswald, they have done no good and it is no business of mine that he has spent his money. If partnership means division of profits but lumping losses we have not yet understood it. I have been in business since 1857 and the intention I had of probably giving him a small annuity will not now be regarded by him as an act of pure generosity when he is told by you that your brother-in-law ought to hold him free from losses, and this on an ex parte statement and not as a referee. It was a terribly injudicious step and explains something I have found it difficult to explain in the tone of Campbell's letters. An injudicious friend may sometimes do you as bad a turn as an evil minded one.

On August 26 Oswald sent a circular to his customers saying the new style of the firm would be Oswald Birchall & Co, and the business will be carried on at the same address as before, Wellington Street, Leeds and at Brick Lane Mills, Bradford, in conjunction with Mr. A. Priestman and Mr J.J. Jagger. "Our works are fitted up with the most modern machinery and the looms are of the most improved and perfect description. We intend to devote our attention mainly to tweeds, fancy coatings, trouserings and sea-side suitings in woollen and worsteds."
The children stayed at Harehills in the summer holidays and were a great success with their grandmother. They returned on September 14. "It was a miserably wet gloomy day and Leeds looked dismal enough with its mantel of smoke, clouds and rain." Dearman was seen of by Campbell and Oswald "for the last time under present conditions".

Eton College boys had a week extra holiday by request of the German Emperor.

In October Dearman dined in Oxford with A.L. Smith, the historian, who was very interested in the common fields at Upton. "He is not only instructing his pupils in ancient land tenures but is writing on the subject. He said to see a farmer who holds land of his own in common fields, and works them, would surprise and delight his pupils. I asked him to come and see us and study the subject on the spot and I would introduce him to the oldest inhabitants."

At the end of the year Dearman had his and Clara's portraits painted by John Collier in London.

Dearman Birchall by Collier   Bishop Ellicott of Gloucester

Clara Sophia Birchall   Eliza Sibson Birchall

1892

On March 1st Mrs Hawkins left, to visit her sister who was married to a colonel in the 17th Lancers in Ireland, and thence to a new position, again looking after motherless children. Dearman says his children "have kept up very well; but it is a great sorrow to everyone of them".

The Bradford Old Bank having refused to loan Oswald Birchall more than £750 on the strength of a guarantee of £500 from his father-in-law Mr Featherstonhaugh, Dearman wrote consenting not to make any further claims on Oswald for the £7,000 he owed him, on payment of the £750 plus his collection of postage stamps (that Jack had wished to purchase from him). Kafka having been let off his debt for £150, and Campbell freed of all the loss on the mill Dearman thought he stood to lose about £12,000 on the winding up of the business.

March 27.   The Bishop confirmed a large party at Upton church, about 50 from Upton and some from Matson and Cranham. The Rector appears to have acted with the greatest energy in preparation for the Confirmation and there were a number of adults including Mrs Archer the coachman's wife.

Marchant the butler gave notice. He feels that having lost his wife he is more free to take a larger place, one partly in London during the season. He feels he could not have his children comfortably in a cottage here; it could be dull.

Berry gave me notice; seems a little discontented and thinks I have not appreciated him. He wants more wages. I expressed regret and fear that he is making a mistake.

April 19.   Beatrice Potter is about to marry Mr Webb a progressive member of the London County Council.

April 30.   I went over to see Eliza. She was brooding on the difficulties we had brought about on ourselves by parting with Mrs Hawkins, and did not endorse any of our plans. Clara drove her Norwegian cobs.

Violet, Linda and Vivian were sent to Weston-super-Mare with their new governess Miss Bindon and Eugénie; the boys went back to Eton, taller and heavier. Dearman's sister-in-law Amy Drummond gave birth to her 10th child, and he and Clara went abroad.

On 12th May, Linda (aged 12) wrote to Clara

Dearest Sissy

I hope you are enjoying yourself. We enjoyed Father's letter very much this morning. Did you see the Drummonds and did Elsie (one of the elder of the seven daughters) talk about the children. I wonder whatever she would say to see us this morning paddling in our brown holland pinnafores on the sands. The very best thing in Weston is "The Baths". They are beautiful.

Weston is not very full now so it is much nicer. Violet and I get up at 7 o'clock and get through as many lessons as we can. What a lovely crossing you must have had if it was like it was here. We have such very nice rooms here, so very different to the Whitby rooms. We went to Anchor Head yesterday and drew. There are a lot of ships on the sea now. I hope you like Berlin very much. With very much love ever your very loving Linda.

In June Dearman was back in London. Duveen wished to buy his whole china collection as he had such demand from America and he now had a very fine shop in New York. John Sinclair dined with them on June 16, and on June 19 Mr & Mrs Wykeham of Tythrop House (the parents of Jack's future wife Adela) made themselves most agreeable and asked Dearman to spend a night with them when they would take him to see the china at Thame House, the seat of his elder brother Herbert Wykeham-Musgrave.

In August they all went to Etretat for a month's sea bathing holiday interspersed with cycling expeditions to Rouen and other places, and ragging Clara. John Sinclair was their first visitor at Bowden on their return; but he "did not pay Clara any marked attention".

Jack and Percy returned to Eton. "They have been the life of the party all the holidays and seem to enjoy nothing so much as being with the family." Dearman then stayed at Tortworth. "Ducie told me he was 63 and he had always taken me to be old enough to be his uncle." By this time, and certainly judging from the Collier portrait, Dearman was looking extremely venerable with his great white side-burns. The Bishop also was getting old. Dearman describes a dinner party at Bowden when the Bishop dropped asleep during dinner, after dinner, and in the drawing room. Mrs Ellicott, however, and their daughter Rosalind sang two duets, and Dr Bower played with great taste and feeling.

Dec 11.   I supped with the Rector (Scobell). We afterwards took a cigarette or two and had a long talk. He told me of his doings but far from showing a vain glorious spirit he was very humble. His ministrations have put another face on Upton, and scarcely a house in the parish but has some representative attending church. He goes visiting all over from 7 to 9 p.m. and he generally gets a cup of tea in some cottage or other. Many men are coming to church and even Communion that never came before. The Bible Class is full, the club full and Dora Scobell's Mothers Meeting a wonderful success. Archer and his wife come arm in arm to every communion. He said he often took 8 hours to prepare a sermon. Thinking it over I wrote and congratulated him on the great and noble work he had done in the parish.

1893

April 13. This is an extraordinary season. We have not had a drop of rain for about six weeks and almost constant sunshine with coldish nights, frost even up to 10°; but the wonderful dryness in the air has prevented the blossom suffering. The country is in a blaze from the pears, plums and even apples. The horse-chestnut on the drive close to the house is in full flower. The gunneras are putting up their noses; wallflowers and lilacs are out. We had asparagus on the 1st April. The land has worked remarkably well and none complain except at prices which are most unprofitable except for hay and we have had constantly to buy for the stables; I have paid £5.15.0 a ton.

The children have been a week at Buckholt without any servant, taking lessons in all useful things. They have had superb weather and the expedition seems to have been a great success. In the afternoon I tricycled up and found them returning from the Roman pavement at Witcombe.

Dearman went to London in May, at the end of which time he had a letter from Linda.

Dearest Father

Thank you very much for the very pretty hats and nice cloaks. We like them very much. The cloaks are so comfortable. They go very well with the new dresses. We are so looking forward to seeing you to-morrow. It seems such a long time ago since we saw you off at the station. Vivian has begun a little Latin because Miss Bindon thinks it will help him so at school. You will be glad to hear that it rained a great deal on Sunday and yesterday. Mr Keen is very glad.

We are just going to ride to Gloucester with the letters. With much love. Ever your very loving daughter

Linda

Dearman returned just in time for the Bath & West of England Show which was at Gloucester on May 31st. Dearman's entries did not, however, do very well. "Our Jersey bull was an utter failure", he says, "and our two samples of butter were never named. The Norwegian ponies being 14 hands could only be shown as hacknies in which they appeared quite out of place and excited some ridicule. Cook should have known what he only found out when there that he was not allowed to drive them except singly."

John Sinclair who had been at the Show, turned up at Bowden in the afternoon and had to sleep in another guest's dressing room. He left next day. There is no comment; but he is back again on June 5th. "His appearance was calculated to set people talking, and there is no doubt he is voicing a 12 year attachment in Clara's ears. She apparently listens with responsive ears." The next day the engagement was official. "A marriage has been arranged between the Rev. John Stewart Sinclair, vicar of St. Dionis, Fulham, grandson of the late Right Hon. Sir John Sinclair, Baronet of Ulbster, Caithness and younger brother of the Archdeacon of London, and Clara, eldest daughter of Mr J.D. Birchall of Bowden Hall, Gloucester."

Dearman's own comment was, "it is very generous of me to receive him so heartily for I cannot bear to reflect on the loss of my child who has been as a wife and most genial companion to me and as a mother to my children these past 8 years."

The children's grandmother Deborah Jowitt was staying at Bowden at the time and she wrote to her daughter Florence Baines.

My darling Florence

John Sinclair was most pleasant and unreserved. He talked so pleasantly and openly, he has quite won all hearts and Clara seems joyfully happy. He has been in love with her for 12 years, but never really proposed to her till last week. It is a blessing he left her to attend to her duties, since it seems, she is as much in love as he is. I was amazed when she told me they intend to be married in August, but now I find Dearman thinks it had better be soon. The trial of losing her would become no better. He is being very unselfish and says there is no one he would like so much as a son-in-law. The children are much interested and are pleased with the excitement. I think they will go on as they are for the present. All are attached to and value Miss Bindon the governess. Vivian goes to school in September and Dearman we know, knows more about housekeeping than any man.

Eliza has written Clara such a sweet, Christian, motherly letter. I think she is a really beautiful unselfish woman. There has been no rain since we arrived at Bowden. Yesterday Susie and I called upon Mrs Archer and Mrs Keen. The former had so much to show, splendid table cloth and tea service, photos and endless histories of her daughter and son-in-law and wonderful baby in Simla. We seemed as though we might stay all day. The gardens are beautiful and the roses splendid. We enjoy the fine strawberries three times a day. The dear children are very nice. Violet is taller than Susie and Linda as tall. They all look well and enjoy rowing on the pond so much they "cannot imagine how they did without it". They rowed me about one afternoon and seemed much pleased. They tidied the boat and put rugs down and it was so comfortable I quite enjoyed it. Susie had a Bible Class with them for half an hour before church this morning and they seemed interested.

With dearest love your own tender
Mother.

In September Theodore Crewdson his brother-in-law came to Gloucestershire with the intention of buying an estate. The first one they looked at, Syde, proved to be exactly what was required. Dearman wrote, "It looked lovely, and we were amazed at the great amount and quality of timber. Theodore seems much smitten with the property which consists of 750 acres."

On Sept 22 Dearman took Vivian to school at Sunningdale accompanied by Theodore Crewdson and his daughter Lily with whom Vivian "talked away".

On the 26th Thomas Dyer, aged 27, arrived as butler, and was to remain for the rest of his long life, and on October 2 Dearman met the honeymooners at Oxton after they had been on a round of smart visits to Sinclair relations in Scotland. They were in the "highest spirits".

Jack was now 16th in seniority at Eton out of over a thousand boys, weighed 12 stone and was 6′ 2″ tall. Percy was also over 12 stone and over 6 foot.

In October Theodore Crewdson bought the whole of the Syde estate including the advowson of the living and perpetual presentation, for what appears now to be the tiny sum of £9,000. So it came about that the two widowed brothers-in-law became neighbours, very different though they were. Theodore was short, ugly and very sporting; Dearman tall, good-looking and aesthetic. Theodore immediately started hunting and enjoyed a run across the Syde estate.

1894

Jack was sent to Florence for the Christmas holidays with a tutor from Cheltenham College. Clara came home and she, her father and Percy had a great talk about professions. To narrow the discussion they eliminated a number that they would not entertain, specially school-masters, manufacturers, surgeons, doctors, civil service, Army and Navy. What remained for discussion was the Church, the Bar, and the Colonies. Percy became a regular soldier, and so one wonders what he must have thought about this kind of talk.

The harassed father discussed governesses with Florence Baines who said she had nothing against Miss Bindon, only she did not seem to have the mastery of the girls and allowed Violet to argue with her. Linda could remember pushing Miss Bindon's boat out into the pond having removed the oars, and then watching her frantic struggles from the bank. On February 2 he interviewed Miss Leonhardt who was dressed uncompromisingly in black, more than middle-aged and a little formidable; but his friends the Venables at Lincoln recommended her. At the same time Dearman thought he could entice the Venables girls to accompany him to Paris; but they would not. However he engaged Miss Leonhardt, at £120 p.a. — she to pay for her own washing — and received congratulations on the appointment from Lady Guise who evidently knew her. On March 2 Violet and Linda were confirmed but Dearman's gout was too bad for him to attend. He said the girls were "deeply interested".

Eliza, who was called Auntie by her nieces, had written to Linda in preparation.

> Lanesfield
> January 29th 1894
>
> My darling Linda
> I remember so well the happiness of receiving you, a dear little baby, in my arms and was so pleased when Dyer placed you in them. You have a very warm place in my heart and I think you have a warm heart and will return it to me. There is no happiness like that derived from love and now I trust you are longing to give a full heart of love to your Saviour. He will in return for your heart fill you with a joy a worldly person knows nothing of. Pray that you may now be enabled to open your heart to Him. He gives so freely and has loved you with such an everlasting love, all trials which will surely come are sanctified. But, dear Linda, should this appear more than you are prepared to seek you are not bound to be confirmed so early as Violet — you might like to take more time to think whether you really wish to give yourself and take up your Cross and follow Christ. It needs real self denial often, it means you must strive to love God with all your heart and your neighbour as yourself. That means a great deal of thought for others and often denying what you most care for. [The end of the letter has not survived; but Linda's reactions are obvious — seed like this did not fall on stony ground in her case.]

There was some more good news for the girls. On April 9th Annie Worsfold arrived as young lady's maid at £20 p.a. She was to remain with them for a great many years. Miss Leonhardt found "both girls were backward especially in history and geography and they had no idea of concentration. Violet is not at all self conscious. Linda is often thinking and asking what she should do. She has a greater sense than Violet of what is fitting. Linda is a great help to Violet and in return she is devoted to Linda. Both are very interesting characters but very different. They have little interest in really good reading. Neither of them have good ears for language and Violet none whatever for music and it was very wise to drop it. Violet has a gift for composition and wrote an amusing essay on the comparative merits of pen and sword. Miss L. has had one fracas with Violet. Neither of them have ever been sulky with her. Violet would do very well if sent to school. Linda is a most charming child in every way." This really shows the great disadvantages girls in these circumstances suffered from lack of a proper education, particularly if we compare this report with those of their brothers who did so very well at school.

This was the year Dearman was High Sheriff of Gloucestershire. The Assizes started on June 30. Mr Justice Hawkins had the reputation of being the most casual judge on the Bench and most severe on the Sheriffs if they failed instantly to attend to the plans he was constantly altering. Dearman waited all the morning at home and his servants at the Bell Hotel when they received a message that the Judge had changed his plans and would go to London in the afternoon, and not return to open the Commission till 12.30 on Monday. Dearman supposed that John Sinclair, his Chaplain, would now not be required to preach his Cathedral sermon till November although he had already arrived specially to preach the following day.

When they did get started the following week Dearman complains of the box he had to sit in with so little room for legs, sword and hat. Sir Henry Hawkins, however, never complained so long as he was protected from draughts, and not a window was allowed to be opened. "We had a wearisom day of nasty cases and the Court was as close, stuffy and disagreeable as hundreds of dirty men and closed windows could make it."

Dearman seems to have been away from home more than ever, and writing rather alarming notes to Violet and Linda. "As you are coming out as Mistress Violet and Mistress Lindaraja you will have to furbish up some suitable head gear and look pretty smart for the Matson affair. I think I mentioned that 14 August is arranged for our garden party. When the answers come you will have to open them, though addressed to me, and send me careful lists of who accepts and who declines.

The roses Keen sent to Arundel House [Clara's house in Fulham] either being picked too full, or packed unsuitably, all fell to pieces and were absolutely worthless."

Dearman's first grandson Ronald was born at Arundel House on September 5th. It was the same day he himself led an expedition of staff from Bowden to Malvern consisting of 26 people. "Only Webber the new gardener stopped to look after the garden, the groom Alfred Jeffries would not go, and Mrs

Godwin was the only person left in the house except Mrs Broomfield and her sisters in the laundry."

A great deal of gratuitous advice was given about names and godparents for the baby. Dearman favoured John Brook and Violet as godmother; but the Archdeacon of London recommended Ronald Sutherland and Lady Glasgow or Lady Caithness as godmother. The parents tactfully picked a compromising course between the two choosing the Archdeacon's names with Brook thrown in, but Violet as godmother. The christening was in a public service in which John baptized five children, the last being his own. Violet undertook her duties with great seriousness, and Dearman stood proxy for Sir John Colquhoun who was detained in Scotland.

The next Assizes were in November and the judge was Mr Justice Matthews. Jack came from Oxford and Percy was sent back from Eton because of the floods. The judge was a Roman Catholic and so there was no state procession to the cathedral; but John Sinclair delivered his sermon. Dearman hired a pair of state horses, 17 hands high, from Wimbush, Belgrave Square, for the occasion, and when he with Clara and John dined with the Judge his equipment was much admired.

The year started off with the High Sheriff's Bal Poudré on January 1st. Evidently Dearman was well pleased with it. "The best Ball ever given in Gloucester. Cypher's orchids etc. etc."

In February Dearman was discussing with Miss Leonhardt, Clara, Florence Baines, Mrs Ancrum and anyone else interested the advisability of sending his daughters to a first-class school for a year before coming out. Mrs Power's school at Eastbourne was decided upon and they were to go in September.

On February 13 Dearman, with Scobell as chaplain because John was too busy to leave his parish in London, met Mr Justice Grantham's train and escorted him to his lodgings. This was after meeting an earlier train in which the Judge did not appear and waiting about at the Bell Hotel. There is no mention of an under-sheriff making these kind of arrangements, as he would have done in later years. It was a very cold night and Scobell had a chill.

The sentences passed by Judge Grantham seemed to Dearman to be heavier than those of Judge Matthews whose sentences had appeared inadequate.

March 4 was Linda's fifteenth birthday. "She had a little party of village children, three Dyers, Joneses, and Patience Barnfield. They were all very nice looking and well behaved little folks."

Dearman was one of the Aldermen on the County Council whose term of office expired on March 16.

Jack and Percy's friends who came to stay at Bowden made him feel uncomfortable. They were either silent or chaffing; no serious attempts at conversation were made. The difference in age between him and his young family was trying to both, and Dearman became more easily offended. Jack now quite often accompanied him to dinner parties around Gloucester and it was not unusual for there to be a séance afterwards which was obviously faked and caused the hosts great amusement. However they seem to have sailed rather near the wind sometimes when for instance it was announced that there was a gentleman walking about who wished to make himself known. A note was passed signed by the well known initials of the late W.P. Price. It said "I am grieved with Alice for what she has done." Dearman appears to have thought these macabre affairs were amusing. Not for long, however; he was soon off to stay with the Dyer-Edwardeses in Nice, and here he seems to come to life in a completely different way. But this book is not meant to be about the South of France, and we have to turn over many pages in the diary, particularly as the rest of the summer was spent mostly in London with a visit to Scotland in the middle.

Then came the summer holidays. Percy went to stay with the Vereys at Twyford for most of August. Henrietta Verey was sister-in-law to John Sinclair's sister Helen Hasell, and her son Hal was at Eton with Percy. The end of August was the season of these crushingly boring garden parties which took place day after day, and for all the same people.

A breath of fresh air is provided, of course, by Dyer-Edwardes, who came to call from Prinknash on his white Egyptian donkey, prettily caparisoned, in order to invite Jack to stay in September to shoot stags. For Violet and Linda

Dearman Birchall as High Sheriff

"Dyer-Edwardes came from Prinknash on his white
Egyptian donkey, prettily caparisoned"

their escape to school at Eastbourne must have been wonderful indeed. It was the kind of school where they kept horses and the girls were free to gallop for miles on the South Downs. Dearman wrote sympathetically after the first week. "Dearest Linda has kept me alive to her movements and I can quite realize her condition of home sickness and interest in her new surroundings alternating."

1896

Dearman was an invalid at the beginning of the year owing to having injured his leg in a fall, and this meant that he had to abandon all engagements like going to stay with the Dyer-Edwardes in Nice.

Tom Dyer-Edwardes was the new High Sheriff and he gave a Costume Ball. It was thought there were far more good costumes because the High Sheriff gave a carte blanche to De Freville, master of the Cotswold Hounds, to invite Cheltenham families. However the supper was said to be very bad, not a turkey or a fowl, only made-up dishes, and the London waiters were atrocious. Dearman heard all the gossip, though he was confined to his room with his leg up. Linda's black cat spent one evening in his room, and showed great skill in capturing a mouse which had been annoying him.

The girls visited their Howard aunts who wrote approvingly to Dearman of their appearance, manners, and bright and cheerful demeanour. He executed a codicil leaving Emily's jewels to be divided between Violet and Linda.

In March Dearman was able to resume attendance at the various lunatic asylum meetings. The Assizes were moved to Cheltenham on account of the prevalence of smallpox in Gloucester. There were supposed to be about 50 cases in a week, and the terror was very great. The shops were losing their custom which went to Cheltenham or Stroud, and many people never went into the City. Dearman was re-vaccinated. He attended an Infirmary meeting, and was told that all the smallpox nurses from London were fully engaged, indeed overworked in private houses. For light relief he called on the Tidswells at Haresfield Court and found their new drawing room by Waller in very good taste and very pretty.

In May he took Percy, who had just passed into Magdalen College Oxford, on a visit to Paris. At a polo match in the Bois, Dearman says he had seen "nothing as beautiful as the fashion and dresses since the Empire fell".

In June Jack entertained the whole family at Oxford including the attractive Noëlle Dyer-Edwardes[85] on a most sumptuous picnic on the river. A somewhat similar picnic was organized for all the domestics at Bowden in Cirencester Park, returning by Syde. The weather was fine and a party of 28 said they had enjoyed it, and did not get back till 10.45 p.m.

Violet and Linda came home in August and were delighted with their new bicycles. They accompanied their father to a cricket match at Barnwood and sat with the patients. At the end of the holidays everyone was sad to part with Vivian (now 12). He had been remarkably good and greatly enjoyed them. The animals at Bowden now included three Iceland ponies and two Highland heifers just bought.

An address was presented to Jack by the village on the attainment of his majority. It was signed by 200 and was brought up by a deputation of four,

---

[85] Noëlle later married the Earl of Rothes. She was rescued from the Titanic when it sank.

Canon Scobell, John Bellows, Job Morris and Smith, foreman on the roads, representing the Village Council.

"We the undersigned residents of Upton St. Leonards desire to offer you our hearty congratulations on attaining your majority. We earnestly trust that you may be enabled to pass through what we hope will be a long and prosperous life in a manner — as your youth has already given promise — worthy of the name your Father has made honourable and beloved."

Percy went up to Magdalen, saying his intention was to become a clergyman. The President wrote to Dearman "I have seen your son. I like his looks and I think he should do well."

In November Dearman wrote to Percy from Brussels. "I hope Jack will go in heartily for the debating society. Nothing but practise will give facility in speaking which is so desirable an accomplishment."

On Dec 5 Dearman had a bad fall on his tricycle at Prinknash. They thought he might have broken his thigh but he had not. Later Mrs Edwardes tried to persuade him to let her take Violet and Linda to parties with Noëlle; but he would not. "I had to decline and am not disposed to give way." As he died the next year, and the girls were put into a year's mourning, they never had much chance of "coming out".

1897

In February Violet and Linda accompanied their father to Hyères. They stayed at the Hotel de L'Hermitage (et Costebelle) and engaged a lady to give them lessons in French speaking; but Violet developed a cough and temperature, and had to have an English nurse. She had pneumonia.

On March 10th they moved to Fuon Santa the Dyer-Edwardes' villa at Nice. Dearman wrote, "Violet bore the journey well. It is unfortunate she thinks she cannot sit with her back to the engine; it is so much more draughty." The next day Dearman says, "We saw the Queen drive in an open landau to the new Hotel Excelsior Regina. There was quite a large body of troops out and the streets were well-lined with spectators. She was dressed in black and white feathers in her bonnet. Princess Beatrice accompanied her. Another carriage contained the Moonshee and his servant, and I think there was a Scotch gillie in this carriage."

Later Dearman reported that Tom Dyer-Edwardes had been much agitated by reading Manning's Life. Mrs E. thought it would set him against Rome; but some arguments there used seemed to him unanswerable and "he is waiting anxiously to see what Gladstone has to say on the subject of the Anglican orders." Tom acted as server to the Revd. W. Penrice, in black cassock, short surplice bordered with deep and handsome lace. "His head, thickly covered with hair, has a circular baldness like the tonsure, and his face with a somewhat severe and melancholy cast, made him look every inch a priest."[86]

They got back to Bowden on April 17th. Clara had a second son on May 27; but on June 11th Dearman died. Jack wrote in his father's diary "Father died today. His illness was not understood by the doctors and afterwards was said to have been typhoid or some low fever. He was not in pain at the end, and fully prepared for the change."

---

[86] Thomas Dyer-Edwardes became a Roman Catholic and left Prinknash to the Benedictines.

Linda Birchall in 1898

EPILOGUE
LINDA BIRCHALL'S DIARY FOR 1898

The situation at Bowden in 1898 was unusual in that Jack the owner was still an undergraduate at Oxford, with another brother Percy at Oxford and the youngest Vivian at Eton, and two sisters Violet and Linda at home.

Jan. 1st. 1898. This morning Violet and I went to church and apart from Canon Scobell were the only congregation. We bicycled to Gloucester afterwards. The roads were disgusting. Went into Watson's and were photographed, *cabinets* and *cartes de visite*. We went to the Parish Tea this evening, coming back about 10.15.

January 13th. Violet and I shopped in Gloucester. We bought the Band of Hope[87] prizes. Jack, Violet and I went a drive with the ponies whom we are going to call Diamond and Jubilee. Jack went to dine at Prinknash.

January 14th. This morning Noëlle came down from Prinknash for lunch. We had Jack's horrid red old "land and water" put into a tart for dinner. It was a joke when he opened it. [It was a hat.]
We went and met Mrs Annesley;[88] she seems very pleasant.

January 15th. We had the Band of Hope treat in the Reading Room. It went off well, prize giving, games and tea. We enjoyed it so much. Canon Scobell was there, and Jack and Vivian also came for part of the time.

Sunday January 16th. I took the Sunday School class. There were sixteen big boys there, and I had not prepared a proper lesson as I did not know I was going to take it.

January 21st. We have had a very melancholy day. Percy went back to Oxford this morning and Jack this afternoon. Percy had to row this afternoon.
Felt very sad and low. I practised hard [the piano].

Linda's daily entries always ended with a note of thankfulness for something which had occurred during the day. On this occasion she simply wrote "that this day is over."

---

[87] An organization to encourage tee-totallers.
[88] The new hired chaperone.

January 26th. We went to Cheltenham and arranged our classes at the College. We saw Miss Beale.[89] We have arranged a French literature class, 10–11. French 11–12. and elocution half an hour after lunch. Literature class difficult but nice, it is the Cambridge class. We have our grammar and elocution alone.

February 2nd. Went to Gloucester in the brougham for my music lesson, the first with Mr. Brewer.[90] I arrived having forgotten my music, awful moment, however Violet brought it after me on her bicycle. Mr. Brewer very kind. I played badly.

Miss Morris[91] came to lunch and was so nice, Noëlle to tea. Played billiards. (D.G) that I had a nice music lesson.

February 12th. Went to a lecture in Cheltenham by Nansen.[92] He is such a splendid man, and his courage and endurance must be marvellous. Lord Ducie took the chair. Read Nansen's book *Farthest North*.

There then followed a short visit to Clara Sinclair in Richmond Park, a day's outing to Cambridge, and a visit to a girls' club, "poor girls, terribly rough".

March 21st. Percy came home this evening. The servants presented him with a dressing case of crocodile and most lovely fittings, for his 21st birthday.

April 7th. Had my last music lesson for this term. I drove the ponies down. They were fearfully fresh and ran into a hedge and also on to the pavement in Gloucester. I could not hold them a bit.

April 16th. Jack and I rode to Cheltenham via Churchdown, Badgeworth and Pollard Oaks; we came back by Churchdown and Barnwood. The cobbs went splendidly.

April 18th. Jack and I rode to Syde to tea with the Crewdsons. Went by Prinknash Hill, Cranham Woods and Caudle Green.

April 21st. Jack and I rode to Bisley via Painswick, and back by Cranham. [The next day Jack returned to Oxford.] It is horrible losing him. Row with

---

[89] Miss Buss and Miss Beale, Cupid's darts do not feel.
How different from us, are Miss Beale and Miss Buss.
[90] A. Herbert Brewer, Organist at Gloucester Cathedral, 1897–1928.
[91] Helena Morris, the artist, (1862–1951). Born at Newnham-on-Severn. Studied in Paris, and at the Gloucester School of Art. Art mistress at local schools. Noted for enterprise and originality.
[92] Fridtjof Nansen, (born 1861). Norwegian scientist, explorer and statesman.

Clara about the Johnstone Stewarts as she wants me to go there as they asked on May 4th: objections, miles to go to see people I don't know; no clothes; don't want to get any new mourning ones. [They were still in mourning for their father.]

April 26th. Violet, Vivian and I bicycled to Berkeley; glorious run, wind with us. Unfortunately when we arrived there we found we were misinformed as to the days of the opening of the castle and it was shut today, so bicycled to Sharpness. We did thirty miles and came back by train.

April 27th. Very depressed. Violet went to London to stay with Clara for a fortnight, and Vivian went back to Eton. Went shopping in Cheltenham. Saw the most lovely Paris model dresses. They are so pretty, muslin with little tucks of lace all down, and then some with a lot of embroidery. Drove in a victoria with Mrs Annesley to tea with Lady Guise at Elmore. She showed us all over the house. We saw the children. Anselm has gone to school. Sir William was at tea. On the way there we saw a poor horse with a cartload of bricks which had tipped over and he was partly hung and nearly strangled. However they released him and just saved him in time.

On May 10th Linda went on a visit to the Arbuthnots at Norton Court near Gloucester, and had a "very jolly time". The return journey is described on May 13th. "I had ordered a trap to meet me at 10 o'clock. It never arrived so Dottie and I walked for three miles and then drove in a sort of a wagon with a labourer. The Norton coachman had been in with Mrs Arbuthnot before and so met us nearly in Gloucester. I came out in a hansom cab. Jack came here for the day rook shooting. Very nice having him."

There then followed another visit to London, this time to the Dyer-Edwardeses at 5. Hyde Park Gate. Linda saw Irving and Ellen Terry acting, ordered a "coming out" dress "white gauze over white satin, with flounces edged with baby ribbon". £13. Church at St. Matthews Westminster "extremely high." "Mr. Gladstone passed away at 5 p.m." The Opera, *Tannhaüser*, "quite delightful". "Faust, a concert at the People's Palace." "Crowds of people called." "Fitted for second ball dress, ivory satin with silver trimmings and orange roses." "Went to the Laundry Girls Club in Fulham; the girls were delightful; we danced with them and talked a great deal."

May 24th. She was back at Bowden, and practising the piano for four hours a day. June brought the balls at Oxford, and her "coming out", which was "better than I thought possible".

June 30th. Percy and I went to Cirencester to see John Sinclair [their brother-in-law] inducted.[93] The dear old Bishop gave a most sweet address. We bicycled back. I never saw such hills.

---

[93] Vicar of Cirencester. He was afterwards Archdeacon.

July 9th. This morning Jack and I tried a pair of cobs Cooke brought up. We drove and rode them, went right through the fields; Jack has bought them for £90 the pair. They are dark bays.

July 13th. Jack and I rode to Cirencester and back on the new cobs, about 32 miles. We lunched with Dillworth Crewdson at Syde and he accompanied us. We went right through the Bathursts' park, down one of the ten rides for 5 miles. We had tea with Clara. They have taken Miss Cripps's house.

July 18th. Jack and I rode cobs. We went over Painswick Beacon, calling at Prinknash on the way. Noëlle came down and we played a great deal of tennis.

July 30th. Jack, Noëlle and I went for a capital ride.

August 1st. Percy, Violet and I drove the ponies to Norton. Coming back, Diamond kicked over the pole, on the Wheatridge; we had great difficulty in stopping them. Poor Jubilee was very badly kicked and broke a vein in his leg. We had to bandage him up tight and then took them out, walking them home. Percy running the trap.

August 5th. Jack, Noëlle and I rode for over three hours beyond Churchdown. We saw hay ricks still smouldering from last night. The farmer has lost ten ricks and five waggons. Jack and I went back with Noëlle to lunch at Prinknash to meet Bishop Winnington Ingram.

Mrs Annesley rushed in this morning saying she was ruined as she had a letter from her bank saying it had failed. It is Hopkinsons Bank.

August 13th. Jack and I rode before breakfast, we went up by Sheepscomb and Cranham. Breakfast at Prinknash. We all went to the cricket at Cheltenham. Gloucestershire beat Warwickshire. We had lunch on the Grand Stand.

August 22nd. All indoor and outdoor servants, except one representative in house, garden, and farm, went to Weston-super-Mare for the day. We washed the dogs.

August 24th. I have come to stay at Prinknash because Noëlle is dull. Jack went to Scotland this evening.

August 27th. We have had the most terrible excitement. Noëlle and I started from Prinknash riding at 10.30. We went to Pollard Oaks field and round there. Noëlle tried to jump a little tiny hedge which she did once, coming back her mare fell and I saw the mare tumble on Noëlle and then it got up and kicked her. At first I thought she must be killed. The kick on her head was about an inch of her temple. I went to the farm 500 yards on and got

Adela Wykeham
(afterwards Lady Birchall)

Jack Birchall

Violet Birchall

Noëlle Dyer-Edwardes
(afterwards Lady Rothes)

someone to carry her in there. I then came home, sending for Mrs Edwardes. The suspense was ghastly waiting for two hours and not knowing in the least how bad she was, perhaps dying.

August 28th.   Violet went to see Noëlle. She is ever so much better.

September 1st.   Everything went wrong. Jack has written to say that I am entirely to blame for Noëlle's accident. Mrs Annesley intensely annoying. Poultry accounts terrible [she kept hens]. Mrs Annesley and I went to an "At Home" at Kimsbury. The worst thing about her is she does nothing but talk about lords and dukes.

September 5th.   Went to see the place of the accident with Noëlle — a tiny little hedge. (D.G.) that I have had a jolly day.

September 6th.   Jack came home. Vivian and I stopped at home to keep him company. A very dull day, practised 1½ hours and did poultry accounts. (D.G.) that there is an end to this day.

September 7th.   Noëlle came down. We had the accident well over. (D.G.) that we have had it over.

September 13th.   Three Choirs Festival. Mrs Wykeham and Adela[94] to stay. We went to the Elijah.

September 28th.   We went to the opening of the Birchall Memorial Institute in Upton in memory of Father. Jack made a splendid speech, also Canon Scobell and Mr Dyer-Edwardes. All very enthusiastic. Jack was praised so much.

October 12th.   We came up to London after bidding Mrs Annesley good bye, a thing which did not give me much pain. Jack met us. He was so kind, and seems interested in his work at Oxford House in the East End.

The next day the sisters went to Germany for two months, where they did a strenuous tour with a chaperone called Miss West. It supposedly proved too much for Linda's highly-strung nature. On December 1st they got back to London.

December 3rd.   This morning Miss West took me to see a doctor, Sir John Williams. He says I am suffering from nervous exhaustion and have to keep to a certan regime for a whole year, no riding, biking, dancing, practising, dinner parties, concerts, theatres, in fact no nothing except three walks a day

---

[94] Jack's future wife.

Indoor staff at Bowden

Upton people

of half an hour each to begin with! I do feel so mad about it. (D.G.) That Miss West gave me such good advice. [It seems extraordinary that no better advice was available.]

December 4th.   Went to St. Peter's Vere Street, Canon Page-Roberts preached a very interesting sermon on inherited depravity.

December 5th.   The Vicarage, Cirencester. To stay with Clara. Mr and Mrs Fred Cripps called; she is Adela Wykeham's sister.

December 17th.   Bowden Hall. Joined Jack, Violet and Miss West on the train at Kemble. Had jolly evening showing Miss West the china. Violet has come home from the Vereys at Twyford; she had a very good Ball last night. Went out for my walks.

December 24th.   Did up Christmas boxes for some of the village people, containing tea, coffee, sugar, bacon, tobacco, cocoa, chocolate, currants, raisins, apples, oranges and crackers.
   The tablet to Father has been put up in Upton church. I don't like the coloured marble against the terracotta background.[95]

December 30th.   This morning I went and invited all the tenants to the Servants' Party which we had this evening. It was very jolly.
   Noel Waller came to tea and to play Fives[96] with the boys.

December 31st.   Windy and wet, but went my morning walks. Percy, Violet and I went up to Prinknash for tea and found Mrs Edwardes and Noëlle there; very pleasant. (D.G.) That I have had a happy year on the whole.

[95] The first of the Christopher Whall windows from the west on the north side of the Lady Chapel in Gloucester Cathedral is also a memorial to Dearman Birchall.
[96] The Birchalls had an Eton Fives court built at Bowden. Jack had been Keeper of Fives at school.

Index

Ackers, B.StJ. (XII) 7, 23, 45, 71, 84, 90, 141, 147, 176, 185, 191
Alexander III, Czar 153
Alexanders, of Aubrey House 89, 126
Alma-Tadema, Sir Lawrence 187
Ancrum, Dr. W. R. 7, 15, 31, 32, 66, 84, 89, 90–1, 94–5, 123, 133, 167, 172, 177, 178, 184, 186
Ancrum, Wayland 74, 172
Annesley, Mrs 231, 233–4, 236
Archer, coachman 123, 133, 138–9, 143, 174, 209, 217
Archer, Mrs 216–7, 219
Armitage, Arthur 84
Armitage, Clara 160
Armitage, George 63, 64
Armitage, J. T. 3
Armley Jail 74
Armley Mill (IX)
Arnold, Matthew (XII), 59
Asylum, County 133, 140, 142, 162
Atkinson, John William 116
Atkinson, nephews 29, 73, 74
Atkinson, Sophia (née Birchall) (X), 2, 10, 34, 42, 126, 128, 171, 203
Atkinson, William 3, 12, 34, 203
Atlay, James Bishop of Hereford 14, 21–2, 32, 69, 72, 77, 84

Bailey, William (murderer) 67
Baines, Arthur 198–9, 203
Baines, Florence see Jowitt
Baker, Thomas Barwick Lloyd (XII) 7, 11, 13, 37 n.133, 166, 172, 184, 192
Baker, Granville Lloyd 13, 16, 37, 122, 133, 142, 189, 190
Baker, Michael Lloyd 204 n.
Barnard, Emily 188 n.
Barnwood Court 60
Barnwood House Asylum, 89, 135, 141–3, 168, 187, 189
Bateman, Lord and Lady 22
Bathurst, Earl 25, 34, 77
Bathurst, Mr and Mrs 19, 30, 32, 46
Bazeley, Rev. William 86, 137 n.168
Bazeley, Selwyn 168
Bazley, Miss Annie 134, 192
Bazley, Gardner 162
Bazley, Thomas (XII), 72, 93, 102, 107, 133–4, 140, 162
Beale, Miss 232 n.
Beaufort, Duke of 7, 12, 27
Bedford, 12th Duke of 174
Bedford Park, 94
Bell Hotel, Gloucester 70–1, 86, 95, 143
Belvoir Castle, 28, 63
Benson, Deborah see Jowitt
Benson, Frank 128, 169
Benson, Robert 196–7

Benson, Robin 138
Benson, William of Montreal 63, 141
Berkeley Canal, 79
Berkeley Hounds, 14, 15, 24, 34, 66
Berlin 150, 158
Bernard, Maida see Mirrielees
Bernard, M. 154, 158
Bethnell Green Museum 54
Bindon, Miss 216, 218–9, 221
Birchall, Clara Jane 1, 2
Birchall, Clara Sophia (IX), 7 n.8, 11, 21, 23, 27, 33–4, 36, 39, 47, 50, 54, 69, 71, 73, 75–7, 85, 89, 92, 94, 98–101, 117, 119, 122–4, 128, 130, 133–4, 136, 139–42, 145–50, 163, 166–7, 171–3, 175, 177–9, 187–90, 196, 198–9, 203, 206, 209, 212, 215–6, 218, 223–4, 229, 232, 237
Birchall, (J.) Dearman, His background (IX); description of by S. M. Howard (X); his collections (X); his family (X); employed Duveen (XI); description of by his daughter Clara (XI); marriage to Clara Brook 1; visits Bowden with Aldam Heaton and Edward Birchall, 10; dislikes Traviata, 10; concerned about Caroline Somerset, 12, 16, feels distrait, 27; attends Amy Brook's wedding, 33; considers buying Cranham Woods, 36, 37; business career (J. D. Birchall & Co.) (IX), 39, 40; partners at Bowden 41; engaged to Emily Jowitt, 47; marriage, 53; letter to his mother-in-law 57; disappointment with Vienna exhibition, 60; opposed to Oswald Birchall's marriage, 69; goes abroad for his gout, 76; birth of eldest son 77; birth of second son, 88; his portrait by F. G. Cotman 91; takes baths at Gastein for 3 weeks, 95; decides to get rid of partner Webb, 95; Spanish tour begins, 105; Ball at Bowden, 135; offer for Upleadon estate, 135; Emily's death, 177; rents house at Dinard, 199; Clara's engagement, 219; takes Percy to Paris, 227; his death, 229
Birchall, Edward, architect (X), (XI), 1, 2, 9, 10, 30, 39, 43, 46, 47–8, 62 n.74, 86, 90, 91, 93, 98, 101, 118, 120, 161, 170–3, 179, 190 n.199, 206
Birchall, Edwin 40 n.69
Birchall, Eliza Sibson (X), 1, 11, 16,

20–1, 29, 34, 42, 47, 50, 52–3, 60–1, 69–73, 80, 83–4, 87, 89–91, 94, 119, 122, 127, 134, 140–2, 147–8, 168–9, 171, 173, 177–9, 183–4, 186–8, 190, 199, 203, 206, 215–6, 219, 221
Birchall, Emily, Clara's description of (XI); her success in examinations (XII); 46, her examinations and acceptance of Dearman's offer of marriage 47; wedding, 53; her journal, 55; writes to her mother, 59; meets Matthew Arnold, 59; her letter to Anna Dora Howard, 60; another, 64; her 22nd birthday, 71; birth of first baby, 77; ill, 80; extracts from her diary (Dec. 1877), 92; birth of daughter, 98; upset by Lily Crewdson's death, 105; letters from Gibraltar 108; studies Latin with Clara, 122; presents Clara at a Drawing Room, 124; her yellow Liberty silk sunflower dress, 135; first visit to Upleadon, 136; her stillborn child, 145; learns Russian, 148; letters from Moscow, 150; her sudden death, 177
Birchall, Jack (Sir John) (XII), birth, 77; 89, 92, 93, 96, 101, 117, 122–3, 127, 130, 137–9, 142–3, 145, 158, 161, 164, 166, 172, 177, 179, 183, 186, 195, 197–8, 204, 206, 210, 217, 220–1, 227, 229, 231, 234
Birchall, Lindaraja, (XII); birth in Gibraltar, 109 et seq., 114, ballad on 115; 116, 120, 123, 131–2, 135, 143, 158, 160, 164, 172–4, 183, 198–9, 206, 216, 218, 222, 224, 227, 229, 231–end
Birchall, Mary 10, 84, 98, 113, 129, 130, 142, 161, 169, 170–1
Birchall, Oswald, 40 n.41, 43, 60–1, 63, 68, 69–70, 76, 82, 91, 95–6, 100–1, 103, 105, 116, 118, 121–2, 124, 132–3, 136, 138, 144, 168, 171, 201, 205, 210, 213, 216
Birchall, Percy (Arthur Percival Dearman) (XII), 88, 89, 96, 117, 120, 122–3, 127, 138, 143, 161, 164, 166, 172, 179, 184, 190–1, 197–8, 206, 212, 217, 220–1, 228, 231, 234
Birchall, Sophia (see Atkinson)
Birchall, Violet (XII), 98, 101, 104, 120, 123, 128, 130, 132, 143,

160, 164, 173, 177, 191, 198, 199, 206, 216, 222–3, 227, 229, 234
Birchall, Vivian (Edward Vivian Dearman) (XII), 177, 188, 198, 206, 216, 218–9, 227, 231
Blomfield, Sir Arthur 15
Bodley, G. F. 136
Bonchurch, 2
Bourne Baker, Mr & Mrs 51, 66, 187
Bowden Hall, (X), 5, 6, 8, 21, 35, 124, 127, 135, 160, 203
Bower, Dr Ernest Dykes 137, 145, 166–7, 177–8, 217
Bowly, Samuel 7, 20, 81, 145 n.
Brewer, Herbert 232 n.
Brockworth bellringers, 73
Brook, Amy (see Drummond)
Brook, Charles, 1, 14, 21, 28, 30–1, 33, 42–3
Brook, Mrs Charles (nee Hirst), 1, 14–5, 21, 28, 30, 33, 42–4, 49, 50–1, 60–2, 71–2, 75, 84, 94, 100
Brook, Clara Jane (see Birchall)
Brook, James William 1, 3, 7, 51, 75, 77, 121
Brook, Lillie 1, 14, 19, 32
Brook, William Leigh (X), 1
Brown, Miss (governess) 79, 85, 94, 98, 101, 116, 119
Brown's Hotel, Dover Street 54, 88, 94, 103, 137
Bruton Knowles, 8, 37, 95, 135
Buccleuch, Duke of 82
Buckholt, 36, 38, 162, 218
Bulley, Frederick 192
Burne-Jones, Edward (XI), 88, 130
Busfield, William 195, 204
Butt, Edward 63–4, 66–7
Byles, J. 37, 203

Cadlands, 67
Campbell, Archibald 21, 40–1, 63, 82, 95, 103, 116, 118, 121, 124, 132–3, 136, 168, 171, 201, 204, 213, 216
Canning, Mrs Gordon 32
Cantalupe, Lord 203
Cartland, Barbara 132
Catarozzi, courier 105, 108–9
Christian, Prince and Princess 22
Cheetham, J. C. 40–1, 63, 65, 82, 213
Clapham, George 8, 13
Clarefield, 77, 122
Clarke, George Somers 18
Clayton, Mrs 16–8, 118
Clifford, Henry & Mrs 15, 20, 61, 76
Clutterbuck, Rev. Charles 39
Colchester, Wemyss 120, 140
Collier, Hon. Sir John (XII), 198, 214
Collinson and Locke, 89

Constable, Mr (Principal Royal Agricultural College) 6, 23, 136
Copenhagen, 149
Cornwall, Rev. A. G. 24, 39 n.
Cotman, Frederick George of Ipswich, 91 n.92, 94, 126
Coutts, Miss Burdett 15, 209
Cranham band, 73
Cranham woods, (XI), 20, 36–7, 39–41, 53, 83, 89, 90
Crewdson, Dillworth 197, 207, 234
Crewdson, Lily 10, 54, 62, 71, 90, 94, 102, 105, 178
Crewdson, Theodore 62, 71, 137, 172, 190, 219, 220
Crossman, Richard Howard, Stafford 62 n.
Curtis–Hayward family of Quedgeley 7, 11, 14, 20–1, 33, 37, 76, 162, 189

Dalton, Rev. T. 198, 203, 212
Darell, Sir Lionel 15
Darwin, Charles 137
Davis, Adeliza 185, 187
Dearman, Sophia (IX), 18
Dearman, John 18
de Ferrieres, Baron 134
d'Epineul, Count 29, 31–2, 35
de Winton, Capt. T. 20, 32, 80, 86, 191
Dickinson, Sebastian 23, 32–3, 70, 96
Dickinson, Mrs (nee Hyett) 13, 31–32
Dinan, 119
Dinard, 119, 199
Diocesan Conference 120
Dorington, Sir J. (XII), 24, 37 n.122, 184, 191
Downe, Viscountess 131 n.
Drummond, Amy 1, 7 n.14–5, 21, 24, 28–33, 37–8, 40–4, 46, 49–51, 60–1, 64, 67, 69–72, 75, 79–80, 82, 85, 88, 91, 98, 123–4, 189, 216
Drummond, Capt. Cecil 28, 30–1, 37, 40–43, 46, 49, 51, 60–1, 64, 67, 72, 81, 85, 91, 100, 123–4, 136, 175–6, 203
Drummond, Edgar 67
Drummond, Lady Elizabeth 33, 41, 61, 67, 69, 82
Drummond, Margaret 126
Ducie, Earl of (XII), 17, 23, 25, 77, 81, 86–7, 176, 206, 217
Duncan, Prof. Martin 75 n.
Dutton, Canon Hon. F. 192
Duveen, Sir J. J. (XI), 74, 88, 217
Dyer-Edwardes, Thomas (XII), 196, 198, 201, 206, 224–5, 227, 229, 223, 236
Dyer-Edwardes, Noëlle 206, 210, 227 n.231, 234–6
Dyer, Laura (Nana) 96, 101, 114,

116–7, 120, 123, 127, 133, 138–9, 143, 145, 158, 171
Dyer, Thomas 219

Eliot, George 94
Ellenborough, Lord & Lady, (XII) 138, 162–3, 175–6, 191
Ellicott, Charles John, Bishop of Gloucester, (XII), 18, 24, 30, 32, 36, 41, 51, 53, 77–8, 99, 101, 126, 128, 181, 215–7, 233
Ellicott, Mrs 7, 18, 21, 27, 30, 32, 34, 36, 41–2, 53, 126–7, 191, 217
Ellicott, Miss 53
Elwes, H. 45, 52, 102
Emeris, Rev. John 37, 43–4, 51, 61, 66, 84, 86, 88, 91, 121, 123, 139, 179, 196, 201, 203–4, 207
Emeris, Fanny 100
Enderby church, Leicester 62 n.
Enderby Hall 14, 22, 28, 32, 37, 42, 49, 50, 71–2, 84, 91, 100, 124, 136
Eton College 195, 203, 207, 212
Eugenie, Empress 27, 32
Evans, Canon 19
Evans, Dr. 17, 80, 100
Evans, Miss 195

Fairford 120
Fearnside (confidential clerk) 40, 68, 95–6, 116, 143
Ferretti, Raffaello 55
Fetherstonhaugh, Lisa (Mrs Oswald Birchall) 43, 69, 70, 91, 216
Fitzhardinge, Lord 45, 77, 174
Foley, Lady Emily 14
Fowler (architect) of Durham, 136
Freeman (solicitor) of Huddersfield 29, 121
Freeman Prof. 143
Fretherne Court 23
Friends Meeting 93

George, Sir Ernest 143
Gibraltar, 107–8, 114
Girdlestone, Canon 178, 183, 195
Girdlestone, Theophilus 195, 197
Gladstone, Prime Minister, 27, 195, 233
Gloucester Cathedral (X), 2, 5, 17, 92, 162, 183
Granada, 106
Graves, Dr. 79, 80, 98, 116, 118, 120, 137
Gray, George Wyndham 136–7, 139, 142, 145, 161, 164, 169, 172, 176, 184–5, 187
Green, Rev. H. H. 11, 13, 16, 18, 26–7, 34, 184, 207
Guise, Lady 221, 233
Guise, Sir W. 17, 80, 84, 91, 135, 186 n.189

…am House, 126–7
…amburg, 148
…anbury of La Mortola, 206–7
…ardwicke Court 11, 14–5, 24, 29, 66, 68, 172, 184
…arehills Grove, Leeds (XI), 46–7, 47 n. 49, 52, 65, 71, 74, 79, 93–4, 103, 147, 174, 192, 213
…arewood Park 5, 103
…arris, Alfred 8, 40, 46, 88, 93, 102, 116
…arris, Anna Elizabeth 8, 18, 46, 86–7
…arris, Anna Jane 8, 77, 99, 173, 182, 188, 195, 201
…arris, Frederick 94, 132
…arris Navigation Co. 94, 117
…arris, Sophia 8, 182, 188, 195, 201
…arvey, Canon & Mrs 16, 19, 31, 91, 162
…asfield Court 51
…atherop Castle 72, 102, 107, 133, 140, 162, 192
…awkins, Mrs Fanny 175, 178–9, 183, 186, 190–1, 196, 198, 205–6, 212, 216
…awkins, Mr Justice 222
…ayward, Rev. H. B. 16, 28 n. 30, 32, 45, 52, 118
…ayward, Mrs (see Somerset, Caroline)
…eaton, (J.) Aldam (XI) 10n. 59, 94, 94 n. 95–6, 98, 101, 116–7, 131, 197, 204
…eaton, Miss Ellen 75, 181
…eaton, Mrs Fanny 52, 75, 116, 212
…eaton, Helen (Mrs Newall) 54, 113, 116, 129, 133
…eaton, Dr John Deakin 52, 75, 116
…icks-Beach, Sir Michael (and Lady Lucy) (XII), 25, 26, 34, 68, 72, 86, 121–2, 162, 196
…icks-Beach, William 90, 106, 172
…ighnam, 37, 93, 183
…irst, Thomas 148
…irst, Joseph 63
…irst, Julius 72, 91, 148
…olford of Dorchester House 196
…oopers of the West 60
…opkinson, Mrs George (nee Blanche Somerset) 11–12, 18, 25
…oward, Anna Dora (nee Jowitt) 60, 62, 64, 115, 162–3, 179, 181
…oward, David 62, 113, 162, 179
…oward, Dora 54, 148–150, 212
…oward, George of Castle Howard 126, 129
…oward, Lady Rachel 160
…oward, Susan (nee Jowitt) (X), 51, 65, 104, 113, 137, 172, 180, 186, 197, 207, 212, 219
…oward, Theodore 51, 65, 137, 179, 212
…ull 74, 88
…unt, Charles Brooke, 6, 8, 11, 27,

44, 183
Huntley church 45
Huxley, Prof. T. H. (XII), 75, 101 n. 137
Hyett, Francis 17, 23
Hyett, W. H. 7, 15, 17, 37, 45, 85, 88
Hyett, Mrs 12

Ilkley, 101, 116, 148, 158, 205
Irvine, Miss 171, 173–5, 177
Irving, Sir Henry 103, 121, 233

Janson, Dearman 70
Japanese cloisonné 53
Jones of Whitley Court 14, 76, 83
Jowitt (family) (IX), (XI), 5, 10
Jowitt, Benson 5, 9, 48–9, 50, 62, 74, 85, 88, 103, 105, 110, 113, 143, 164, 172, 179, 198, 213
Jowitt, Mrs Benson (Carrie) 5, 10, 48, 49, 85, 103, 198
Jowitt, Deborah (nee Benson) 9, 10, 34, 39, 47, 51, 62, 76, 79, 90, 94, 105, 121, 123, 137, 176, 179–80, 190, 204, 207, 213, 219
Jowitt, The Earl 99 n.
Jowitt, Esther Maria 174, 198 n.
Jowitt, Florence (Mrs Baines) 46, 48, 53, 62, 68, 76, 79, 89, 93, 98, 103, 114, 123, 133, 161, 163, 177, 180–2, 185, 193, 196, 198, 203, 207, 219, 221, 224
Jowitt, Henry 39
Jowitt, John 9, 10, 19, 34, 39, 46–7, 50, 51, 62, 74, 76, 79, 85, 90, 93–4, 103, 113, 121, 123, 137, 164, 174, 176, 179–80, 190, 202
Jowitt, Walter 27
Jowitt, Rev. William 86, 99
Junior Carlton Club 5, 17

Kafka, Emil 140, 144, 147, 174, 176, 204–5, 216
Keen, William 63, 77–8, 82, 85, 89–90, 101, 139, 165, 172–3, 183, 222
Kelso, Capt. 162–3, 176
Kemp, John 23 n. 92
Kent, Duke of 207
Kerr, Russell 193

Lanesfield, Cheltenham 140, 147, 169
Law, Very Rev. Henry, Dean of Gloucester 19, 30, 36, 64, 77, 139, 162
Lawson, Malcolm 128
Leatham, Edward & Mrs. 74, 90, 91
Lees, George 197
Leeds Mercury 55
Leighton, Lord 88
le Jeune, Miss 55
Lempriere, Colonel and Mrs. 107–8, 162–3

Leonhardt, Miss 221–2, 224
Lewis's Private Hotel, Jermyn Street 16
Lindley, John 17 n.
Lyndhurst church 130
Lypiatt Park 24, 122, 184
Lysons, Canon Samuel 32, 52
Lysons, Lorenzo 93

McCheane, Rev. James 1, 103
Macnamara, Mrs. 114
Manners, Lady Adeliza 176
Manning, Archbishop 70
Marling, Mr 73–4, 80
Marnock, Robert (XI), 65 n. 77
Marshall, Emma 122, 174
Meltham Mills (X) 1
Millais, Effie 127
Millais, Sir John Everett 25, 190
Miller, Samuel Birchall 26
Mirrielees, Archibald 151, 153–4
Mirrielees, Maida (Mrs Bernard) 47–8, 54, 80, 89, 96, 111, 113, 120, 126, 130–1, 138, 142, 151, 154–6, 158, 160, 169, 178, 196, 203
Miserden, 45, 74, 90
Moody and Sankey 175–6
Morley, Prof. Henry 78 n.
Morris, Helena 232 n.
Morris, Job and Mrs. 191, 198, 228
Morris, William (XI), 126, 130
Morris, William & Co. 10
Moscow 150–5

Nankin 42, 131
Naples 55, 57, 173
Napoleon III 104
Needham, Dr 89, 168, 184, 192
Nevill, Lord 5, 187
Newall, Frederick 129, 133
Newington, Dr 5, 7, 71, 75
New Zealand 137
Nice 54, 206, 224, 229
Nightingales 26–7, 41
Nut Hill 65, 130, 132

Oakley Park 89
Oxley, Louis 16, 36
Oxton Hall, Tadcaster 40, 86, 93, 129, 172, 182
Ozleworth 39

Painswick 6, Beason (XI) 14, 28, 85, 122
Palgrave, F. T. 128
Palmieri, Marchese 55, 57
Paris 28, 95, 173, 227
Parker, Edward of Browseholme 129
Parklands 73, 101, 189
Parry, Sir Hubert 162, 201
Parry, Thomas Gambier (XI), (XII), 7, 15, 21, 24–26, 32, 36–7, 46, 71, 100–2, 120, 130, 133, 144, 160, 172, 183, 201

Patience (Aesthetic Opera) 137
Paxton, Sir J. 17
Percival family of Meredith, 136, of
    Kimsbury 166–7
Perini, courier 54, 59, 94
Playne, Mrs Arthur 204 n.
Playne, Mr (High Sheriff) 27, 37
Poland 150
Pollock, Sir Frederick 127
Potter, Beatrice (Mrs Sidney Webb)
    (XII), 62 n. 204, 216
Potter, Richard 62
Prevost, Archdeacon 20
Prevost, Col. & Mrs 7
Price, W. P. (of Tibberton) 7, 26,
    45, 80, 88, 133, 136, 142, 189,
    224
Princes' Gardens, No 20 122–3
Prinknash Park (XI), 14, 20, 27, 37,
    45, 90, 93, 137–8, 176, 185, 204

Quakers (IX)
Quakers' Yard Colliery 94, 117
Quedgeley 95

Rea, Elizabeth 161, 177, 179, 186,
    198
Rice, Misses of Matson House, 84,
    132 n. 140, 168, 173
Ritualists 24, 41
Robins Wood Hill 14, 45
Rolt, John 30, 39, 87
Roman dresses 173
Ross, Sally 64, 123
Rossetti, Christina 181
Rossetti, D. G. (IX), (XI)
Royal Agricultural College, 89–90,
    136
Ruskin, John (IX), (XII), 103, 172–3
Rutland, 6th Duke of (XII), 25, 28,
    33, 41
Ryrie, Rachel 123, 127

Saintbridge House, 20
Salome, Antoine de 8
Sandford, Rev. G. 109, 113
Sandfords of the Isle 63–4
Sanger, Prof. Frederick 62 n. 105
Sanlini of Rome 59
Satsuma 46, 53
Saye & Sele, Lord & Lady 14
Scarborough 186–7
Scarbrough, Countess of 28, 33, 49,
    65, 82
Scarcroft (X), 8, 147
Scobell, Rev. Canon Edward 204,
    216–7, 224, 228, 231, 236
Scobell, Sanford and Edith 132–3,
    141, 203
Scott, Sir Gilbert (X), 36, 149
Sedding, J. D. 103, 130

Severn, Arthur 173
Severn Bore 96
Seymour, Sir J. 19, 28, 30
Shaw, Norman (IX), (XII), 10, 62,
    89, 94, 116, 130, 132
Sheepscombe church 45, 51
Shorthorns 90
Siamese twins 7
Sinclair, Clara (see Birchall)
Sinclair, Helen (Mrs Hasell) 120,
    124, 224
Sinclair, Janet 124, 130, 140, 162–3,
    209
Sinclair, Rev John 124, 126–7,
    130–1, 138, 140–2, 162–3, 209,
    217–9, 223, 233
Sinclair, Ronald 222–3
Sinclair, William 204, 209
Somerset, Caroline [Mrs Hayward]
    12, 14–8, 21, 23–4, 28, 30, 32,
    34, 36, 44, 52, 118, 168–9, 181
Somerset, Lord Edward 22
Somerset, Georgiana 11, 15–6, 23,
    29, 31–2, 35, 44
Somerset, Colonel Henry 16–7, 19,
    35
Somerset, Mrs Henry 7, 15, 18, 31,
    35
Somerset, Lord William 20
Somervell, Florence 207
Sorrento 57
Sowerby's glass works 133
Spence, Very Rev. Henry, Dean of
    Gloucester, 192
Springfield House, Leeds (IX)
Standish House 62 n.
Stanton, Sir E. 207
Stanton, James 7, 13, 83, 174
Starkey, Frederick and Mrs (nee
    Snow) 142, 162–3
Stewart, Capt. Arthur of Saintbridge
    12, 14, 16, 20, 21, 44
Studley Royal 102
Sudeley, Lady 162, 176
Sumner, Judge Charles and Mrs. 11,
    16, 21, 32
Sykes, William 118, 120–1
Sykes, Charles 123

Tangiers 108, 110
Temperance Society 90, 142
Tenby 137
Tennyson 184 n.
Terry, Ellen 121, 233
Teulon, S. S. 45
Tinling, Canon and Mrs 18–9, 24,
    41, 130
Tinling, Rose 37
Tollemache, Algernon 126–7
Tothill, Richard 45, 51, 69, 75, 85–6,
    90, 114, 123, 129, 164, 167–8,

    171, 174–5, 179, 183, 186
Tricycling 103, 124, 128, 130

Upleadon Court Farm (XI), 1
    139, 145, 147, 166, 176, 183
Upton St. Leonards (XI), 5, 3

Van, Miss 8, 12, 32, 34, 50, 6
    76–7, 79
Veitch, (Exeter) 15, 25–6, 101
Venables, Canon Edmund
    family 3, 19, 27, 36, 47, 8
    162–3, 221
Venables, Mrs 89
Verey, Rev. Cecil H. 132
Verey, Hal (Lt.Col H. E.) 22
Verey, Lady (Henrietta) 224, 2
Verey, Lindaraja (see Birchall)
Victoria, Queen 27, 70, 79,
    206–7, 229
Von Holst 77

Wakefield, Amy 54, 138
Wales, Prince of 18, 82, 87–8
Waller, F. S. 92, 101 n. 134
Waller, F. W. 101, 198, 227
Warburg, M. M. 40–1, 63, 68,
    80, 82, 85, 95, 100, 116,
    121, 124, 132–3, 136, 143,
    213
Warde, Mrs 137
Warneford Trust 78
Warre, Dr Edmond Headmast
    Eton 198
Warsaw 150
Waterhouse, Alfred 90
Webb, T. P. [partner in J
    Birchall & Co.] 3, 21, 40–1, 6
    76, 81–2, 95, 100, 116–7,
Wedderburn, Sir David 83, 91
Wedderburn, Lady 45, 46
Wellesley, Colonel 108
Wells, Sir Spencer 170
Wesley, Dr S. S. 26
Whistler J. McN. 89, 126
Whitcomb, George 36–7, 40
White, Maude 120
Whitwell, Crommelin (Duche
    Bedford) 174
Whitwell, Robert 174
Wilde, Oscar (XII), 104, 128
Williamson, Prof. A. W. 65 n.
Wilson, Capt. 54–5
Witts, Rev. Broome 72, 189
Wykeham, Adela 235–6
Wykeham, Mr & Mrs Philip
    236
Wykeham-Musgrave, Herbert
    Thame Park 217

Yorke Mr R. 51, 168